Human Rights in a Multilevel Constitutional Area

—

Global, European and Hungarian Challenges

NÓRA CHRONOWSKI

Human Rights in a Multilevel Constitutional Area

—

Global, European and Hungarian Challenges

NÓRA CHRONOWSKI

L'Harmattan
Paris

The research was supported by the
"Bolyai János Scholarship" of the Hungarian Academy of Sciences.

ISBN 978-2-343-13759-9

Volumes may be ordered at a discount from
L'Harmattan Könyvesbolt, Kossuth Lajos utca 14-16
H-1053 Budapest, Hungary
T.: +36-1-267-5979
harmattan@harmattan.hu
webshop.harmattan.hu

CONTENTS

PREFACE

More than fifteen years ago I started my PhD research on EU constitutionalism and the Europeanisation of national constitutional law. I had had the hypothesis that the economic-then-political integration triggers the approximation of national constitutional standards, the decline of sovereignty-reasoning and the rise of seeking for a more and more enhanced protection of common constitutional values of human rights, dignity, rule of law and democracy. One can say that I was a young optimist back then, however, some of my ideas were supported by the tremendous efforts in Europe to create a new treaty called constitution, and integrate the various levels of the European human rights standard.

The first two decades of the 21st century brought however more challenges than solutions. Thus, I decided to analyse some of these challenges from the viewpoint of human rights protection and other constitutional principles. As Gábor Halmai wrote in his book in 2014: "Ultimately, the globalization of constitutional law implies that constitutionalism is no longer the sole prerogative of nation states, but emerges instead as a set of standards for an international community that is in the process of taking shape." (Halmai 2014, 6) This statement inspired me to apply continuously the multilateral approach to constitutional evaluation, and discuss the principles, institutions, instruments and proceedings from global, European and domestic perspective.

I thank my colleagues, András Jakab, Balázs Majtényi, Georgina Naszladi, András László Pap, József Petrétei, Zoltán Szente, Emese Szilágyi, Tamara Takács, Márton Varju and Attila Vincze for their cooperation and openness to discuss my often discursive ideas, or just ensuring me about their friendship.

I am grateful to the Hungarian Academy of Sciences for the Bolyai János Research Scholarship that I was granted twice to investigate the current human rights challenges. I am also grateful to the Eötvös Loránd University Faculty of Law for supporting my visiting research in the TMC Asser Institute in The Hague where I completed this book. The three years I have spent as research fellow in the Institute for Legal Studies HAS Centre for Social Sciences also gave me a lot of inspiration and support.

And, the foremost thank and gratitude goes to my family, my husband Zoltán and my two dear little sons, Zoli and Bence who heartened me during the long years of research and were always on the board to help and gave me rays of hope that I am able to accomplish this mission.

The Hague, 30 April 2017

INTRODUCTION

Problems discussed in this book are set out on three levels: global, European and local. From these perspectives, especially Hungarian challenges and pitfalls are analysed. However, these levels and problems are not completely separated, as in a multilevel constitutional area the horizontal challenges are interrelated and intersected; each level may also vertically influence the success or the fault of an attempt at another level. During the discussion references and feedbacks will be made to each level. In the meantime, I strongly believe that no constitutional question is worthwhile to discuss in splendid isolation, through the prism of solely the national legal system. Global and European constitutionalism is still the most useful frame of argumentation in this regard.

Globalisation is a fact, and it has inevitable influence on constitutional and human rights law. While the globalisation of business is a very fast movement, human rights are far slowly "globalising", and their protection is still first and foremost the duty of the states. The first part of the book is devoted to a global challenge of human rights protection: the issue of business and human rights. The dilemma for responsible business is how to respect and support human rights in complex social, political and economic contexts – particularly where these human rights are being violated. The main objective of the business and human rights discussion is to expand the international human rights obligations to multinational enterprises, transnational companies and other business entities. For the success of the business and human rights concept, it is necessary to shift focus on non-state actors, NGOs and corporations as – at least – secondary subjects of international law.

The years of 2010s brought a period of frustrating crises to the European Union. There are still no adequate responses to the financial and monetary crises, refugee crisis, exit aspirations of certain member states and the increasing constitutional crises in Central Europe. In addition, the broad scope of crises veils somehow the backsliding in fundamental rights protection level in the states making an illiberal turn. Under the given circumstances further efforts for an integrated and balanced European system of human rights protection is extremely important. Two entities, first the Council of Europe and later the European Union made significant attempts to find a harmonised best level, but the mission is not accomplished yet.

From the aspect of the development of the European human rights standard, the accession of the Union to the European Convention on the Protection of Human Rights and Fundamental Freedoms (ECHR) is of great significance, as it realizes the consolidation of human rights protection in Europe. The accession is inevitable – even if the Court of Justice of the European Union (CJEU) stopped it for a while –, because the Treaty on European Union stipulates the obligation (not just the possibility) for the Union to access. The first chapter on European human rights protection evokes the antecedents of the EU's accession to the ECHR – especially the relationship between the case-law of the Strasbourg and Luxembourg courts, and then summarises the state and advantages of the accession.

The Charter of Fundamental Rights of the European Union has become part of the primary sources of Union law in December 2009. This reform has been of key importance from the aspect of the (constitutional) development of the Union. The second chapter on European challenges aims to collect arguments for direct applicability by assessing the significance and effect of the Charter so far, and underpins its strong relations to the general values of the European Union. First, I try to evaluate the actual situation with its deficiencies and controversies in respect of the EU values, the rule of law mechanism, the effect of the Charter and the recent case law of the CJEU and finally argue for the removal of the legal limitations from the way of direct application, considering also its difficulties and advantages, with special regard to member states risking the common EU values, such as Hungary.

Since 2010 the Hungarian constitutional developments have attracted widespread attention throughout Europe. Criticism and concerns, welcome and self-justification – various explanations surrounded the new constitutional identity building. After a relatively rapid period of constitution making the new 'Fundamental Law of Hungary' (it is the official translation of its title) came into force on 1st January 2012, but the constitutional patchwork was not finished. Six adopted amendments have shaped and shaded the new constitutional architecture, and of course not with equal significance, but all influenced the present landscape. In the background, a practically unlimited constitution amending power – a two-third majority in the parliament – acted during 2012–14, when most of amendments were adopted.

Developments in Hungarian constitutional law after 2010 suggest that the era in Hungarian constitutionalism characterized by a commitment to the rule of law has been replaced by an era where the law is regarded as an instrument available to government to rule. Under the new constitution, the constraints which follow from the rule of law have been habitually overridden or ignored by the government acting in parliament. The Constitutional Court's attempts, to continue the legacy of pre-2010 constitutional practice, were reproached by the government delimiting the powers of the Court or overruling its decisions in formal amendments of the Constitution's text.

After a short introduction and overview of replacing the 'old with new' architecture in the Hungarian Constitution, the first chapter on the Hungarian constitutional crisis analyses the relationship between the new Hungarian constitution and the normative values of the European Union with special regard to the legally binding Charter of Fundamental Rights that articulates the general values into individual rights. To ground this comparison and evaluation, the notion of EU values will be clarified and their impact on member states' constitution-making will be outlined. After this, the focus is shifted to the question, to what extent the new Fundamental Law of Hungary is compatible with the shared values of the European Union, with special regard to its fundamental rights standard. In the following chapter, I undertake to examine in terms of some European constitutional values how much did the Constitutional Court of Hungary endeavour to enforce European standards in the course of interpreting the Fundamental Law and how much did it try to contribute in the European Network of (Constitutional) Courts.

The 'rule by law' governance and the frequently amended new constitution of 2011/12 also reformulated the frameworks for the protection of human dignity and social solidarity. The decline of the standards in this field is spectacular and visible. The third chapter about the Hungarian situation intends to draw attention to the dangers of this path which may even lead to challenging European solidarity. For this purpose, a short section is devoted to the principle of social solidarity and its implementation in Hungary in the pre-2010 practise. The Constitutional Court in the late 1990's was even willing to strike down austerity measures for the protection of social rights closely tying them to the protection of equal human dignity. Although social solidarity was an underdeveloped societal practice for several reasons, the Constitutional Court strongly committed to the protection of human dignity and this way guaranteed a higher profile for social (solidarity) rights, especially in case of social care based on needs. Then, to a contrast this, the 'non-solidary' system of the Fundamental Law and the new directions of the constitutional case law is discussed. The recent case law of the Constitutional Court reaffirms the initial concerns, that dignity supported by solidarity got lost in the post-democratic transitions in the past seven years.

The last chapter evaluates the constitutional rules in the context of national identity and ethnicity, with special regard to those articles which are of discriminative nature and may lead to social exclusion. The first point is that – while the former Hungarian constitution was neutral regarding the values and applied the political nation concept – the new constitution does not clearly identify the political community to which it shall be applied, due to an inconsistent and controversial use of the concepts of political nation and cultural nation in the text. Using the category of nation in a cultural sense, the text allows for both a narrower and a wider meaning of membership than the category of political nation. Thus, because the definition of the 'nation' is rather controversial, it is unclear whether ethnic minorities fall under the same norms of political solidarity as the Hungarian majority. The second point is that the rights associated with the social solidarity might be interpreted restrictively. The possibility of penalizing homelessness or distributing social benefits compared to the 'usefulness of one's activity to the community' – again, combined with the ethnocentric nation concept – may in practice lead to social exclusion and indirectly sanction systematic discrimination against the largest Hungarian ethnic group, the Roma people, the members of which are most likely to live in poverty.

GLOBAL CHALLENGES – BUSINESS AND HUMAN RIGHTS

Introduction – global constitutionalism

Globalisation is a fact, and it has inevitable influence on constitutional and human rights law. While the globalisation of business is a very fast movement, the constitutional human rights are far slowly "globalising", and their protection is still first and foremost the duty of the states. The dilemma for responsible business is how to respect and support human rights in complex social, political and economic contexts – particularly where these human rights are being violated. The main objective of business and human rights discussion is to expand somehow the international human rights obligations to multinational enterprises, transnational companies and other business entities. For the success of the business and human rights concept, which does not even belong to the international soft law to date, it is necessary to shift focus on non-state actors, NGOs and corporations as – at least – secondary subjects of international law.

The concept of global constitutionalism accepts the convergence of national constitutional configurations in case of those states that share the same constitutional values, i.e. belong to the same constitutional families.[1] According to *Law* and *Versteeg*, this convergence is characterised by constitutional learning (i.e., in the course of attempting to learn from one another, countries are likely to imitate one another), constitutional competition (i.e., the need to attract and retain capital and skilled labor gives countries an incentive to offer similarly generous constitutional guarantees of personal and

[1] David S. Law and Mila Versteeg: The Evolution and Ideology of Global Constitutionalism, *California Law Review* Vol. 99, 2011, 1164–1166.

economic freedom), constitutional networks (i.e., reward countries for adopting the same type of constitutional regime that others have already adopted), and constitutional conformity (i.e., countries face pressures to conform to global constitutional norms in order to win acceptance and support).[2] The content of the national constitutions of democratic states converges in three aspects. First, they refuse the legislative supremacy – or the sovereignty of the parliament – and accept some form of the judicial (constitutional) review. Second, they are committed to the protection of fundamental human rights by prescribing explicit or implicit proportionality clauses. Third, they respect the rule of law guaranties.[3]

The results or effects of globalisation in constitutional law are that one the one hand the core of the constitutional human rights can be identified as part of the majority of national constitutions, and on the other hand the growth of the generic rights became a general trend, in other words the rights creeped over the past decades.[4] This tendency must be influenced by the evolution of international human right law, i.e. constitutional fundamental rights and international human rights have strong interrelation – the latter are the basis of the former, because states do not enact the rights, but recognise them.

---

[2] Ibid. 1173–1187.

[3] Mark TUSHNET: The Inevitable Globalization of Constitutional Law, in *Harvard Law School, Public Law & Legal Theory Working Paper Series*, Paper № 09-06 1–2. and A. E. Dick HOWARD: The Essence of Constitutionalism, Constitutionalism and Human Rights: America, Poland, and France, in Kenneth W. THOMPSON and Rett R. LUDWIKOWSKI (eds.): *A Bicentennial Colloquium at the Miller Center*, 1991, Lanham, MD, University Press of America, 3–41.

[4] Law and Versteeg has created a rights index composed of 60 constitutional human rights. While in 1946 the constitutions contained 19 rights in average, in 2010 this number has increased to 33, which means 70 % growth. LAW and VERSTEEG 'The Evolution and Ideology' 1190.

1 Concept of Business and Human Rights

Business and human rights (BHR) is seemingly a recent movement, however its roots can be found in the concept of Corporate Social Responsibility (CSR).[5] Thus it is not a completely new initiation, although still a recognised challenge since the late 1980's. In the last decades a range of research projects, books and articles applying multidisciplinary approach were devoted to the topic.[6] The main objective of BHR discussion is to expand somehow the (international) human rights obligations to multinational enterprises

---

[5] The term "corporate social responsibility" came into common use in the late 1960s and early 1970s. CSR is a form of corporate self-regulation integrated into a business model. CSR policy functions as a built-in, self-regulating mechanism whereby a business monitors and ensures its active compliance with the spirit of the law, ethical standards, and international norms. Originally CSR was considered to be voluntary and distinct from law. Today the CSR normativity is increased by the influence of human rights law, labour rights, environmental and anti-corruption rules. See also Karin BUHMANN: Business and Human Rights: Analysing Discursive Articulation of Stakeholder Interests to Explain the Consensus-based Construction of the 'Protect, Respect, Remedy UN Framework', *International Law Research* 2012, Vol. 1, № 1, 88–102.

[6] See e.g. Klaus M. LEISINGER: Business and human rights, in *The Future of Sustainability* (ed. Marco KEINER), Springer, 2006, 117–151.; Richard FALK: Interpreting the Interaction of Global Markets and Human Rights, in *Globalization and Human Rights* (ed. Alison BRYSK), University of California Press, Berkeley, Los Angeles, London, 2002; Marion WESCHKA: Human Rights and Multinational Enterprises: How Can Multinational Enterprises Be Held Responsible for Human Rights Violations Committed Abroad? *ZaöRV* Vol. 66, 2006, 625–661.; Florian WETTSTEIN: *Multinational Corporations and Global Justice,* Stanford University Press, Stanford, California, 2009; Sarah JOSEPH: *Corporations and Transnational Human Rights Litigation,* Hart Publishing, Oxford and Portland, Oregon, 2004; Janet DINE: *Companies, International Trade and Human Rights,* CUP, Cambridge, 2007; Radu MARES (ed.): *The UN Guiding Principles on Business and Human Rights: Foundations and Implementation,* Martinus Nijhoff Publishers, Leiden, Boston, 2012; John G. RUGGIE: *Just Business: Multinational Corporations and Human Rights,* Norton, New York and London, 2013; Tamara TAKÁCS: Human rights in trade: The EU's experience with labour standards conditionality and its role in promoting labour standards in the WTO, in J. WETZEL (ed.): *The EU as a 'Global Player' in the Field of Human Rights,* Routledge, 2012, 97–112. See also Institute for Human Rights and Business, http://www.ihrb.org/ and Business & Human Rights Resource Center, http://www.business-humanrights.org/Home

(MNEs), transnational companies (TNCs) and other business entities. It is more than the CSR as softly tries to create enforceable duties for companies beyond the self-regulation, and establish the grounds of their accountability for human rights violations. In constitutional legal terms it leads to the old question of third party effect of human rights on the one hand and extraterritorial jurisdiction of the national courts on the other. As a related problem, the constitutional background of the application of international law by the courts can also be mentioned.

To understand BHR, one can choose a top down approach, and analyse the actions and instruments of the United Nations and – at least in regional context – the follow-up actions of the European Union, which are to date of voluntary nature, and even not belong to the international soft law, but they may be assessed as a kind of policy. The other choice is the bottom up approach, from the side of the national feedbacks to the international standards and the relation of international human rights and domestic fundamental rights obligations, determined by the constitutional design of the states.

Both mentioned approaches may be influenced by the concept of global constitutionalism, which accepts the convergence of national constitutional configurations in case of those states that share the same constitutional values, i.e. belong to the same constitutional families.[7] This chapter applies both the top down and bottom up approach and tries to evaluate the outcomes of the BHR policies and strategies in the light of global constitutionalism.

2 Top down approach

The core problem is how the individual's inviolable and unalienable fundamental rights can be guaranteed in a globalised community, if we presume that a kind of 'world democracy' may come into existence. In other words, as *Galgano* formulated, the question is how

---

[7] LAW and VERSTEEG 'The Evolution and Ideology' 1164–67.

can the features of democracy, having developed within a national framework, be adapted to a post-state system of governance?[8] Surely essential is the access to effective fundamental right protection with efficient remedies for the legitimisation of international law and international public order.

According to *Tomuschat*, the international community has attained the positive international protection of human rights in three theoretical and historical stages. The first step is reaching a consensus with respect to the necessity of protection and the scope of the rights to be protected. The second stage is international codification, putting it into a treaty and national adoption. The third stage is establishing and operating a mechanism for the enforcement of rights. Even the universalist approach admits that whilst the first two steps have, by and large, been taken successfully, the third – and perhaps most important phase – has not yet been accomplished.[9] In addition, the system of international protection must be treated as a dynamic system; it has to be continuously adjusted to the changing state of global reality (handling terrorism, crime, flow of data, environmental disasters, pandemics, economic and financial crises, ethnic tensions, etc.).

As the UN Human Rights High Commissioner formulates the phenomenon in respect of business, "The global developments over the past decades have seen non-state actors such as transnational corporations and other business entities play an increasingly important role both internationally, but also at the national and local levels. The growing reach and impact of business enterprises have given rise to a debate about the roles and responsibilities of such actors with regard to human rights. International human rights standards have traditionally been the responsibility of governments, aimed at regulating relations between the state and individuals."[10]

---

8 Francesco Galgano: *Globalizáció a jog tükrében* [Globalisation through the prism of law], HVG-ORAC, Budapest, 2006, 7, 9.

9 Christian Tomuschat: *Human Rights: Between Realism and Idealism*, Oxford University Press, Oxford, 2003, 3.

10 http://www.ohchr.org/EN/Issues/Business/Pages/BusinessIndex.aspx

In *Ruggie's* words, "The root cause of the business and human rights predicament today lies in the governance gaps created by globalization – between the scope and impact of economic forces and actors, and the capacity of societies to manage their adverse consequences. These governance gaps provide the permissive environment for wrongful acts by companies of all kinds without adequate sanctioning or reparation. How to narrow and ultimately bridge the gaps in relation to human rights is our fundamental challenge."[11]

Many scholars pointed out that MNEs can infringe human rights directly or indirectly. The infringement is direct, if the enterprise uses child or forced labour, does not guarantee safety and health precautions, or establishes inhuman working conditions (like in sweatshops), discriminates on the bases of gender, race, sexual identity, belonging to ethnic, religious minority on the workplace, pollutes the environment, etc. Indirectly, typically during armed conflicts or by supporting autocratic or totalitarian regimes MNEs can be complicit in or benefit from human rights violations committed by host states.[12]

At the same time, it also worth to keep in mind that the increased economic development goes hand in hand with improvement in human rights; and the role of the MNEs (their investments and operation) is inevitable in this respect. They not only contribute to the socioeconomic welfare but promote the efficient exercise of civil and political rights as well.[13]

This dual effect shall be taken into consideration in constructing the international and constitutional legal instruments in the field of accountability of business enterprises for human rights.

---

[11] John RUGGIE: Protect, Respect and Remedy – A Framework for Business and Human Rights, *Innovations* Vol. 3, № 2, spring 2008, 189–212, 189. http://www.mitpressjournals.org/doi/pdf/10.1162/itgg.2008.3.2.189

[12] WESCHKA 'Human Rights and Multinational Enterprises' 626–627.; David WEISSBRODT: Business and Human Rights, *University of Cincinnati Law Review* Vol. 74, 2005, 57–58.; LEISINGER 'Business and human rights' 117ff.

[13] FALK 'Interpreting' 61. and William H. MEYER: *Human Rights and International Political Economy in Third World Nations: Multinational Corporations, Foreign Aid, and Repression*, Praeger, Westport, 1998, 108.

2.1 Assessment of UN instruments for responsible business

With the increased role of corporate actors, nationally and internationally, the issue of business' impact on the enjoyment of human rights has been placed on the agenda of the United Nations. Over the past decade, the UN human rights machinery has been considering the scope of business' human rights responsibilities and exploring ways for corporate actors to be accountable for the impact of their activities on human rights.[14]

For initiating universal attempts, instruments and strategies it was necessary to recognise that the human rights treaties just provide for indirect human rights responsibilities of businesses. The first efforts to define direct responsibilities of companies were more or less unsuccessful, or too 'soft', however good lessons to learn. Amongst these the drafts of the UN Commission on Transnational Corporations have to be mentioned that tried to create a code of conduct for companies from the 1970s,[15] as well as the OECD Guidelines[16] and ILO Tripartite Declaration[17] that promoted responsible business in their sphere of competence.[18]

The UN Global Compact – a voluntary framework for responsible business with the objective of sustainable, stable and inclusive

---

[14] Business and human rights – UN High Commissioner for Human Rights. http://www.ohchr.org/EN/Issues/Business/Pages/BusinessIndex.aspx

[15] See e.g., United Nations Draft International Code of Conduct on Transnational Corporations, 23 I.L.M 626 (1984)

[16] The OECD Guidelines for Multinational Enterprises are far reaching recommendations for responsible business conduct that 44 adhering governments – representing all regions of the world and accounting for 85% of foreign direct investment – encourage their enterprises to observe wherever they operate. The Guidelines were updated in 2011 for the fifth time since they were first adopted in 1976. See more at http://www.oecd.org/daf/inv/mne/oecdguidelinesformultinationalenterprises.htm

[17] The ILO's search for international guidelines in its sphere of competence resulted, in 1977, in the adoption by the ILO Governing Body, of the Tripartite Declaration of Principles concerning Multinational Enterprises and Social Policy (MNE Declaration). See http://www.ilo.org/empent/Publications/WCMS_094386/lang--en/index.htm

[18] Weissbrodt 'Business and Human Rights' 62–63.

global economy – was proposed by Secretary-General *Kofi Annan* in 1999 and it was launched in 2000. It contains a set of legally non-binding values on general human rights duties of businesses, labour standards, environmental protection and – since 2004 – anticorruption.[19] As UN Secretary-General *Ban Ki-moon* introduced the instrument, "The Global Compact asks companies to embrace universal principles and to partner with the United Nations. It has grown to become a critical platform for the UN to engage effectively with enlightened global business."[20] A unique feature of the Global Compact is that participation not only commits the company as a whole, but specifically its leadership. However, its effect is limited because of the lack of clarity regarding the definitions and distinctions on the duties of businesses and states; furthermore there are neither clear standards for monitoring and evaluation of corporations' conduct, nor repercussions for failing to adhere to the principles.[21]

It is not accidental that there is no international convention on the basic human duties yet, as such an international obligation

---

[19] The UN Global Compact asks companies to embrace, support and enact, within their sphere of influence, a set of core values in the areas of human rights, labour standards, the environment and anti-corruption: Human Rights, Principle 1: Businesses should support and respect the protection of internationally proclaimed human rights; and Principle 2: make sure that they are not complicit in human rights abuses. Labour Principle 3: Businesses should uphold the freedom of association and the effective recognition of the right to collective bargaining; Principle 4: the elimination of all forms of forced and compulsory labour; Principle 5: the effective abolition of child labour; and Principle 6: the elimination of discrimination in respect of employment and occupation. Environment Principle 7: Businesses should support a precautionary approach to environmental challenges; Principle 8: undertake initiatives to promote greater environmental responsibility; and Principle 9: encourage the development and diffusion of environmentally friendly technologies. Anti-Corruption Principle 10: Businesses should work against corruption in all its forms, including extortion and bribery.

[20] http://www.unglobalcompact.org/

[21] WEISSBRODT 'Business and Human Rights' 63.; Denis G. ARNOLD: Transnational Corporations and the Duty to Respect Basic Human Rights, *Business Ethics Quarterly* Vol. 20, № 3, July 2010, 3–4. Available at SSRN: http://ssrn.com/abstract=1612296
See also http://www.unglobalcompact.org/AboutTheGC/index.html

presumably would cause more damage than advantage to human rights law, providing governments with excuses to limit the exercise of human rights.[22] The human duties have fallen into two categories. The first category comprises 'vertical' duties in the relation of the individual and the state, which might be enforced by the government. The second category comprises horizontal duties in relations of the individual with other members of the society. Vertical duties usually appear in national constitutions, however separately from constitutional rights, i.e. the exercise of the rights is independent from the fulfilment of the duties. 'Horizontal' duties are usually not written into the constitution, as the constitution transforms these into vertical duties, as authorises the state to specify and enforce them, and thus intervene into the organic relations of the society. In 2003, the UN Sub-Commission on the Promotion and Protection of Human Rights – building upon the previous initiatives regarding corporate social responsibility – approved a draft declaration on human social responsibilities (i.e., corporate human rights duties),[23] but finally the Human Rights Council (HRC) had not even considered the Norms. The draft was harshly criticised by the stakeholders because of its scope, vagueness, uncertain legal status and force, etc. As *Arnold* assessed, "the Norms fail to provide a plausible and defensible account of those duties and in so doing undermine, rather than enhance, efforts to ensure that corporations contribute to the fulfillment of those basic human rights necessary for a decent standard of living for all."[24]

In 2005, *John Ruggie,* professor of Harvard University was appointed as a Special Representative to the Secretary-General of the United Nations (SRSG) with a mandate to investigate a number of important questions relating to the obligations of business for the

---

[22] See John H. Knox: Horizontal Human Rights Law, *The American Journal of International Law* № 1, 2008, 1–3.

[23] Draft Norms on the Responsibilities of Transnational Corporations and Other Business Enterprises with Regard to Human Rights, E/CN.4/Sub.2/2003/12 (2003) http://www1.umn.edu/humanrts/links/NormsApril2003.html

[24] Arnold 'Transnational Corporations' 9. See also Leisinger 'Business and human rights' 2.

realisation of fundamental rights. As *Knox* emphasized, that time the application of human rights law to corporations was highly contested: human rights groups (NGOs) and corporations differently approached whether corporations have, or should have, direct obligations under human rights law.[25] *Bilchitz* pointed out, that the mandate of the SRSG arose from the failure by the HRC a year earlier to adopt the above mentioned Norms, as many of the states was on the opinion that BHR issues deserve further investigation. The SRSG was initially appointed for a two year period and was provided with a broad mandate that defined the terms of reference for his activities.[26] The HRC endorsed unanimously Ruggie's reports, first in 2008 and finally in 2011. As *Mares* assessed, "While the Norms chose a more direct path to corporate accountability, to a large extent relying on international treaties and monitoring, and national regulations, the SRSG conceived a broader and less centralised template aimed at leveraging the responsibilities and roles of various social actors and relying on legal and other rationalities to move markets towards a more socially sustainable path."[27] The SRSG process created a reflexive law forum employing argumentative strategies and succeeded in generating a great consensus among the stakeholders. It was convincing enough for MNEs as well that a soft institutionalisation of business responsibilities for human

---

[25] John H. Knox: The Ruggie Rules: Applying Human Rights Law to Corporations, in *The UN Guiding Principles on Business and Human Rights: Foundations and Implementation* (ed. Radu Mares), Martinus Nijhoff Publishers, Leiden, Boston, 2012, 51–83, 51. Available also at http://www.globalgovernancewatch.org/docLib/20110829_Ruggie_Rules.pdf

[26] David Bilchitz: The Ruggie Framework: An Adequate Rubric for Corporate Human Rights Obligations? *SUR international journal on human rights* Vol. 7, № 12, June 2010, 199–229, 199–201.
http://www.surjournal.org/eng/conteudos/pdf/12/miolo.pdf

[27] Radu Mares: Business and Human Rights After Ruggie: Foundations, the Art of Simplification and the Imperative of Cumulative Progress, in *The UN Guiding Principles on Business and Human Rights: Foundations and Implementation* (ed. Radu Mares), Martinus Nijhoff Publishers, Leiden, Boston, 2012, 1–50, 1.

rights would reduce economic risks flowing from business related human rights abuse.[28]

As a result of the SRSG's activity, there is now greater clarity about the respective roles and responsibilities of governments and business with regard to protection and respect for human rights. Most prominently, the emerging understanding and consensus have come as a result of the UN 'Protect, Respect and Remedy' Framework on human rights and business, which was elaborated by the SRSG. On 16 June 2011, the UN HRC endorsed Guiding Principles on Business and Human Rights for implementing the UN 'Protect, Respect and Remedy' Framework (hereinafter: the Framework), providing – for the first time – a global standard for preventing and addressing the risk of adverse impacts on human rights linked to business activity.[29] Along with the Framework, also Guiding Principles were issued to assist governments and corporations in the implementation.

The Framework rests on three pillars. The first is the state duty to protect against human rights abuses by third parties, including business enterprises, through appropriate policies, regulation, and adjudication. The second is the corporate responsibility to respect human rights, which means that business enterprises should act with due diligence to avoid infringing on the rights of others and to address adverse impacts with which they are involved. The third is the need for greater access by victims to effective remedy, both judicial and non-judicial. Each pillar is an essential component in an inter-related and dynamic system of preventative and remedial measures: the state duty to protect because it lies at the very core of the international human rights regime; the corporate responsibility to respect because it is the basic expectation society has of business in relation to human rights; and access to remedy because even the most concerted efforts cannot prevent all abuse.[30]

---

[28] BUHMANN 'Business and Human Rights: Analysing' 98–99.

[29] http://www.ohchr.org/EN/Issues/Business/Pages/BusinessIndex.aspx

[30] Guiding Principles on Business and Human Rights: Implementing the United Nations "Protect, Respect and Remedy" Framework, Report of the Special Repre-

2.2 Actions of the EU for enhanced corporate social responsibility

The European Commission adopted a new CSR strategy in 2011, and encourages enterprises to base their approach to corporate social responsibility on internationally recognised CSR guidelines and principles.[31] This is especially the case for larger enterprises and for enterprises seeking to adopt a more formal approach to CSR. For companies seeking a formal approach to CSR, especially large companies, authoritative guidance is provided by internationally recognised principles and guidelines, in particular the updated OECD Guidelines for Multinational Enterprises, the ten principles of the United Nations Global Compact, the ISO 26000 Guidance Standard on Social Responsibility, the ILO Tripartite Declaration of Principles Concerning Multinational Enterprises and Social Policy, and the United Nations Guiding Principles on Business and Human Rights. This core set of internationally recognised principles and guidelines represents an evolving and recently strengthened global framework for CSR. European policy to promote CSR should be made fully consistent with this framework. As *Erkollar* and *Oberer* evaluated the EU's CSR strategy: "The European Commission was a pioneer in developing a public policy to promote corporate social responsibility, defining in their 'European Alliance' (2006) the support of multistakeholder CSR initiatives, research and education on CSR, and the support of small and medium-sized companies in their CSR activities, as priority areas for the European Union to focus on, accompanied by an applicable legislation and collective agreements between social partners. With it's new strategy on CSR (2011) the European Commission emphasized the need for the establishment

sentative of the Secretary-General on the issue of human rights and transnational corporations and other business enterprises, John Ruggie, 21 March 2011.

[31] European Commission: An Analysis of Policy References made by large EU Companies to Internationally Recognised CSR Guidelines and Principles, March 2013, http://ec.europa.eu/enterprise/policies/sustainable-business/files/csr/csr-guide-princ-2013_en.pdf

of sector-based platforms for enterprises and stakeholders to make commitments and jointly monitor progress, the improvement and tracking of levels of trust in businesses, the creation of guidelines for the development of future self- and co-regulation initiatives and the improvement of company disclosure of social and environmental information."[32]

The BHR issues are involved into (or subordinated to) the broader CSR strategy at EU level and has to date no overarching character. The European Commission has published practical human rights guidance for enterprises in three business sectors (employment and recruitment agencies, oil and gas, information and communication technology). These guides are the outcome of an intensive multi-stakeholder process, and are consistent with the UN Guiding Principles on BHR. They take particular account of the experience of EU companies, but aim to be as globally applicable as possible. The guides are not intended to be legally binding.[33]

The EU also requested member states to develop national action plans to support implementation of the UN Guiding Principles.

3 Bottom up approach – constitutional impediments

The system of international human rights protection may be criticized more harshly from a perhaps somewhat partialist and instrumentalist approach. It must keep in mind that beyond the trends of globalisation, universalism and constitutional convergence, also "reverse globalisation",[34] particularisation and constitutional diver-

[32] Alptekin Erkollar – BJ Oberer: Responsible Business: The European Union is Driving Forward the European Strategies on Corporate Social Responsibility, *Journal of EU Research in Business* Vol. 2012, 1–15, 15. http://www.ibimapublishing.com/journals/JEURB/2012/360374/360374.html

[33] http://ec.europa.eu/enterprise/policies/sustainable-business/corporate-social-responsibility/human-rights/index_en.htm

[34] For the term, see Seyla Benhabib: *Another Cosmopolitanism, with the Commentaries by Jeremy Waldron, Bonnie Honig, Will Kymlicka* (ed. Robert Post), Oxford University Press, Oxford, 2006, 51.

gence processes can also be observed in the global world. *Donnelly* pointed out that internationally recognised human rights create obligations for states, and international organisations call upon states to account for their fulfilment. If everybody has the right to *x*, in contemporary international practice it means: every state is authorized to and responsible for the application and protection of the right to *x* in its own territory. The Universal Declaration of Human Rights is the common standard of achievements for all peoples and nations – and for the states representing them. Covenants create obligations only for states and the international human rights obligations of states exist only in relation to persons falling under their jurisdiction. Although human rights legal norms have internationalized, their transposition has remained almost exclusively national. Contemporary international and regional human rights regimes are supervisory mechanisms monitoring the relationship between states and individuals. They are not alternatives to the essentially state concept of human (fundamental) rights.[35] For example, in Europe (within the framework of the Council of Europe) the European Court of Human Rights (ECtHR) examines the relationship between states and citizens or residents on the basis of subsidiarity. The position of the Inter-American Court of Human Rights is the same.[36] The central role of states in contemporary international human rights structures is also indisputable with respect to the content of recognized rights. The most important participatory rights are typically (though not generally) limited to citizens. There are several obligations – e.g. in the area of education and social safety – which may be undertaken only with respect to residents and they apply to aliens only if they fall under the jurisdiction of the state. Foreign states do not have an internationally recognized

[35] Jack Donnelly: The Relative Universality of Human Rights, *Human Rights Quarterly* Vol. 29, № 2, May 2007, 281–306.

[36] See also Nicolás Zambrana Tévar: Shortcomings and Disadvantages of Existing Legal Mechanisms to Hold Multinational Corporations Accountable for Human Rights Violations, *Cuadernos de Derecho Transnacional* Vol. 4, № 2, Octubre 2012, 398–410, 403.

human right obligation, for instance, to protect victims of torture in another country. They are not free to go beyond the means of persuasion in the case of foreign victims of torture. Contemporary norms of sovereignty prohibit states from applying means of coercion abroad against torture or any other human right violation.[37]

For the success of the BHR concept it is necessary to shift focus on non-state actors, NGOs and corporations as – at least – secondary subjects of international law. From this perspective was the Ruggie Framework criticized by *Bilchitz,* because considering the limits of international human rights law enforcement, corporations should have binding obligations for the realisation of fundamental rights. Non-binding instruments – such as the Framework – do not assist in the development of customary international law in the area of BHR and may even hamper progress. Corporations should not only respect human rights, i.e. avoid their violation, but also actively contribute to the realisation of human rights (positive duties).[38] Corporate accountability also cannot be effectively dealt with through existing methods; as *Vega, Mehra* and *Wong* stated, "While [the Framework and the Guiding Principles] contain positive elements, they fall short of creating an effective mechanism for addressing the many corporate human rights violations that continue by not providing a remedy in the international arena when national systems are unavailable or ineffective."[39]

Even in the European Union, which has an intensively evolving fundamental rights framework,[40] are significant obstacles that hamper the efficient application of the UN Framework for BHR. A con-

---

[37] Jack DONNELLY: *Universal Human Rights in Theory and Practice,* Cornell University Press, New York, 2003, 8, 14, 33–34.

[38] BILCHITZ 'The Ruggie Framework' 199ff.

[39] Connie de la VEGA, Amol MEHRA and Alexandra WONG: Holding Businesses Accountable for Human Rights Violations – Recent Developments and Next Steps, *Dialogue on Globalisation,* Friedrich Ebert Stiftung 2011, 1. http://library.fes.de/pdf-files/iez/08264.pdf

[40] Nóra CHRONOWSKI: Integration of European Human Rights Standard – the Accession of EU to the ECHR, in *Efektywność europejskiego systemu ochrony praw człowieka* (red. Jerzy JASKIERNIA), Adam Marszałek, Toruń, 2012, 957–975.

ference on CSR was organised during the Swedish EU presidency in November 2009, where remarkable conclusions were drawn about the problems with the functioning of the UN Framework. In respect of the states' obligation to protect human rights, the incoherence of the member states legislation (e.g. on issues of trade, investment, overseas development and corporate law) was seen as presenting a fairly uneven playing field within the Union of 28 states even before relations with other states, such as Brazil, Russia, India or China. The accountability mechanisms relating to the overseas operations of EU-domiciled companies was also mapped, and cited as an important first step in understanding some of the state-based gaps that might exist. In the field of corporate responsibility to respect, business requires states to play their appropriate role in order to help create additional demand. The issue of avoiding complicity in the human rights abuses perpetrated by others was also seen as being key feature here. As to the remedies, it was concluded that greater awareness of and adherence to existing international human rights mechanisms and greater access to effective remedies, both legal and non-legal is needed.[41]

It can be added that also the national constitutions and constitutional jurisprudence should be more open to consequences of the global world order by giving up the regulative and applicative models related to and rooted in the traditional concept of state sovereignty. In the following three major questions of constitutional design – the third party effect, the application of international law and the extraterritorial jurisdiction of the courts – will be discussed which should be re-evaluated or even revisited for enhanced realisation of businesses' responsibility for human rights violations.

[41] Ministry for Foreign Affairs Sweden, Protect, Respect, Remedy – a Conference on Corporate Social Responsibility (CSR), Stockholm 10–11 November 2009, Conference Report, 5–8. available at http://www.ihrb.org/pdf/Protect_Respect_Remedy_Stockholm_Nov09_Conference_Report.pdf

3.1 Third party effect (Drittwirkung)

Constitutions of the democratic states governed by the rule of law traditionally contain fundamental rights catalogue in line with international human rights law. These rights shall be normative and effective, i.e. enforceable before the courts of law. The effect of fundamental rights can be vertical or horizontal. It is impossible to reproduce in the framework of this book the rich legal literature on the complex problem of horizontal effect (Drittwirkung),[42] thus just the main points of the concept are highlighted in the context of BHR.

The vertical effect of the fundamental rights stems from the historical function of the rights, which is to protect the individuals against the state organs and limit the public power.[43] The international human rights law, as well as the UN BHR Framework relies on the states to guarantee the effective fundamental rights protection; and claims against the states can be brought to international human rights courts after exhausting the domestic remedies, i.e. if the given state fails to protect the rights.

The horizontal effect of fundamental rights means that they prevail also between individuals; and influence or determine the legal relations of private actors. This horizontal or third party effect can be direct or indirect.[44] According to the theory of indirect horizontal effect, the fundamental rights norm of the constitution is not applicable directly in private law relations; it is only used as an interpretative guide to determine private law relations among in-

[42] See, e.g. Hans Carl NIPPERDEY: Die Grundprinzipien des Wirtschaftsverfassungsrechts, *Deutsche Rechtszeitschrift* Vol. 5, 1950, 193–198, Ernst STEINDORFF: *Persönlichkeitsschutz im Zivilrecht,* Müller, Heidelberg, 1983, 12., Claus-Wilhelm CANARIS: Grundrechte und Privatrecht, *Archiv für die civilistische Praxis* 184(3), 1984, 201–246., György KISS: *Alapjogok a munkajogban* [Fundamental Rights in Labour Law], JUSTIS, Pécs, 2010, 125–184.

[43] József PETRÉTEI: *Az alkotmányos demokrácia alapintézményei* [Basic Institutions of Constitutional Democracy], Dialóg Campus, Budapest–Pécs, 2009, 440.

[44] Eric ENGLE: Third Party Effect of Fundamental Rights (Drittwirkung), *Hanse Law Review* Vol. 5, № 2, 2009, 165–166.

dividuals inter se. Thus, indirect horizontal effect exists when private law obligations are interpreted with regard to fundamental rights. It is the duty of the state, i.e. the legislator to create the rules of private (trade, investment, etc.) law in compliance with the constitutional and also international human rights so as the principles of the civil code to transmit the idea of human rights (dignity, equality, freedom, privacy, etc.); and thus the courts of law can interpret the private law regulation in the light of the constitutional (and international human rights) values. The theory of direct horizontal effect represents that the fundamental rights enshrined in the constitution are applicable in the private relations of the individuals. This results that private or labour law contracts infringing fundamental rights are invalid.[45] Direct horizontal effect implies that an individual has, in his action against another private party, a claim based directly on a constitutional right, which overrides an otherwise applicable rule of private law.[46] This idea would however transform the private law claims into human rights disputes, and the private law regulation would lose its function.[47] Thus the most widely used and followed concept in national constitutional practice is the idea of the indirect horizontal effect of constitutional rights.[48] Without contesting the concerns on the direct horizontal effect it must not born in mind that MNEs and TNCs are very special, powerful and influential private actors, thus with regard to their overwhelming dominance over the individuals and even the states, the application

---

45 Petrétei 'Az alkotmányos demokrácia' 441.

46 Olha O. Cherednychenko: Fundamental rights and private law: A relationship of subordination or complementarity? *Utrecht Law Review* Vol. 3, № 2, 2007, 4–5.

47 Petrétei 'Az alkotmányos demokrácia' 441.

48 That is the case in large majority of EU member states. Only the Portuguese and Greek constitutions allow direct horizontal effect. The European constitutional case law seems to differentiate between rights in respect of their indirect horizontal effect. Leonard F. M. Besselink: General Report, in *The Protection of Fundamental Rights Post-Lisbon: The Interaction between the Charter of Fundamental Rights of the European Union, the European Convention on Human Rights and National Constitutions* (ed. Julia Laffranque), Tartu University Press, Tallinn, 2012, 91–93.

of direct horizontal effect of fundamental rights would be reasonable to their relations.[49]

3.2 Application of international law by national courts

The national constitutions usually contain provisions on international law and international community, reaffirming the acceptance and respect of internationally agreed values, amongst the international human rights norms. Thus these kinds of constitutional provisions preliminary commit and restrain the national governments for and by the common international values.[50] However, the constitutional declaration in itself does not guarantee that the international human rights law is applied and enforced effectively in a given country, because the enforcement depends on and influenced by the way of implementation (monist or dualist approach), the level and effectiveness of protection of the relevant constitutional provisions (by constitutional court or courts of law with constitutional review powers) and the exact content of those provisions (e.g. they refer to international law in general, or distinguish the sources of international law, firmly express the rank of the international law in the domestic legal system etc.), and finally the general attitude of the courts of law to the application of international treaties, internation-

[49] It is worth to mention that the courts, even the European Court of Justice are very careful with the recognition of indirect horizontal effect. See e.g. Viking, Laval (on right to collective action, allowing indirect horizontal effect) and Dominguez (on right to paid annual leave, not granting clearly the horizontal effect) cases (C-438/05 International Transport Workers' Federation and Finnish Seamen's Union v Viking Line ABP and OÜ Viking Line Eesti, Judgment of the Court of 11 December 2007; C-341/05 Laval un Partneri Ltd v Svenska Byggnadsarbetareförbundet, Svenska Byggnadsarbetareförbundets avdelning 1, Byggettan and Svenska Elektrikerförbundet, Judgment of the Court of 18 December 2007; C-282/10 Maribel Dominguez v Centre informatique du Centre Ouest Atlantique and Préfet de la région Centre, Judgment of the Court of 24 January 2012)

[50] Tom Ginsburg, Svitlana Chernykh and Zachary Elkins: Commitment and Diffusion: Why Constitutions Incorporate International Law, *University of Illinois Law Review*, 2008, 101–137. http://works.bepress.com/zachary_elkins/1

al courts' judgments, universal customary international law, peremptory norms *(ius cogens)* and general principles of law recognized by civilized nations. Or as *Cram* explained: "When considering the migration of human rights norms into the judicial sphere, two initial observations may be made. The first is that while some constitutions oblige national courts to engage with norms in international human rights law, the precise status that is given to these norms varies considerably from constitution to constitution. Second, by comparison with explicit constitutional references to international human rights laws, there is a conspicuous lack of any equivalent constitutional exhortation to give effect to / consider / take account of national human rights norms."[51]

The judicial dialogue – i.e., considering and applying international and foreign court decisions, drawing the consequences of international courts' judgments by national courts – may support the international BHR principles as well. The question is whether the international and national courts do really have a dialogue, or they continue their parallel monologues?[52]

Dialogue is when two (or more) participants in equal position, are seeking agreement by exchange of views, generally in order to achieve some joint outcome. The precondition of the dialogue is the near identical or similar position of the participants, which primarily occurs on the level of powers and influence, and from this perspective, assumes identical weight. The dialogue is actually a specific form of debate; therefore it shall be distinguished from the general discussion and consultation as well. As a specific form of the debate, some criteria may be outlined that characterise the dialogue and without this framework the parties would misunderstand each other. First, the dialogue assumes a common goal, or if

---

[51] Ian Cram: Resort to foreign constitutional norms in domestic human rights jurisprudence with reference to terrorism cases, *Cambridge Law Journal* Vol. 68, № 1, March 2009, 119.

[52] Nóra Chronowski and Erzsébet Csatlós: Judicial Dialogue or National Monologue? – the International Law and Hungarian Courts, *ELTE Law Journal* Vol. 1, № 1, 2013, 7–28.

you prefer, a common subject on which the dialogue is going on. The dialogue may never end in itself. Second criterion is the commitment to the common goal. All the participants want to achieve the common goal, which is to eliminate or reduce the conflict, and the debate or the individual interests shall be subordinated to this goal. Regularity is also an important feature of the dialogue. The dialogue is rarely a single exchange of views, because the interests of the participants are usually complex. The fourth characteristic in a dialogue is that the parties strive to be conclusive and effective. All of them are interested in the conflict resolution, and therefore they are willing to 'sacrifice', i.e., to give up some parts of their own interests in order to reach a mutual compromise outcome, because this is usually more preferable for everyone than enforcing their individual interests. Finally the mutuality must be mentioned, which should characterize all of the participants. The mutuality covers also concession, empathy, tolerance, etc. The meaning of a dialogue is not overcoming each other, but to achieve a common goal. A focal question is, whether and to what extent do the national courts consider the judgments of international or foreign courts. Do they just simply refer them, or do they reflect on them by overruling their own, former jurisprudence? The latter would prove the existence of judicial dialogue and contribute to the efficiency of international human rights law, the former, however, is not enough to satisfy the criteria of the dialogue.[53]

Applying the general features of the dialogue to the courts, one can conclude that the basic condition – the equal position – is given if we consider the powers and status of e.g. the ECtHR, the constitutional courts and ordinary courts of last instance. As to the common goal and the commitment to that – first and second specific conditions – it may be supposed that the analyzed courts are to protect fundamental rights and common constitutional values, but these are very far and abstract common goals. The concrete goal of

[53] For a different and wider concept of constitutional dialogue, see Tímea Drinóczi: Constitutional dialogue theories – extension of the concept and examples from Hungary, *Zeitschrift für öffentliches Recht* Vol. 68, № 1, 2013, 87–110.

each court is to solve a given case, safeguard e.g. the ECHR or the constitution in line with its function, and the way they reach this goal is influenced by the circumstances of the given case, the references of the parties concerned, and the presumption of the judges regarding the *ratio decidendi*. The latter also interferes with the regularity, because the national courts usually refer to international sources only if it supports the reasoning or has stronger convincing force than the purely domestic legal based argumentation. Fourthly, the courts have no conflict with each other, thus – although they respect each others statements and rulings – they need not to be conclusive and effective in this respect. Sometimes the domestic courts seem to be rather careful or reticent with the interpretation of international treaties as they maybe try to avoid a potential future conflict with the international tribunal authorised for authentic interpretation of the given treaty. Of course if all role-players – i.e. courts – agree that the conflict can be traced back to a given piece of domestic law infringing a normative international commitment, and the procedural conditions are available (their procedures were initiated, at least one of them has power to eliminate the concerned norm, they have appropriate procedural ties among each other), the international and domestic courts may cooperate effectively by referring each others' decisions. Finally, in the 'dialogue' of the courts, the mutual respect can be observed and rivalry is really rare phenomenon, but it is also true, that courts are not compelled to mutual concessions. Thus, as a final conclusion, it can be stated that the domestic courts apply the international law if they have to or they want to decorate their reasoning with it, but it is still far from a constructive dialogue, and organic inclusion of international law, principles and practices into the jurisprudence. Only a few constitutions encourage the courts explicitly to use international or foreign precedents; and on global stage still the domestic constitutional argumentation is decisive rather than borrowing or transplantation. Significant jurisdictions, such as the US courts follow exceptionalist practice and refuse the use of foreign judgments almost completely.[54] This attitude of the courts may reduce the effect of the legally non-binding UN BHR Framework on human rights litigation.

3.3 The problem of extraterritoriality

The problem of extraterritoriality related to the rule that international law holds states responsible for human rights violations, and not MNEs or TNCs. The states as duty bearers have to guarantee that business enterprises do not infringe the human rights in the territory where they operate. First and foremost the host state (where the MNE operates or the potential human rights violation occurs) should establish guarantees against the human rights violations by their national laws and law enforcement mechanism. However, because of the dominance and mobility of the MNEs, as well as the needs, means, economic interests or state of development of the given country, the offered human rights guarantees are often insufficient in the host state. E.g. it is very typical in developing countries that the governments fail to take actions against MNEs for human rights violations, because they need foreign investment, jobs, technical enterprise or they simply do not have resources (financials, legal procedures, non-corrupt judiciary, etc.) to sanction human rights abuses although would be willing to do so.[55] For these reasons, it is a logical step on the side of the victims of human rights violations caused by MNEs that they – seeking for redress and compensation – try to sue corporations for their activities performed abroad in the home states, i.e. in the country where the given business enterprise is domiciled. According to *Weschka,* it is true that home states are not currently liable in international human rights law for failing to prevent, punish, or otherwise regulate the delinquencies of their TNCs' overseas operations, but the home states

---

54 Gábor Halmai: *Perspectives on Global Constitutionalism, The Use of Foreign and International Law,* Eleven, The Hague, 2014, 186–191.

55 Weschka 'Human Rights and Multinational Enterprises' 628–629., Joseph 'Corporations and Transnational' 9–10., Tévar 'Shortcomings' 399–401.

have high human rights records, developed procedures, non-corrupt and functioning court system, and international law also "recognises the right of home states to exercise extraterritorial jurisdiction over their nationals committing wrongs abroad".[56] Thus the national courts have the chance to rule on MNEs' overseas human rights abuses, and enforce human rights norms 'horizontally'.

Numerous suits were filed mainly in common law countries, before United States, Canadian, Australian and United Kingdom courts against parent companies.[57] The most successful legal instrument for transnational human rights litigation seemed to be undoubtedly the US Alien Tort Statute (ATS) 1789 that had been dormant for nearly two centuries before lawyers began creatively using it in the 1980s to bring international human rights cases in US courts. The ATS grants jurisdiction to federal courts to hear tort claims by aliens alleging violations of the 'law of the nations'.[58] However, the ATS in itself cannot help to solve the problem of liability of the MNEs, because courts take several features into consideration in respect of transnational litigation,[59] such as the doctrine of separation of powers, the state action doctrine, the political question, sovereign immunity and international comity considerations, the 'corporate veil' as well as *'forum non conveniens'*.[60]

In the landmark *Kiobel* decision (2013) the US courts greatly restricted the scope of ATS and limited the US courts' jurisdiction in foreign human rights cases.[61] US Court of Appeal for the Second

---

[56] WESCHKA 'Human Rights and Multinational Enterprises' 629., see also JOSEPH 'Corporations and Transnational' 11–12.

[57] JOSEPH 'Corporations and Transnational' 15., Olivier DE SCHUTTER: Transnational Corporations and Human Rights: An Introduction, *Global Law Working Paper* 01/05, Symposium – Transnational Corporations and Human Rights, NYU School of Law, 2005, 7.

[58] TÉVAR 'Shortcomings' 408., JOSEPH 'Corporations and Transnational' 10, 17.

[59] HALMAI 'Perspectives' 236–239.

[60] WESCHKA 'Human Rights and Multinational Enterprises' 629–631., TÉVAR 'Shortcomings' 409.

[61] *Kiobel v. Royal Dutch Petroleum Co.*, Decided April 17, 2013, 133 S. Ct. 1659 (U.S. 2013)

Circuit ruled that the ATS is inapplicable to corporations because corporate liability is not a discernible norm of customary international law. The Supreme Court heard arguments over whether the Alien Tort Statute could apply to corporations, and later expanded the case to consider whether the law could be invoked in similar cases against anyone. The judgment finally was controlled by the 'presumption against extraterritoriality', which means that the Congress is presumed not to intend its statutes to apply outside the US unless it provides a 'clear indication' otherwise. The Supreme Court explained that, even where the claims 'touch and concern the territory of the United States, they must do so with sufficient force to displace the presumption against extraterritorial application'. The Court also discussed corporations, stating that corporations are often present in many countries, but a 'mere corporate presence' in the United States is insufficient.[62]

However, so long as at least some portion of the relevant conduct occurred within the US, ATS cases may still be sustainable. Altogether, the Kiobel decision makes it far more difficult for the human rights activists to sue US corporations based on the corporation's

---

Petitioners, Nigerian nationals residing in the United States, filed suit in federal court under the Alien Tort Statute, alleging that respondents – certain Dutch, British, and Nigerian corporations – aided and abetted the Nigerian Government in committing violations of the law of nations in Nigeria. The ATS provides that "[t]he district courts shall have original jurisdiction of any civil action by an alien for a tort only, committed in violation of the law of nations or a treaty of the United States." 28 U.S.C. §1350. The District Court dismissed several of petitioners' claims, but on interlocutory appeal, the Second Circuit dismissed the entire complaint, reasoning that the law of nations does not recognize corporate liability.

62 A few days after Kiobel, the Court vacated and remanded a Ninth Circuit decision that had allowed extraterritorial ATS claims to proceed [*Rio Tinto PLC v. Sarei*, 569 U.S. ---, 2013 WL 1704704 (April 22, 2013)]. In Rio Tinto, foreign plaintiffs sued foreign defendants who had 'substantial operations in this country', including 'assets of nearly $13 billion – 47% of which are located in North America'. Even this degree of corporate presence was not enough to overcome the presumption of extraterritoriality when the alleged torts had occurred outside the United States.

overseas activities.[63] As the post-Kiobel rulings of the US courts[64] show – although the door is not closed completely on using the ATS – plaintiffs can mostly rely on asserting parallel claims under federal laws that are expressly extraterritorial but limited to their own narrow circumstances.

4 Conclusions

The ways of development may be (1) an ambitious initiative for a 'Business and human rights Treaty' and (2) strengthening the legal characters of national action plans on BHR.

As to the first path, it is not a mere fantasy. As de Schutter reports, "On 26 June 2014 the Human Rights Council (HRC) adopted a resolution calling for the establishment of an open-ended intergovernmental working group (IGWG) 'to elaborate an international legally-binding instrument to regulate, in international human rights law, the activities of transnational corporations and other business enterprises'. The resolution was tabled by Ecuador and South Africa, and it was co-sponsored by Bolivia, Cuba, and Venezuela. Although strongly supported by an impressive coalition of civil society organizations who formed a 'Treaty Alliance' in support of a binding treaty and despite gaining support from a plurality within the Human Rights Council, the proposal was highly divisive: within the 47-members-large HRC, it was supported by 20 member states and opposed by 14 states (including the United States and

---

[63] Rich SAMP: Supreme Court Observations: Kiobel v. Royal Dutch Petroleum & the Future of Alien Tort Litigation, http://www.forbes.com/sites/wlf/2013/04/18/supreme-court-observations-kiobel-v-royal-dutch-petroleum-the-future-of-alien-tort-litigation/

[64] See *Sarei v. Rio Tinto, Al-Shimari v. CACI or Balintulo v. Daimler* cases commented by Marco SIMONS: Post-Kiobel roundup: Apartheid case is not dismissed, but may soon be; some positive decisions from other courts (September 10, 2013), http://www.earthrights.org/blog/post-kiobel-roundup-apartheid-case-not-dismissed-may-soon-be-some-positive-decisions-other

the Member States of the European Union), whereas 13 member states of the HRC abstained."[65]

The achievements of the first session of the IGWG held in Geneva during 6–10 July 2015 were summarised by Lopez and Shea: "This first session, which was relatively well attended, raised expectations, especially from a wide array of civil society organizations, despite concerns of a likely boycott of the process by Western states. After all was said and done, the first session could be described as a qualified success. Although state participation was low and many discussions proved more political than legalistic, there was some meaningful progress. (…) Over the course of the week, there were eight panels addressing the following topics: (i) implementation of the UNGPs; (ii) principles of the treaty; (iii) scope of enterprises covered by the instrument; (iv) scope of human rights covered by the instrument; (v) obligations of states to guarantee respect of human rights, including extraterritorial obligations; (vi) enhancing the responsibilities of corporations to respect human rights, including prevention, mitigation, and remediation; (vii) legal liability of corporations; and (viii) access to remedy."[66]

Although many are pessimistic and remind to the failures of the 1970s and the 2003 proposal by the UN Sub-Commission for the Promotion and Protection of Human Rights for the adoption of a set of Norms on the Human Rights Responsibilities of Transnational Corporations and Other Business Enterprises, de Schutter believes that we can maybe learn from the mistakes committed in the past, and examines "the legal as well as political feasibility of four potential options for a legally-binding international instrument in the area of business and human rights. The four options: (i) to clarify and strengthen the states' duty to protect human rights, including extraterritorially; (ii) to oblige states, through a framework conven-

---

[65] Olivier De Schutter: Towards a New Treaty on Business and Human Rights, *Business and Human Rights Journal* Vol. 1, 2016, 41–67, 41-42.

[66] Carlos Lopez and Ben Shea: Negotiating a Treaty on Business and Human Rights: A Review of the First Intergovernmental Session, *Business and Human Rights Journal* Vol. 1, 2016, 117–126, at 111 and 113.

tion, to report on the adoption and implementation of national action plans on business and human rights; (iii) to impose direct human rights obligations on corporations and establish a new mechanism to monitor compliance with such obligations; and (iv) to impose duties of mutual legal assistance on states to ensure access to effective remedies for victims harmed by transnational operations of corporations."[67] De Schutter argues that a hybrid instrument building on elements of the first and the fourth option may be the best way forward both in terms of political feasibility and improving access to effective remedies for victims.[68]

Of course, the strive for a BHR Treaty may fall short many ways, the developments in the field might be also triggered by the advocacy and sustained evaluation of national action plans (NAPs) on business and human rights. The HRC thus encouraged the states to elaborate their NAPs.[69] In 2017 there are 13 adopted NAPs, and the range of other in progress.[70] "Every NAP process affirms the UNGPs' essential tenet that human rights apply within the business sector and indicates a political commitment to bring domestic laws, policies, and practices into alignment with this norm."[71]

To sum up, BHR is still a policy instead of a legal framework, although by further development a really efficient instrument could it be as response to the challenges of globalisation on human rights. The limits of the United Nations' BHR concept are on the one hand

---

67 De Schutter 'Towards a New Treaty' 41.

68 De Schutter 'Towards a New Treaty' 44.

69 Human Rights Council, 'Human Rights and Transnational Corporations and Other Business Enterprises', A/HRC/RES/26/22 (15 July 2014), https://documents-dds-ny.un.org/doc/UNDOC/GEN/G14/083/82/PDF/G1408382.pdf?OpenElement

70 http://www.ohchr.org/EN/Issues/Business/Pages/NationalActionPlans.aspx, https://business-humanrights.org/en/un-guiding-principles/implementation-tools-examples/implementation-by-governments/by-type-of-initiative/national-action-plans

71 Claire Methven O'Brien, Amol Mehra, Sara Blackwell and Cathrine Bloch Poulsen-Hansen: National Action Plans: Current Status and Future Prospects for a New Business and Human Rights Governance Tool, *Business and Human Rights Journal* Vol. 1, 2016, 117–126, at 117.

the deficiencies of international human rights enforcement mechanisms, and on the other hand some constitutional dogmas on direct third party effect of human rights, the rigid and unimaginative application of international law by national courts, and excluding extraterritorial jurisdiction in human rights cases. Thus, for the success of "principled pragmatism"[72] of UN BHR Framework and policy, some paradigms of national constitutional law should be changed, or at least the domestic courts should make a better use of the constitutional convergence.

[72] For the term, see 'Just Business' – Ruggie on Business and Human Rights at the UN. http://businesshumanrightsireland.wordpress.com/2013/05/13/just-business-ruggie-on-business-and-human-rights-at-the-un/

EUROPEAN CHALLENGES OF HUMAN RIGHTS PROTECTION

Introduction - human rights protection and the European Union

The years of 2010s brought a frustrating crisis era to the European Union. There are still no adequate responses to the credit crunch, refugee crisis, exit striving of certain member states and the constitutional crises in Central Europe. In addition, the plenty of crisis veils somehow the backsliding of fundamental rights protection level in the states making an illiberal turn. As András Sajó assessed in 2003,

> 'The collapse of oppressive regimes in Eastern Europe raised high hopes. It was believed that the strong desire to get rid of communist authoritarianism and the wish to enjoy the advantages of a market economy would result in new societies committed to the rule of law and constitutionalism. It was also believed that the emerging societies would create institutions that would undo past injustices and be concerned about preventing the development of new injustices. Skeptics, on the other hand, argued that the social and economic conditions require a process of transition that does not favor such noble improvement, and that the cultural and structural traditions of these societies are not favorable to the rule of law and market fairness, nor are they sympathetic to human rights.'[73]

Now it seems that defeatists were right. Ironically, those member states labelling themselves as illiberal are still highly relying on the benefits from the unique liberal value community that is committed to rule of law, democracy and human rights. In other words, the European Union is keeping to finance – on the basis of the mutual trust – these derogatory members as well. These governments gain from the deficiencies of European value protection system.

---

[73] András Sajó: Erosion and Decline of the Rule of Law in Post-communism: an Introduction, in András Sajó (ed.): *Out of and Into Authoritarian Law*, Kluwer Law International, the Hague, London, New York, 2003, x.

Still, the Union is not inactive: to strengthen the rule of law in the EU, the European Commission put forward a new EU framework in March 2014[74] that was inspired by the experiences of the Hungarian constitutional crisis among others. In doing so, the Commission aimed to more effectively address any situation where "there is a systemic threat to the rule of law" within any member state. The framework is designed to complement existing means of protecting the EU's rule of law. These include infringement procedures limited to a breach of a specific provision of EU law) pursuant to Article 258 of the Treaty on Functioning of the European Union (TFEU); and the "last resort" or "nuclear option"[75] preventive and sanctioning mechanisms provided for in Article 7 of the Treaty on European Union (TEU). The purpose of the framework is to enable the Commission to find a solution with the EU country concerned so as to prevent the emergence of a systemic threat to the rule of law.

However, this is a soft and careful political tool of persuasion just being tested on Poland. To preserve the rule of law and to prove a systemic threat to EU values of Article 2 TEU[76] an effective legal instrument seems to be necessary that goes beyond the limited infringement procedures. The systemic threat cannot proved by member state based investigations, because the country threatening the common European values will cautiously and preliminary undermine the domestic checks and balances.

---

[74] Communication from the Commission to the European Parliament and the Council, A new EU Framework to strengthen the Rule of Law, COM/2014/0158 final, 11 March 2014

[75] This exaggerated term was used by Manuel Barroso, former president of the European Commission. According to Armin von Bogdandy, this qualification was unwise and stuck. See Armin von BOGDANDY: How to protect European Values in the Polish Constitutional Crisis, http://verfassungsblog.de/how-to-protect-european-values-in-the-polish-constitutional-crisis/

[76] Article 2 TEU: "The Union is founded on the values of respect for human dignity, freedom, democracy, equality, the rule of law and respect for human rights, including the rights of persons belonging to minorities. These values are common to the member states in a society in which pluralism, non-discrimination, tolerance, justice, solidarity and equality between women and men prevail."

In my opinion, Article 7 procedures of the TEU should not be put aside being completely ineffective,[77] instead, they should be strengthened and underpinned with legal buttresses. And the European Union already has a legal means, first, its potencial accession to the ECHR, and second, the Charter of Fundamental Rights (Charter).[78] The respect of fundamental rights and freedom is equally important value as the rule of law, thus their protection should go hand in hand.

Article 6 of the Treaty on European Union (TEU) contains the fundamental rights standard of the Union, the three pillars of which are constituted by the Charter of Fundamental Rights, the European Convention for the Protection of Human Rights and Fundamental Freedoms[79] (hereinafter ECHR), and the recognition of fundamental rights as general principles of the Union's law. The fundamental rights standard is binding on both the institutions and member states of the Union. The definition of the pillars of fundamental rights protection of the EU is closely connected with the basic principles laid down in Article 2 TEU (especially with the requirements of democracy, the rule of law and respect for human dignity), the objectives set by Article 3 TEU and the democratic principles enumerated in Title II TEU. This definition is also interlinked with the accession criteria outlined in Article 49 TEU, as it serves as a clear-cut point of orientation for states wishing to accede. On the whole, it may be stated that Article 6 TEU gives expression to the "anthropocentric" dimension of the Union, restricts integrative power with regard to its content and vests the Union

---

[77] Balázs FEKETE and Veronika CZINA: Article 7 of the Treaty on European Union – is it really a nuclear weapon? http://hpops.tk.mta.hu/en/blog/2015/04/article-7-of-the-treaty-on-european-union

[78] András JAKAB: The EU Charter of Fundamental Rights as the Most Promising Way of Enforcing the Rule of Law against EU Member States, in C. CLOSA and D. KOCHENOV (eds.): *Reinforcing Rule of Law Oversight in the European Union,* Cambridge University Press, Cambridge, 2017, 187.

[79] Convention for the Protection of Human Rights and Fundamental Freedoms, Rome, 4 November 1950.

with the modern attributes of material and constitutional rule of law.

The entry into force of the Treaty of Lisbon (TL), on the one hand, satisfied the long-existing need of the integration to have – similarly to its member states – its own binding catalogue of fundamental rights. On the other hand, it authorized the Union – also similarly to its member states – to become involved as a party in the rights protection mechanism of the ECHR. The provisions contained in paragraphs (1) and (2) of Article 6 TEU appeared first in the Treaty establishing a Constitution for Europe,[80] which was adopted in 2004 but did not come into effect in the lack of ratification by some of the member states, these provisions were raised to the level of primary legislation only on the entry into force of the TL. At the same time, paragraph (3) of Article 6 does have its antecedents in primary legislation.

Paragraph (3) is aimed at laying down – at the level of basic principle – that human rights shall form part of the Union's law. Furthermore, it defines two factors that could serve as standards when defining the extent and content of human rights: the constitutional traditions common to the member states and the ECHR.

Article 6 (3) appears first – in a somewhat different formulation – in the Single European Act[81] (SEA) adopted in 1986, which, as regards its political and economic objectives, aimed to implement closer integration through the extensive transformation of the founding treaties. The Preamble to the SEA laid down member states' commitment to fundamental rights by declaring that: the Single European Act was created in order that member states may "work together to promote democracy on the basis of the fundamental rights recognized in the constitutions and laws of the Member States, in the Convention for the Protection of Human Rights and Fundamental Freedoms and the European Social Charter, notably freedom, equality and social justice". This text – in a similar formulation, but

[80] Treaty establishing a Constitution for Europe, OJ C 310, 16. 12. 2004, 1.

[81] Effective from 1 January 1987.

with extended content – became incorporated into the text of Point F of the Maastricht Treaty on European Union, then – renumbered but in the same formulation – into the Treaty of Amsterdam, while its newest formulation forms part of the Lisbon Treaty as well. The original text of the paragraph reads as follows: "The Union shall respect fundamental rights, as guaranteed by the European Convention for the Protection of Human Rights and Fundamental Freedoms signed in Rome on 4 November 1950 and as they result from the constitutional traditions common to the Member States, as general principles of Community law."

The Lisbon Treaty changed the above formulation only in one respect: instead of the expression "Community law" it uses the term "Union's law". This is explained by the fact that the European Union, vested with legal personality on the entry into force of the Lisbon Treaty, has replaced and is a legal successor to the European Community, therefore, the expression "Community law" applied earlier has given way to the term "Union law". However, an even more important change in content is that while on the basis of the earlier terminology the implementation of human rights was guaranteed only in the laws of the three European Communities (in other words, only in the former first pillar of the EU), the present formulation – due to the elimination of the earlier pillar system by the Lisbon Treaty – extends this guarantee to the whole of the Union's law (thus, to the areas of the former second and third pillars as well), that is to say, to all legal acts of the European Union.

Two points of comparison with regard to the genesis of Article 6 (3) are the constitutional traditions common to the member states and the provisions of the ECHR. Out of them, it was first the constitutional traditions of Member States, then later the provisions of the ECHR that infiltrated the case-law of the Court of Justice of the European Union (ECJ). The genesis of the paragraph dates back to the case-law accumulated by the ECJ in the 1960s. As the first milestone of the first range – the constitutional traditions common to the member states – one may mention the Stauder case,[82] where the concept of fundamental rights serving as general principles of Community law appeared. In this case the Court was to make a ruling on a decision of the Commission.[83] In accordance with the above-mentioned decision, member states were entitled to sell butter to certain beneficiaries at a reduced price under certain welfare schemes. In order to prevent fraud, the decision prescribed the presentation of certain documents including – in accordance with the German translation – a "coupon indicating the name" of those concerned. A beneficiary claimed that this requirement was in conflict with the provision of the German Basic Law relating to human dignity and challenged the decision before the German Administrative Court (Verwaltungsgericht Stuttgart). After all, the Court did not consider the case from the aspect of conflict between Community law and a fundamental right contained in the national constitution, but concluded that the Community legal rule had been erroneously translated and it was only the German version of the Commission decision that referred to the indication of the beneficiary's name, in other languages only reference to the identification of the person concerned was laid down. Therefore, in the Court's opinion, the Community regulation did not contain a provision capable of prejudicing the fundamental rights of persons. However, the judgment also stated that fundamental rights of persons formed part of the general principles of Community law, respect for which shall be guaranteed by the Court. The application of the common constitutional traditions of member states as general principles is given an even more striking expression in the opinion of the Advocate-General connected with the judgment.[84] In accordance with the opinion given by Advocate-General Roemer, "it is a view shared by numerous authors that general qualitative concepts of national

[82] Judgment of the Court of 12 November 1969 in Erich Stauder v Ville d'Ulm – Sozialamt. Case 29/69 [ECR (Collection of Supreme Court Decisions) 1969, 419].
[83] Commission Decision (69/71/EEC) of 12 February 1969.
[84] See Dirk EHLERS: *Fundamental Rights and Freedoms*, De Gruyter, Berlin, 2007, 12.

constitutional law, in particular fundamental rights recognized by national law, must be ascertained by means of a comparative evaluation of laws, and such concepts, which form an unwritten constituent part of Community law, must be observed in making secondary Community law."[85]

As a next step – still preceding the Solange-I decision of the German Constitutional Court, in the preliminary ruling procedure relating to the Internationale Handelsgesellschaft case[86] – the Court held that the protection of fundamental rights inspired by the constitutional traditions common to the member states must also be ensured within the framework of the structure and objectives of the Community. According to the basic facts of the Internationale Handelsgesellschaft case, a system of deposits was introduced by Community law with regard to the export of certain goods, in accordance with which if a licensee did not deliver the goods during the period of validity of the export licence, he would forfeit the deposit. The German Administrative Court held that the system of deposits ran counter to the principles of freedom of action and of disposition laid down by the German Basic Law, in its view, the Regulation of the Council and the Commission in question constituted excessive intervention in these freedoms. The Court held that the system of deposits was necessary for the proper calculability of export and import processes. Furthermore, the Court stated that the validity of measures adopted by the institutions of the Community can only be judged in the light of Community law; otherwise, the legal basis of the Community itself would be called in question. Despite the fact that the Court reiterated its statement made in the Stauder case (that fundamental rights formed part of the general legal principles of Community law), it pointed out that fundamental rights formulated by national law could not affect the validity of

[85] See Opinion of Advocate-General Roemer of 29 October 1969 in Erich Stauder v Ville d'Ulm – Sozialamt, Case 29/69 [ECR 1969, 419].

[86] Judgment of the Court of 17 December 1970 in Internationale Handelsgesellschaft mbH v Einfuhr- und Vorratstelle für Getreide und Futtermittel, Case 11/70 [ECR 1970, 1125].

Community law. At the same time, an examination should be made as to whether there exist any principles in Community law that are analogous to the national regulation in question, and protection of these rights should be derived from the constitutional traditions of the member state.

In connection with the maximum standard and regard for the constitution of a specific member state, mention should be made of the Hauer case.[87] In Hauer the Court made a decision within the framework of a preliminary ruling procedure concerning the Council Regulation regulating wine production. Under the regulation, national authorities were prohibited from granting authorization for new planting of vines on plots of land suitable for vine-growing. The claimant in the original case argued that the Community measure infringed the right to property and the freedom to pursue a trade or profession guaranteed by the German Basic Law as it restricted them disproportionately. The Court reiterated its position expounded in its previous judgments that fundamental rights form an integral part of the general principles of the law, the observance of which is ensured by the court. In safeguarding those rights, the latter is bound to draw inspiration from the constitutional traditions common to the member states, so that measures which are incompatible with fundamental rights recognized by the constitutions of those states are unacceptable in the Community. It further confirmed that the court shall have regard to international treaties for the protection of human rights. At the same time it explained that the introduction of special criteria for assessment stemming from the legislation or constitutional law of a particular member state would, by damaging the substantive unity and efficacy of Community law, lead inevitably to the destruction of the unity of the common market and the jeopardizing of the cohesion of the Community.[88]

---

[87] Judgment of the Court of 13 December 1979 in Liselotte Hauer v Land Rheinland-Pfalz, Case 44/79 [ECR 1979, 3727].

[88] A further example for defining standards and rejecting national constitutions is the Grogan case (Judgment of the Court of 4 October 1991 in The Society for the Protection of Unborn Children Ireland Ltd v Stephen Grogan and others,

With regard to the other train of legal development – the ECHR – the Court primarily pointed out that in safeguarding fundamental rights, the Court must have regard to international treaties for the protection of human rights on which the member states have collaborated or of which they are signatories. Thus it defined the second most important source in respect of the fundamental rights of the Community. This significant rule was laid down in the judgment in the Nold case.[89] This judgment was passed within the framework of proceedings taken by a wholesale dealer in coal for the annulment of a Commission decision,[90] in which the applicant complained that the decision imposed unfavourably discriminatory conditions on him and violated his right to enterprise. In its judgment the Court expounded, on the one hand, that besides the constitutional traditions common to the member states, international treaties for the protection of human rights – on which the member states have collaborated – can also supply guidelines which should be followed within the framework of protection of fundamental rights under Community law. On the other hand, it stressed that "the Court [...] cannot therefore uphold measures which are incompatible with fundamental rights recognized and protected by the Constitutions of those States".[91] This careful formulation gained more strength later on and expanded most vigorously in the direction of the ECHR. As a matter of course, in its judgment passed in the Rutili case,[92] the Court expressly and specifically referred to the ECHR in the range of international treaties. By today, the recognition of inter-

C-159/90 [ECR 1991, I-4685]). For more detail, see Joseph Weiler: Fundamental Rights and Fundamental Boundaries: on Standards and Values in the Protection of Human Rights, in Nanette A. Neuwahl and Allan Rosas (eds.): *The European Union and Human Rights*, Martinus Nijhoff, The Hague, Boston, London, 1995, 56–60.

89 Judgment of the Court of 14 May 1974 in Nold, Kohlen- und Baustoffgroßhandlung v Commission of the European Communities, Case 4/73 [ECR 1974, 491].

90 73/94/ECSC: Commission Decision of 21 December 1972 authorizing new terms of business of Ruhrkohle AG (OJ L 120, 7. 5. 1973, 14)

91 Ibid. Point 13

92 Judgment of the Court of 28 October 1975 in Roland Rutili v Ministre de l'intérieur, Case 36/75 [ECR 1975, 1219].

national treaties has acquired the meaning of having extensive regard for the jurisprudence of the European Court of Human Rights and adopting certain interpretational frameworks.[93] The content and formulation of the Article is significant also because it becomes obvious on comparison with a review of case-law that it implements the codification of the case-law of the Court of Justice of the European Union.[94]

1 Integration of European human rights standard – the accession of EU to the ECHR

Article 6 of the Treaty on European Union (TEU) contains the fundamental rights standard of the Union, the three pillars of this standard are the Charter of Fundamental Rights, the European Convention for the Protection of Human Rights and Fundamental Freedoms (ECHR), and the recognition of fundamental rights as the general principle of Union law. The definition of the pillars of human rights protection of the EU is closely connected with the basic principles laid down in Article 2 of the TEU (especially with the requirements of democracy, rule of law and respect for human dignity), the objectives defined by Article 3 of the TEU and the democratic principles enumerated in Title II of the TEU. This definition is also interlinked with the accession criteria outlined in Article 49 of the TEU, as they serve as unambiguous points of orientation for states wishing to accede. On the whole it may be stated that Article 6 of the TEU gives expression to an "antropo-centric" dimension of the Union, restricts integrative power with regard to its content and vests the Union with the modern attributes of material and constitutional rule of law.

From the aspect of the development of the human rights standard, the accession of the Union to the ECHR is of great significance, as

---

[93] See EHLERS 'Fundamental Rights' 12.

[94] See more in Márton VARJU: *European Union human rights law,* Edward Elgar Publishing, Cheltenham, 2014.

it realizes the integration of human rights protection in Europe. The accession is inevitable, because the Treaty on European Union in its Article 6 para. (2) stipulates the obligation (not just the possibility) for the Union to access.

1.1 Antecedents of accession

1.1.1 The relationship between the case-law of the Strasbourg and Luxembourg courts

In the display of interaction between the ECHR and the human rights protection of the Union – both during the initial steps and at present - the case-law of the ECJ and the ECtHR have played a significant role. Alongside the parallels between the judgments of the two courts, tensions may also arise between them, as it is of importance which court can exert a greater influence on the case-law of the other.[95]

With regard to the two types of case-law, the ECJ was the first to take steps in the direction of having regard to the ECtHR with its longer past and considering it more and more the source of the "general principles of Community law" contained in the TEU.[96] The approximation of the ECJ to the ECHR can be traced by providing

---

[95] BLUTMAN László: *Az Európai Unió joga a gyakorlatban*, HVG-ORAC, Budapest, 2010, 478–479. See also CHRONOWSKI Nóra, DRINÓCZI Tímea, KOCSIS Miklós, ZELLER Judit: 6. cikk, in OSZTOVITS András (ed.): *Az Európai Unióról és az Európai Unió működéséről szóló szerződések magyarázata 1*, Complex, Budapest, 2011, 46–78.

[96] Cf. Johan CALLEWAERT: Unionisation vs. conventionisation. The Relationship between EU Law and the European Convention on Human Rights and its Impact on the Domestic Legal System of the EU Member States, in Conference on the Europeanisation of Public International Law: The Status of International Law in the EU and its Member States, Universiteit van Amsterdam, 2005 September 2, Collection of Documents, 42., SZALAYNÉ SÁNDOR Erzsébet: Konvergenz der Grundrechte und Grundfreiheiten in der Europäischen Union, in CHRONOWSKI Nóra (ed.): *Adamante Notare – Essays in Honour of Antal Ádám on the Occasion of His 75th Birthday*, PTE ÁJK, Pécs, 2005, 533.

an overview of a number of cases. In the Carpenter case[97] the ECJ, interpreting Community law expressly in the context of Article 8 of the ECHR, established the plaintiff's right to respect for family life. As a further example one may cite the Connolly case,[98] concerning which the ECJ defined the scope of Community level protection of the freedom of expression with reference to Article 10 of the ECHR and the case-law of the ECtHR.[99] On the other hand, one may also find examples where the ECJ has left it for the national court to apply or adopt European Union law within the frames provided by the ECHR. Such examples include the Pupino case,[100] which is also worth mentioning because the ECJ came to interesting conclusions about which legal documents were binding on member states in the spirit of loyalty to the Community (now the obligation of sincere cooperation contained in Article 4 para (3) of the TEU).[101] The case of *Pupino* illustrated that the Court of Justice continues to adhere closely to Strasbourg case-law even in the new areas of European Union law covered by the former "third pillar" (Justice and Home Affairs).

Based on the above-mentioned cases one may draw the conclusion that the ECJ has followed the case-law of the ECtHR,[102] and concerning the definition of the content of fundamental rights of the Community (now European Union) it has attributed "special significance" to the ECHR.[103] However, it should also be noted that,

[97] C-60/00. Mary Carpenter v Secretary of State for the Home Department, Judgment of the Court of 11 July 2002 [ECR 2002, I-6279]

[98] C-274/99. Bernard Connolly v Commission of the European Communities, Judgment of the Court of 6 March 2001 [ECR 2001, I-1575]

[99] Szalayné 'Konvergenz' 533–534.

[100] C-105/03. Criminal proceedings against Maria Pupino, Judgment of the Court (Grand Chamber) of 16 June 2005 [ECR 2005, I-5285]

[101] Nikolaos Lavranos: UN Sanctions and Judicial Review, in Jan Wouters, André Nollkaemper and Erika de Wet (eds.): *The Europeanisation of International Law, The Status of International Law in the EU and its Member States,* T.M.C. Asser Press, The Hague, 2008, 201.

[102] Blutman 'Az Európai Unió joga' 479.

[103] Thus ECJ accorded special significance to the Convention amongst international human rights treaties in Hauer case decided in 1979. See 44/79. Liselotte

although by the general principle of human rights protection the ECJ has recognized the rights guaranteed by the ECHR and the fact that the ECHR also forms part of the traditions of the member states, it has never declared that it would be bound by the ECHR or the case-law of the ECtHR before the accession.[104]

In connection with this, the question soon arose as to whether the rights guaranteed by the ECHR could be given the *same interpretation* in the context of European Union law as in the context of international law. A difference in interpretation could not be considered lucky for several reasons. On the one hand, it would not be advantageous from a theoretical aspect, since in this case the content of rights and the scope of their protection would differ merely because of accidental circumstances (e.g. in the case of business undertakings operating in the same state, the prohibition of cartels would be governed by the international law interpretation of the ECHR, while in the case of undertakings functioning in different states, the Union law interpretation would be applicable). On the other hand, there are also practical arguments in favour of parallelism in so far as it would mean a much clearer situation concerning human rights if they were interpreted in one single way.[105]

Judgments based on differing interpretations have resulted from, for instance, Article 6 of the ECHR, which lays down the guarantees of court procedures within the framework of the right to a fair trial. While in the Orkem case[106] the ECJ did not regard the "right to silence"[107] an element of guarantee, the ECtHR treated it as an in-

Hauer v Land Rheinland-Pfalz, Judgment of the Court of 13 December 1979 [ECR 1979, 3727]. This has been its consistent position since then. See e.g. C-94/00. Roquette Frères SA v Directeur général de la concurrence, de la consommation et de la répression des fraudes, and Commission of the European Communities, Judgment of the Court of 22 October 2002 [ECR 2002, I-9011] point 25.

104 Carl Lebeck: The European Court of Human Rights on the relation between ECHR and EC-law: the limits of constitutionalisation of public international law, *Zeitschrift für öffentliches Recht* Vol. 62, 2007, 207.

105 Callewaert 'Unionisation' 44.

106 374/87. Orkem v Commission of the European Communities, Judgment of the Court of 18 October 1989 [ECR 1989, 3283.]

107 No one may be compelled to give evidence against himself.

tegral part of Article 6.[108] In this instance the ECJ subsequently reviewed its own case-law, approximating it to the interpretational frames of the ECtHR, therefore, the interpretational practice of the Strasbourg Court has an impact on Union law. Several judgments of the CJEU – cf. Roquette Fréres case,[109] Booker Aquacultur case[110] – show that the CJEU emphatically did not deviate from the interpretation given by the ECtHR because of the "special significance" attributed to it.[111]

The steps taken by the CJEU have been answered by the ECtHR too, since in several cases one may observe the approximation of the ECtHR to the case-law of the CJEU and the approximation of the ECHR to the Charter. One may cite as an example the Goodwin case[112], concerning which the ECtHR ensured a greater degree of protection to the marriage of transsexuals than contained in Article 12 of the ECHR with express reference to Article 9 of the Charter.[113] Mention should also be made of the Pellegrin case,[114] concerning which the ECtHR interpreted the right to a fair process citing the case-law of the Court of Justice.[115] Article 12 of the ECHR on the prohibition of discrimination is another example relating to law-making, which was clearly affected by the ongoing preparations for the Charter.[116]

In connection with the above, the essential question arises as to what extent the human rights jurisdiction of the ECtHR can be

---

108 Cf. *Funke v. France* Judgment of 25 February 1993 Series A no. 256

109 C-94/00. Roquette Frères SA v Directeur général de la concurrence, de la consommation et de la répression des fraudes, and Commission of the European Communities, Judgment of the Court of 22 October 2002 [ECR 2002, I-9011]

110 C-20/00. and C-64/00. Booker Aquacultur Ltd (C-20/00.) and Hydro Seafood GSP Ltd (C-64/00.) v The Scottish Ministers joint cases, Judgment of the Court of 10 July 2003 [ECR 2003, I-7411]

111 See more in Blutman 'Az Európai Unió joga' 478–479.

112 *Goodwin v. United Kingdom* [GC], no. *28957/95*, ECHR 2002-VI.

113 By doing so, the ECtHR was the first European court referring specifically to the provisions of the Charter. See Callewaert 'Unionisation' 49-50.

114 *Pellegrin v. France* [GC], no. 28541/95, ECHR 1999-VIII

115 Szalayné 'Konvergenz' 533.

116 Callewaert 'Unionisation' 50.

recognized over Union legislation prior to the Union's accession to the ECHR. Since the end of the 1990s several cases have arisen which show readiness on the part of the ECtHR to scrutinize Union law applying the standard of the ECHR. Such cases include the Matthews case[117] and the Cantoni case[118] as well as the Bosphorus case.[119] Concerning the latter the ECtHR affirmed the scrutiny of Union law from the point of view of human rights; at the same time, it also admitted that it applied the ECHR as a standard with respect to Union law only insofar as there were deficiencies in the Union's own provisions or practice relating to human rights protection. Having regard to this latter decision, if drawing a parallel, one may speak of a "Solange"-type decision on the part of the ECtHR, as it steps up as a protector of human rights only if the protection provided by Union law is insufficient.[120]

In the Bosphorus case the ECtHR reiterated that states participating in the ECHR were entitled to transfer specific powers falling within the scope of their sovereignty to international and supranational organizations. The supranational organization on which the power has been conferred is not accountable under the ECHR until it also becomes a party to it.[121] Under Article 1 of the ECHR, a contracting party is accountable for all acts and omissions of its responsible organs, regardless of whether the act or omission in question occurred based on the party's national law or because of the need to comply with its international obligations. The ECtHR has pointed out that the exemption of contracting parties from responsibility as a result of the transfer of competences in the areas concerned

---

[117] 24833/94. *Matthews v. United Kingdom* Reports 1999-I. See also case of *Senator Lines GmbH v. The 15 Member States of the European Union,* Admissibility Decision of 10 March 2004 no. 56672/00

[118] *Cantoni v. France* Judgment of 15 November *1996* no. 17862/91, Reports 1996, 1617.

[119] *Bosphorus Hava Yollari Turizm Ve Ticared Antonim Sirketi v. Ireland* [GC], no.45036/98, ECHR 2005-IV.

[120] Lavranos 'UN Sanctions' 202.

[121] *Bosphorus Hava Yollari Turizm Ve Ticared Antonim Sirketi v. Ireland* [GC], no.45036/98, ECHR 2005-IV. 152., see also *Matthews v. the United Kingdom* [GC], no. 24833/94, ECHR 1999-I. 32.

would be incompatible with the aim and subject-matter of the Convention, because it would endanger the application and effectiveness of the guarantees contained in the ECHR.[122] "In the Court's view, State action taken in compliance with such legal obligations is justified as long as the relevant organisation [EC/EU] is considered to protect fundamental rights, as regards both the substantive guarantees offered and the mechanisms controlling their observance, in a manner which can be considered at least equivalent to that for which the Convention provides [...]. By »equivalent« the Court means »comparable«: any requirement that the organisation's protection be »identical« could run counter to the interest of international co-operation pursued [...]. However, any such finding of equivalence could not be final and would be susceptible to review in the light of any relevant change in fundamental rights' protection. If such equivalent protection is considered to be provided by the [international or supranational] organisation, the presumption will be that a State has not departed from the requirements of the Convention when it does no more than implement legal obligations flowing from its membership of the organisation. However, any such presumption can be rebutted if, in the circumstances of a particular case, it is considered that the protection of Convention rights was manifestly deficient. In such cases, the interest of international co-operation would be outweighed by the Convention's role as a »constitutional instrument of European public order« in the field of human rights [...]."[123]

Concerning the case the ECtHR reviewed the development of fundamental rights protection by the Community (now Union), its substantive legal guarantees and the applicability of the Community (Union) control mechanism from the aspect of the protection of individual rights. In consideration of all of the above, the ECtHR found, that "the protection of fundamental rights by EC law can be

[122] Bosphorus ibid. 153.
[123] Bosphorus ibid. 155–156.

considered to be, and to have been at the relevant time, »equivalent« [...] to that of the Convention system."[124]

In summary, it may be stated that the relationship between the two Courts in the field of human rights protection was characterised by close cooperation even before the accession. The ECJ conceded that the ECtHR shall have the final say concerning the interpretation of human rights laid down by the ECHR. At the same time, the ECtHR established the presumption (subject to rebuttal in individual cases) that the level of protection provided to fundamental rights by Union law could be considered equivalent to the level of protection ensured by the ECHR.[125]

1.1.2 *The development of primary legal foundations*

The accession has been discussed in Europe since 1979, when the European Commission first presented a memorandum on the accession of the EC to the ECHR.[126] In 1982 and in 1985 the European Parliament asked the Commission to start formal negotiations on the accession. On neither occasion however did the Commission receive the support of all the EC Members to do so, that is why finally submitted a formal proposal to the Council in 1990. The Council asked the Court of Justice to give its opinion[127] on whether accession was in conformity with the Treaty on the European Community. In 1996 the Court found that the European Community lacked authority to join the ECHR.[128]

---

[124] Bosphorus ibid. 165.

[125] Egbert MYJER: Csatlakozhat-e az Európai Unió az Emberi jogok és alapvető szabadságok védelméről szóló Európa Tanács-i Egyezményhez? *Magyar Jog* № 3, 2007, 174.

[126] European Commission – Memorandum on the accession of the European Communities to the European Convention for the Protection of Human Rights and Fundamental Freedoms (4 April 1979), Bulletin of the European Communities, Supplement 2/79.

[127] See TFEU Art. 218(11) [TEC Art. 300(6)].

[128] Opinion 2/94 of the Court on Accession by the Community to the European Convention for the Protection of Human Rights and Fundamental Freedoms (28

The ECJ ruled, that

> principle of conferred powers must be respected in both the internal action and the international action of the Community. [...] No Treaty provision confers on the Community institutions any general power to enact rules on human rights or to conclude international conventions in this field. [...] Accession to the Convention would [...] entail a substantial change in the [...] Community system for the protection of human rights in that it would entail the entry of the Community into a distinct international institutional system as well as integration of all the provisions of the Convention into the Community legal order. Such a modification of the system for the protection of human rights in the Community, with equally fundamental institutional implications for the Community and for the Member States, would be of constitutional significance and would therefore be such as to go beyond the scope of Article 235. It could be brought about only by way of Treaty amendment.[129]

The consequences of the EC becoming a member of another international organization were presumably regarded as problematic by the Court of Justice; therefore, it ruled that Article 235 of the TEC [later Article 308, now Article 352 of the TFEU] did not constitute a suitable legal basis for accession.[130]

Then it was more than half a decade later, during the process of Union constitution-making, that the Working Group of the European Convention (February 2002- July 2003) in charge of matters relating to fundamental rights formulated the idea that the Convention should make a political decision on the need to accede. The main political and legal arguments in favour of accession – also debated during European constitution-making – included the following:

(1) As the Union reaffirms its own values through its Charter, its accession to the ECHR would give a strong political signal of the coherence between the Union and the European human rights system taken in a wider sense. (2) Accession to the ECHR would

March 1996) [ECR 1996, I-1759]

[129] Opinion 2/94 of the Court on Accession by the Community to the European Convention for the Protection of Human Rights and Fundamental Freedoms (28 March 1996) [ECR 1996, I-1759] points 24, 27, 34. and 35.

[130] Blutman 'Az Európai Unió joga' 484.

give citizens an analogous protection vis-à-vis acts of the Union as they presently enjoy vis-à-vis all the member states, which is particularly justified by the fact that member states have transferred substantial competences to the Union. (3) Accession would be the ideal tool to ensure a harmonious development of the case law of the Strasbourg and Luxembourg Courts in human rights matters.[131] It would not affect the autonomy of Community (or Union) law or the authority of the European Court of Justice, nor would it lead to hierarchical relations between the two Courts, since the Luxembourg Court would remain the sole supreme arbiter of questions relating to the Community (Union) legal order and the ECtHR, as a specialised court, would exercise some type of external control over the international law obligations of the Union resulting from accession to the ECHR. Consequently, the position of the Court of Justice would be analogous to that of national constitutional or supreme courts in relation to the Strasbourg Court at present. However, when analysing the relationship between the two courts, the question of hierarchical relations between the CJEU and ECtHR cannot be avoided. This is so because if Union citizens are not granted the required rights protection in proceedings before the CJEU – similarly to the situation when they are not granted adequate rights protection by their member states – nothing will prevent them from having recourse to the Strasbourg Court with reference to the ECHR. Since the Union would be bound by the ECHR, the interpretation of the ECtHR would also be binding on it. All this would eventually result in the human rights case-law of the ECtHR taking precedence over the respective case-law of the CJEU; therefore, a process of unification would be likely to take place in European human rights protection. Naturally, homogenization would have positive

---

[131] Callewaert emphasized relate to harmony, that the effectiveness of fundamental rights must not be reduced by needlessly increasing the plurality and relativism of their definition and content. Legal uncertainty is incompatible with the notion of fundamental rights. Johan Callewaert: The European Convention on Human Rights and European Union Law: A Long Way to Harmony, *European Human Rights Law Review* № 6, 2009, 783.

effects on human rights protection, at the same time, it would eliminate from human rights jurisdiction the phenomenon best described as "integration sensitivity", which has always characterised the jurisprudence of the CJEU. During the interpretation of fundamental rights, the ECtHR would not be able to have regard to the Union's current objectives and structure (which are – conspicuously – accorded a significant role in the practice of the CJEU) or the degree of integration, since the very same human rights standard should be applicable to the Union and other contracting states of the ECHR. However, all these problems could be solved by the provision of the Charter referring to interpretation in conformity with the ECHR, which allows derogation from the requirement of identical content and scope of fundamental rights only in a positive direction: only insofar as the Union *acquis* guarantees a higher level of protection. (4) Beyond the direct relationship, the Union will also be able to appear as a party in proceedings conducted before the ECtHR in Strasbourg in cases indirectly connected with Community (or Union) law, in other words, in connection with member states' compliance with their obligations relating to the Community (Union).

On the other hand, the problem was also raised that the opening of the Strasbourg Court would have two practical-technical drawbacks: the prolongation of proceedings and the excessive workload of the ECtHR. As a result of the fall of the Iron Curtain, which opened up the possibility of legal remedy to the citizens of former Communist states as well, the Strasbourg Court has clearly come close to the limits of its capacity. The possibility of referring Union proceedings to the ECtHR would render the situation even more complicated.[132] In spite of all this – in view of the long past the ECtHR can look back on in matters relating to the protection and interpretation of fundamental rights – Strasbourg could make a significant contribution to the Union's system of fundamental rights protection and connect it into the European system.

[132] Edgar Stieglitz: *Allgemeine Lehren im Grundrechtsverständnis nach der EMRK und der Grundrechtsjudikatur des EuGH*, Nomos Verlagsgesellschaft, Baden-Baden, 2002, 227.

In consideration of all of the above, on the recommendation of the Convention, the *EU Constitution* also laid down the *authorisation* enabling the Union to accede to the ECHR.[133] As a result, at the time of signing the EU Constitution in 2004, it became clear that because all member states of the Union were parties to the ECHR, accession – alongside the recognition of the legally binding force of the Charter – would be the most obvious possibility to improve human rights protection.

1.1.3 *Preparation by the Council of Europe for the EU's accession*

Right from the beginning it was clear that the actual realization of accession was a political issue falling within the competence of the Council of Europe and it required unanimity with regard to the conditions and reservations. In order to accomplish it, the ECHR itself had to be amended because in accordance with its provisions only states were allowed to accede to it. At the time of the creation of the ECHR there were no prospects of the participation of a supranational organization.

The Steering Committee for Human Rights of the CE, (hereinafter referred to as CDDH) summarized the legal and technical questions of EC/EU accession in a study as early as 2002.[134] The Committee expressly refrained from taking a political position on the accession and also avoided the examination of questions falling within the decision-making competence of the EC/EU. The study distinguished between three levels of provisions to be amended: (a) amendments to the text of provisions already contained in the

133 Treaty Establishing the Constitution for the Eurpean Union Art. I-9(2) and Protocol 32.

134 Study of technical and legal issues of a possible EC/EU accession to the European Convention on Human Rights. Report adopted by the Steering Committee for Human Rights (CDDH) at its 53rd meeting (25-28 June 2002) DG-II(2002)006 [CDDH(2002)010 Addendum 2]

ECHR and its additional Protocols, (b) supplementary provisions, the interpretation or content of which would change (e.g. national or citizen), and (c) any technical and administrative changes not pertaining to the text of the Convention (such as the budgetary contribution of the EC/EU). Apart from the above, the study also made mention of the ancillary agreements that would be affected by the accession (e.g. the European Agreement relating to Persons Participating in Proceedings of the European Court of Human Rights and the Sixth Protocol to the General Agreement on Privileges and Immunities of the Council of Europe.)[135] The questions of a new additional protocol to be attached to the ECHR and of an accession treaty to be concluded between the EC/EU and the CE member states were still regarded as alternatives by the CDDH study. The Committee would have preferred the latter with a view to avoiding the lengthiness of the double procedure and ratification. (However, bearing in mind the excessive workload of the ECtHR and the need for procedural reform, it subsequently realized that adopting a new additional protocol would be inevitable.) In 2002 it was still uncertain whether the EC or the EU would accede to the ECHR, therefore, the study reckoned with both possibilities, at the same time, it made a reference to the Laeken Declaration, which, at the time of the definition of the mandate of the European Convention, provided for the establishment of the EU as a legal person in international law. In other words, during the preparatory process the CE tried to comment continuously on the trends of development of the EU and of human rights protection in the Union.

From the point of view of the modification of the text of the ECHR the primary question was Article 59, which enabled only states to ratify the Convention. Furthermore, provisions of the ECHR referring to a state or states also needed to be changed.[136] It also had to be clarified in what way the EC/EU was to participate in the Committee of Ministers supervising the enforcement of the judgments

[135] DG-II(2002)006 [CDDH(2002)010 Addendum 2] Chapter I point I. 2-3.

[136] ECHR Arts. 10(1), 11(2), 17, 27(2)-(3), 38(1.a), 56(1) and (4), 57(1)

of the ECtHR.[137] A question of even greater significance was that after the accession, apart from the possibility of the EC/EU being sued independently before the ECtHR, based on what procedure the EC/EU should intervene in proceedings taken against its member state(s), and how the EC/EU could later become involved as co-defendant in the proceedings of the ECtHR. As for inter-state affairs (Article 33 of the ECHR), the question arose as to whether this procedure could be resorted to for the purpose of enforcing Article 7 of the TEU (namely, where a member state has seriously infringed the principles of democracy, rule of law, liberty or respect for human rights and fundamental freedoms). According to the study, in the final analysis, this decision depends on the agreement reached between the EC/EU and its member states.[138] Finally, mention should be made of the fact that the CDDH study considered it desirable to set up the office of a Strasbourg judge representing the EC/EU, because it would be advantageous from the point of view of equal representation of each legal system and legitimacy of decisions. In consideration of the above reasons, it is not possible to support the theoretical counter-argument claiming that there would be no need for a judge elected in respect of the EC/EU as there were judges on the Court elected in respect of each of the member states. Similarly, ad hoc participation by the EC/EU in the work of the Strasbourg Court does not seem a good solution either (ad hoc EC/EU judge), regarding the fact that a) it would have to be decided for each case whether it involved Community law or not, which may cause difficulties in practice, b) ad hoc appointments would complicate the Court's procedure and they would be an extra burden for the Court, c) as ad hoc judges are not elected by the Parliamentary Assembly, there would be a problem of legitimacy with respect to the EC/EU judge. The CDDH also thought that consideration should also be given to the question of whether it would be necessary to introduce a special procedure under which the ECJ

---

137 DG-II(2002)006 [CDDH(2002)010 Addendum 2] Chapter II part A)

138 DG-II(2002)006 [CDDH(2002)010 Addendum 2] Chapter II part B)

would be authorised to request a preliminary ruling on the interpretation of the ECHR from the European Court of Human Rights. An advantage of this would be that it would assist in avoiding divergences in case-law. On the other hand, it would have the disadvantage of creating an imbalance between the EC/EU and the other Contracting Parties to the Convention, the supreme courts of which would not be able to benefit from a system of references, furthermore – and this is an even more powerful counter-argument – it would lead to a prolongation of the proceedings.[139]

Based on the preparatory work of the CDDH, the Committee of Ministers of the EC adopted numerous measures in order to ensure the effective implementation of the ECHR both at the national and European levels. Protocol № 14 of the ECHR was prepared within this framework. It inserted a new paragraph 2 in Article 59 of the Convention stating that the European Union was allowed to accede to the Convention. This concise "opening clause" became included in the ECHR through Protocol № 14 with a view to the draft Constitution of the EU in response to the "enabling authorisation" formulated by the European Convention. However, "opening up" the ECHR to the EU is only the starting point of the accession process. In order to achieve this aim, there is a need to further modify the ECHR and to sign an accession treaty with the EU. At the time of the formulation of Protocol № 14 it was still not possible to conduct talks on questions of detail relating to the accession, since the EU had no authority to do so.[140] Due to the failure to ratify the Constitution of the EU, the elaboration and adoption of the Luxembourg Treaty and the prolonged ratification of Protocol № 14 of the ECHR (as a result of which it entered into force only on 1 June 2010), the CDDH was not able to continue work relating to the preparation of the accession until 2010. Accession talks began on 15 March 2011.

[139] DG-II(2002)006 [CDDH(2002)010 Addendum 2] Chapter II part C)

[140] Myjer 'Csatlakozhat-e' 170–171.

1.2 The legal basis of the accession

EU accession to the ECHR had two conditions in public international law. One was the authorisation of the EU enabling it to accede to the Convention, in other words, ensuring a legal basis for this in the founding treaty, which in turn was preconditioned on the EU being a legal person in international law [The last sentence of paragraph 3 of Article 1 of the TEU states: "The Union shall replace and succeed the European Community."] Article 6 of the Constitution of the European Union explicitly laid down the EU's legal personality and the Lisbon Treaty adopted this solution: Article 47 of the TEU declares that the Union shall have legal personality.

In accordance with para 2 of Article 6 of the TEU, the EU, being a legal person, may accede to the ECHR, so, the authorisation does not enable it to become a member of the Council of Europe. This one-sided authorisation imposes an obligation on the Union and its institutions; at the same time, it does not enable the ECtHR to check on the decisions of the ECJ, since this will become possible only following the formal accession.[141] The conditions pertaining to the accession are specified in the Protocol (№ 8) attached to the Lisbon Treaty.

The other condition was the amendment of the ECHR in order to enable the EU to accede to it, since under the original version only states could become parties to the ECHR. This obstacle was removed by Protocol № 14 of the ECHR, which entered into force on 1 June 2010. In addition, Protocol № 14 also carries out the reform of the ECtHR, which, in spite of not being a comprehensive reform, renders the control mechanism sustainable in the medium run.[142]

---

[141] Rainer Arnold: Fundamental Rights in the European Union, in Nadiezda Siskova (ed.): *The Process of Constitutionalisation of the EU and Related Issues*, Europa Law Publishing, Amsterdam, Groningen, 2008, 37.

[142] On the reform see Szalayné Sándor Erzsébet: Új távlatok az európai alapjogvédelemben, Hatályba lépett az Egyezmény 14. Kiegészítő Jegyzőkönyve, *Közjogi Szemle* № 3, 2010, 33.

1.2.1 The accession process

In accordance with Article 1 of Protocol № 8 attached to the Lisbon Treaty,[143] the agreement relating to the accession of the Union to the ECHR provided for in Article 6(2) of the Treaty on European Union shall make provision for preserving the specific characteristics of the Union and Union law, in particular with regard to: (a) the specific arrangements for the Union's possible participation in the control bodies of the European Convention; (b) the mechanisms necessary to ensure that proceedings by non-member states and that individual applications are correctly addressed to member states and/or the Union as appropriate.

According to Articles 2-3 of the Protocol, the agreement shall ensure that accession of the Union shall not affect the competences of the Union or the powers of its institutions. Furthermore, it shall ensure that nothing contained in the agreement affects the situation of member states in relation to the European Convention, in particular in relation to the Protocols attached to it, measures taken by member states derogating from the European Convention in accordance with Article 15 of the Convention and reservations to the European Convention made by member states in accordance with Article 57 of the Convention. None of the provisions mentioned in Article 1 affect Article 344 of the Treaty on the Functioning of European Union, under which EU member states undertake not to submit a dispute concerning the interpretation or application of the Treaties to any method of settlement other than those provided for in the Treaties. Consequently, it is not possible to resort to Article 33 of the ECHR pertaining to inter-state affairs.

The above were confirmed by member states in the Declaration on Article 6(2) of the Treaty on European Union.[144] The declaration states: "The Conference agrees that the Union's accession to the

143 Protocol (№ 8) Relating to Article 6(2) of the Treaty on European Union on the Accession of the Union to the European Convention on the Protection of Human Rights and Fundamental Freedoms.

144 Declaration 2 on Article 6(2) of the Treaty on European Union

European Convention for the Protection of Human Rights and Fundamental Freedoms should be arranged in such a way as to preserve the specific features of Union law. In this connection, the Conference notes the existence of a regular dialogue between the Court of Justice of the European Union and the European Court of Human Rights; such dialogue could be reinforced when the Union accedes to that Convention."

On 7 July 2010, official talks began between the European Commission and the Council of Europe on the European Union's accession to the European Convention for the Protection of Human Rights and Fundamental Freedoms. The negotiators of the European Commission and the members of the ad hoc Working Group of the Steering Committee for Human Rights of the Council of Europe (CDDH-UE) have conducted regular talks since 7 July 2010 in order to elaborate the accession treaty. The Committee of Ministers of the Council of Europe has appointed 30 June 2011 as the final date for concluding talks.[145]

Theoretical and technical questions to be clarified during the accession process – on the basis of Protocol № 8, Declaration № 2 and the CDDH study of 2002 – include which Protocols of the Convention the EU is going to join, in what form the EU will participate in the organs of the Council of Europe, what will characterize the relationship between the ECJ and the ECtHR, the basic principle of which is co-ordination. The specific features of Union law must be preserved, and dialogue and cooperation must prevail in legislation and the application of law. Furthermore, it must be ensured that accession would not affect the relationship of member states to the ECHR, the competences of the European Union and in particular, the ECJ's exclusive jurisdiction to interpret EU law and also that, if necessary, both the EU and the member state would be enabled to appear as parties before the ECtHR (co-defendants, joinder of parties).[146]

---

145 Szalayné 'Új távlatok' 36., 39. On the deadline see also the document of CDDH № (2010)008. on 3 June 2010.

146 See more Szalayné 'Új távlatok' 36–37.

After the end of this process the accession treaty shall be signed by the 47 Contracting States of the ECHR and the EU and it will be ratified by the member states of the Council of Europe (including EU member states) in accordance with Article 59 (1) of the Convention.

In accordance with the second subparagraph of Article 218 (8) of the Treaty on the Functioning of the European Union, the Union's accession to the ECHR requires a unanimous decision of the Council and the consent of the European Parliament [Point a) ii of Article 218 (6)]. The decision concluding this agreement shall enter into force after it has been approved by the member states in accordance with their respective constitutional requirements [second subparagraph of Article 218 (8)].[147]

1.2.2 *The position taken by the CJEU and the ECtHR concerning accession*

During the process of direct preparations for the accession, the CJEU emphasized the following.[148] The accession of the EU, being a regional integration organization, may take place in special circumstances that are different from the conditions laid down for the accession of states. In accordance with Article 6 of the TEU, accession cannot extend the competences of the Union, and having regard to Protocol № 8, which has a binding force equivalent to that of the Treaties, the accession treaty must provide for preserving the special features of the Union and Union law. A special feature of the Union and its legal order is that, as a general rule, it affects individuals only through interposed national means of implementa-

[147] SZALAYNÉ 'Új távlatok' 39.

[148] Discussion document of the Court of Justice of the European Union on certain aspects of the accession of the European Union to the European Convention for the Protection of Human Rights and Fundamental Freedoms, Luxembourg, 5 May 2010. curia.europa.eu/jcms/upload/docs/application/pdf/2010-05/convention_en_2010-05-21_12-10-16_272.pdf

tion and application of law. Therefore individuals who wish to have their fundamental rights protected against the acts of the Union must usually apply to the national authorities and, in particular, to the courts of the member states. If in a specific case the individual is not satisfied with the protection ensured at the national level, on having exhausted the possibilities of application for legal remedy at the national level, he may take action against the member state concerned before the ECtHR. Through such an action an individual can also indirectly challenge a Union act when challenging the national provision implementing it. With regard to the Union's accession to the ECHR, this special feature of the Union legal system must be considered in the context of the principles governing the functioning of the control mechanism established by the ECHR, having particular attention to the principle of subsidiarity.

In January 2011 the presidents of the ECtHR and the Luxembourg Court made the first joint communication on the application of the Charter of Fundamental Rights and the EU's accession to the ECHR.[149] In the communication the presidents of the two Courts confirmed the above. They stressed that the preliminary ruling procedure under Article 267 of the TFEU could not be regarded a legal remedy to be exhausted before the applicant was allowed to apply to the ECHR. They also emphasized that such procedure should be put in place which did not require the amendment of the ECHR and took account of the characteristics of the two judicial systems. As the presidents of the Strasbourg and Luxembourg Courts stated in their joint communication, "it is guaranteed that the review exercised by the ECHR will be preceded by the internal review carried out by the CJEU and that subsidiarity will be respected". They took the view that the results of their discussion can usefully be made known in the context of the negotiations on accession ongoing between the Council of Europe and the EU. The courts are determined to continue their dialogue on these questions which are

---

149 See www.echr.coe.int/NR/rdonlyres/02164A4C-0B63-44C3-80C7-FC594EE16297/0/2011 Communication_CEDHCJUE_EN.pdf

of considerable importance for the quality and coherence of the case-law on the protection of fundamental rights in Europe.

1.3 Draft Accession Agreement and the CJEU

As the final report on the negotiations[150] summarizes:

> The CDDH-UE held in total eight working meetings with the European Commission between July 2010 and June 2011. The CDDH submitted a report to the Committee of Ministers on the work carried out by the CDDH-UE, with draft legal instruments appended, on 14 October 2011.
> On 13 June 2012, the Committee of Ministers gave a new mandate to the CDDH to pursue negotiations with the EU, in an ad hoc group ("47+1"), with a view to finalising the legal instruments setting out the modalities of accession of the EU to the Convention.
> The "47+1" group held five negotiation meetings with the European Commission. At the 5th negotiation meeting, the participants agreed on the draft revised instruments at the negotiators' level.
> The draft revised instruments on the accession of the EU to the ECHR consist of a draft Agreement on the accession,[151] a draft declaration by the EU, a draft rule to be added to the Rules of Committee of Ministers for the supervision of the execution of the judgments, and of the terms of friendly settlements in cases to which the EU is a party, a draft Model of Memorandum of Understanding, and a draft explanatory report to the Accession Agreement. They all form a package and are equally necessary for the accession.
> Firstly, before signature, an opinion of the CJEU would be sought on the compatibility of the draft agreement with the EU Treaties.

[150] Fifth negotiation meeting between the CDDH ad hoc negotiation group and the European Commission on the accession of the European Union to the European Convention on Human Rights, 47+1(2013)008rev2, Strasbourg, 10 June 2013, http://www.echr.coe.int/Documents/UE_Report_CDDH_ENG.pdf

[151] Draft revised agreement on the accession of the European Union to the Convention for the Protection of Human Rights and Fundamental Freedoms, 47 + 1(2013)008rev2

To bothersome surprise and disappointment of many, the main findings of the CJEU in Opinion 2/13[152] were the following:[153]

1. The review which the Court of Justice is called upon to carry out in the context of the Opinion procedure is closely circumscribed by the Treaties; therefore, if it is not to encroach on the competences of the other institutions responsible for drawing up the internal rules necessary in order to make an accession agreement operational, the Court must confine itself to examining the compatibility of that agreement with the Treaties and satisfy itself not only that it does not infringe any provision of primary law but also that it contains every provision that primary law may require. It follows from this that the assessments relating to those internal rules are irrelevant to the examination of a request for an Opinion and do not therefore call into question the admissibility of that request.
2. The fact that the European Union has a new kind of legal order, the nature of which is peculiar to the European Union, its own constitutional framework and founding principles, a particularly sophisticated institutional structure and a full set of legal rules to ensure its operation, has consequences as regards the procedure for and conditions of accession of the European Union to the European Convention on Human Rights (ECHR). It is precisely in order to ensure that that situation is taken into account that the Treaties, notably Article 6(2) TEU, Protocol No 8 relating to Article 6(2) TEU on the accession of the Union to the ECHR, and the Declaration on Article 6(2) TEU, make accession subject to compliance with various conditions. In performing the task conferred on it by the first subparagraph of Article 19(1) TEU, the Court of Justice must review, in the light, in particular, of those provisions, whether the legal arrangements proposed in respect of the European Union's accession to the ECHR are in conformity with the requirements laid down and, more generally, with the basic constitutional charter, the Treaties. For the purposes of that review, it must be noted that the conditions to which accession is subject under the Treaties are intended, particularly, to ensure that accession does not affect the specific characteristics of the European Union and EU law.

[152] CJEU 18 December 2014, Opinion 2/13, Accession of the European Union to the European Convention for the Protection of Human Rights and Fundamental Freedoms

[153] Summary – Opinion of the Court (Full Court), 18 December 2014, http://eur-lex.europa.eu/legal-content/EN/TXT/HTML/?uri=CELEX:62013CV0002_SUM&from=EN

3. The accession of the European Union to the European Convention on Human Rights (ECHR) as envisaged by the draft agreement is liable adversely to affect the specific characteristics of EU law and its autonomy.
   In the first place, in so far as Article 53 of the ECHR essentially reserves the power of the High Contracting Parties to lay down higher standards of protection of fundamental rights than those guaranteed by the ECHR, that provision should be coordinated with Article 53 of the Charter of Fundamental Rights of the European Union, as interpreted by the Court of Justice, so that the power granted to Member States by Article 53 of the ECHR is limited — with respect to the rights recognised by the Charter that correspond to those guaranteed by the ECHR — to that which is necessary to ensure that the level of protection provided for by the Charter and the primacy, unity and effectiveness of EU law are not compromised. However, there is no provision in the agreement envisaged to ensure such coordination.
   In the second place, the approach adopted in the agreement envisaged, which is to treat the European Union as a State and to give it a role identical in every respect to that of any other Contracting Party, disregards the intrinsic nature of the European Union. In so far as the ECHR would, in requiring the European Union and the Member States to be considered Contracting Parties not only in their relations with Contracting Parties which are not Member States of the European Union but also in their relations with each other, including where such relations are governed by EU law, require a Member State to check that another Member State has observed fundamental rights, even though EU law imposes an obligation of mutual trust between those Member States, accession is liable to upset the underlying balance of the European Union and undermine the autonomy of EU law.
   In the third place, by failing to make any provision in respect of the relationship between the mechanism established by Protocol No 16 to the ECHR (which permits the highest courts and tribunals of the Member States to request the European Court of Human Rights to give advisory opinions on questions of principle relating to the interpretation or application of the rights and freedoms guaranteed by the ECHR or the protocols thereto) and the preliminary ruling procedure provided for in Article 267 TFEU, the agreement envisaged is liable adversely to affect the autonomy and effectiveness of the latter procedure. In particular, it cannot be ruled out that a request for an advisory opinion made pursuant to Protocol No 16 by a court or tribunal of a Member State that has acceded to that protocol could trigger the procedure for the prior involvement of the Court of Justice, thus creating a risk that the preliminary ruling procedure provided for in Arti-

cle 267 TFEU might be circumvented, a procedure which is the keystone of the judicial system established by the Treaties.

4. The envisaged agreement on the accession of the European Union to the European Convention on Human Rights (ECHR) is liable to affect Article 344 TFEU. The procedure for the resolution of disputes provided for in Article 33 of the ECHR could apply to any High Contracting Party and, therefore, also to disputes between the Member States, or between those Member States and the European Union, even though it is EU law that is in issue. The fact that Article 5 of the draft agreement provides that proceedings before the Court of Justice are not to be regarded as a means of dispute settlement which the Contracting Parties have agreed to forgo in accordance with Article 55 of the ECHR is not sufficient to preserve the exclusive jurisdiction of the Court of Justice, given that Article 5 of the draft agreement merely reduces the scope of the obligation laid down by Article 55 of the ECHR, but still allows for the possibility that the European Union or Member States might submit an application to the European Court of Human Rights (ECtHR), under Article 33 of the ECHR, concerning an alleged violation thereof by a Member State or the European Union, respectively, in conjunction with EU law. Thus, the fact that Member States or the European Union are able to submit an application to the ECtHR is liable in itself to undermine the objective of Article 344 TFEU and, moreover, goes against the very nature of EU law, which requires that relations between the Member States be governed by EU law to the exclusion, if EU law so requires, of any other law. In those circumstances, only the express exclusion of the ECtHR's jurisdiction under Article 33 of the ECHR over disputes between Member States or between Member States and the European Union in relation to the application of the ECHR within the scope ratione materiae of EU law would be compatible with Article 344 TFEU.
5. The arrangements for the operation of the co-respondent mechanism laid down by the envisaged agreement on the accession of the European Union to the European Convention on Human Rights (ECHR) do not ensure that the specific characteristics of the European Union and EU law are preserved. First, the draft agreement provides that if the European Union or Member States request leave to intervene as co-respondents in a case before the European Court of Human Rights (ECtHR), they must give reasons from which it can be established that the conditions for their participation in the procedure are met, and the ECtHR is to decide on that request in the light of the plausibility of those reasons. In carrying out that review, the ECtHR would be required to assess the rules of EU law governing the division of powers between the European Union and its Member States as well as the criteria for the attribution of their acts or omissions, in order to adopt a final

decision in that regard which would be binding both on the Member States and on the European Union. Such a review would be liable to interfere with the division of powers between the European Union and its Member States. Secondly, the draft agreement provides that if the violation in respect of which a High Contracting Party is a co-respondent to the proceedings is established, the respondent and the co-respondent are to be jointly responsible for that violation. That provision does not preclude a Member State from being held responsible, together with the European Union, for the violation of a provision of the ECHR in respect of which that Member State may have made a reservation in accordance with Article 57 of the ECHR. Such a consequence is at odds with Article 2 of Protocol No 8 relating to Article 6(2) TEU on the accession of the Union to the ECHR, according to which the accession agreement is to ensure that nothing therein affects the situation of Member States in relation to the ECHR, in particular in relation to reservations thereto.

Thirdly, the draft agreement provides for an exception to the general rule that the respondent and co-respondent are to be jointly responsible for a violation established, by virtue of which the ECtHR may decide that only one of them is to be held responsible for that violation. A decision on the apportionment as between the European Union and its Member States of responsibility for an act or omission constituting a violation of the ECHR established by the ECtHR is also one that is based on an assessment of the rules of EU law governing the division of powers between the European Union and its Member States and the attributability of that act or omission. Accordingly, to permit the ECtHR to adopt such a decision would also risk adversely affecting the division of powers between the European Union and its Member States.

6. The arrangements for the operation of the procedure for the prior involvement of the Court of Justice provided for by the envisaged agreement on the accession of the European Union to the European Convention on Human Rights (ECHR) do not enable the specific characteristics of the European Union and EU law to be preserved.

   In the first place, it is necessary for the question whether the Court of Justice has already given a ruling on the same question of law as that at issue in the proceedings before the European Court of Human Rights (ECtHR) to be resolved only by the competent EU institution, whose decision should bind the ECtHR. To permit the ECtHR to rule on such a question would be tantamount to conferring on it jurisdiction to interpret the case-law of the Court of Justice. Yet the draft agreement does not contain anything to suggest that that possibility is excluded.

In the second place, the agreement envisaged excludes the possibility of bringing a matter before the Court of Justice in order for it to rule on a question of interpretation of secondary law by means of the prior involvement procedure. If the Court of Justice were not allowed to provide the definitive interpretation of secondary law, and if the ECtHR, in considering whether that law is consistent with the ECHR, had itself to provide a particular interpretation from among the plausible options, there would most certainly be a breach of the principle that the Court of Justice has exclusive jurisdiction over the definitive interpretation of EU law. Accordingly, limiting the scope of the prior involvement procedure, in the case of secondary law, solely to questions of validity adversely affects the competences of the European Union and the powers of the Court of Justice in that it does not allow the Court to provide a definitive interpretation of secondary law in the light of the rights guaranteed by the ECHR.

7. The envisaged agreement on the accession of the European Union to the European Convention on Human Rights (ECHR) fails to have regard to the specific characteristics of EU law with regard to the judicial review of acts, actions or omissions on the part of the European Union in common foreign and security policy (CFSP) matters. As EU law now stands, certain acts adopted in the context of the CFSP fall outside the ambit of judicial review by the Court of Justice. That situation is inherent to the way in which the Court's powers are structured by the Treaties, and, as such, can only be explained by reference to EU law alone. Nevertheless, on the basis of accession as provided for by the agreement envisaged, the European Court of Human Rights (ECtHR) would be empowered to rule on the compatibility with the ECHR of certain acts, actions or omissions performed in the context of the CFSP, and notably of those whose legality the Court of Justice cannot, for want of jurisdiction, review in the light of fundamental rights. Such a situation would effectively entrust the judicial review of those acts, actions or omissions on the part of the European Union exclusively to a non-EU body, albeit that any such review would be limited to compliance with the rights guaranteed by the ECHR. Jurisdiction to carry out a judicial review of acts, actions or omissions on the part of the European Union, including in the light of fundamental rights, cannot be conferred exclusively on an international court which is outside the institutional and judicial framework of the European Union.
8. The agreement on the accession of the European Union to the European Convention on Human Rights is not compatible with Article 6(2) TEU or with Protocol No 8 relating to Article 6(2) TEU on the accession of the Union to the European Convention on Human Rights.

1.4 Conclusion

After the landmark opinion of the CJEU, many commentators still call for the accession. According to Besselink, Claes and Reestman: "And yet it is fully within the Court's powers to give a negative opinion. It is, however, not in the power of the Court to decide what to do next. So, the decision whether to accede to the ECHR is not for the Court to determine. This is ultimately for the member states to decide, either qua members of the Council as the EU treaty-making power, or qua member states as masters of the EU Treaties in the framework of the amendment procedure – this follows from Article 218(11) TFEU (though the European Parliament and Commission will inevitably be involved in both instances)."[154]

But – as usual – there are less optimistic commentaries as well.[155] Tobias Lock explains: "the Court of Justice's demands will not be easily satisfied and if they are, the question arises of whether the concessions that would have to be made might result in exactly the opposite of what accession was originally meant to achieve: a reduction in the human rights protection in Europe. Thus it is appropriate to ask whether accession is still desirable in light of Opinion 2/13."[156]

However, the overwhelming crisis-argumentation (i.e. refugee-, Brexit- and rule of law crisis) pushed the question to the background of the European political agenda, I am still hopeful that the accession will proceed. The Charter of Fundamental Rights provides for a satisfactory solution to the problem of the relationship between the Charter and the ECHR. The Charter takes the Convention as setting out the minimum level of protection, while making it clear

[154] Leonard BESSELINK, Monica CLAES and Jan-Herman REESTMAN: A Constitutional moment: Acceding to the ECHR (or not), *European Constitutional Law Review* Vol. 11, № 1, 2015, 2–12, 2.

[155] S. PEERS: The EU's Accession to the ECHR: The Dream Becomes a Nightmare, *German Law Journal* Vol. 16, 2015, 222.

[156] Tobias LOCK: The future of the European Union's accession to the European Convention on Human Rights after Opinion 2/13: is it still possible and is it still desirable? *European Constitutional Law Review* Vol. 11, № 2, 2015, 239–273, at 267.

that the Charter itself may provide for a more extensive level of protection. That solution is compatible with the Convention and reflects the principle of subsidiarity governing the relationship between the Convention and the national legal systems. It is furthermore intended to promote harmony between the two instruments and to avoid competition between them. The Charter expressly states that the meaning and scope of the Charter rights corresponding to the rights guaranteed by the Convention should be interpreted consistently with Convention rights.[157] Article 53 of the Charter contains a "horizontal" clause on non-reversal, which involves the recognition of the other legal mechanisms, in particular national constitutions and the international texts on the protection of human rights and fundamental freedoms, from the time that they are ratified by the member states. On the basis of this recognition, the principle used is that of the most favourable provision: the level of protection guaranteed by the Charter may not be lower than the level offered by the provisions of the texts cited, within their respective fields of application.

These provisions of the Charter and the approximated case law of the two European Courts trigger the integration of the European human rights standard. The common standards of human rights protection result a European network of human rights producing network-effects (the more users the more utility, and the more utility is attempting to other potential users). The mutual dialogue of judges leads to the constitutional borrowing and migration in the field of the fundamental rights cases. The multilevel protection and interpretation of generic rights may lead to a race to the top and the beneficiaries of the system are the individuals.

---

[157] Jean-Paul Costa: The Relationship between the European Convention on Human Rights and European Union Law – A Jurisprudential Dialogue between the European Court of Human Rights and the European Court of Justice, Lecture at the King's College London, 7 October 2008, in Background Documentation, Fundamental Rights Protection in EU Law under the Lisbon Treaty, ERA, Trier, 22-23 April 2010.

2 Fully binding EU Bill of Rights for the member states – a potential tool in constitutional crisis management

The Charter of Fundamental Rights of the European Union has become part of the primary sources of Union law based on Article 6 (1) TEU. This reform has been of key importance from the aspect of the (constitutional) development of the Union. Ensuring the legal binding force of the Charter did not mean a change in the division of competences between the Union and the member states. This follows, on the one hand, from the guarantees relating to the field of application defined in Article 51 of the Charter and, on the other hand, from the statement made by the Court of Justice of the European Union (CJEU) that fundamental rights protection guaranteed by the Union cannot have the effect of extending the competences of the Community defined by the founding treaties,[158] which was also reinforced by the second subparagraph of Article 6(1) of the TEU. Thus to date the Charter does not replace the national systems for fundamental rights protection, instead it just complements them. The Charter addresses first and foremost the EU institutions. Member states are subject to their own constitutional bill of rights, and they have to respect the Charter only insofar as they apply Union law. This logic system is challenged sometimes by the CJEU on the one hand, by the ambiguous interpretation of the "acting within the scope of" criterion, and on the other hand by national courts whose questions in the preliminary ruling procedures seem to indicate an existing need for enhancing the scope of the Charter beyond the application of Union law. However, this soft, case law based expansion of scope is somehow uncertain.[159] Thus, the EU law still does

---

[158] Judgment of the Court of 17 February 1998 in Lisa Jacqueline Grant v South-West Trains Ltd., C-249/96 [ECR 1998, I-621]

[159] Michael DOUGAN: Judicial review of Member State action under the general principles and the Charter: defining the "scope of Union law", *Common Market Law Review* Vol. 52, 2015, 1201–1246.; Bernhard SCHIMA: EU fundamental rights and Member State action after Lisbon: putting the ECJ's case law in its context, *Fordham International Law Journal* Vol. 38, 2015, 1097, 1113–1114.

not contain effective mechanism to compel member states to respect fundamental rights in general.

It is worth to mention that already in November 2013 the European Commission started to collect impulses and ideas which may contribute to shaping of the European Union's justice policy over the coming years. The forum of the debate on EU justice policies was the *Assises de la Justice*, and the discourse encompassed the potential development of civil, criminal and administrative law, the rule of law and fundamental rights in the EU.[160] To stimulate the debate five discussion papers were made available. Discussion paper on Fundamental Rights posed the question whether the rights guaranteed in the Charter should be directly applicable in the member states in all cases, by abolishing the limitations of Article 51 of the Charter.[161] That time I already welcomed and urged the direct applicability of the Charter in the member states.[162] Amongst the interventions of the dialogue one can find the outlines of the rule of law mechanism, but the full direct effect of the Charter was not fostered.[163, 164]

Thus in the present contribution I emphasise again the importance of the direct applicability by collecting some new arguments and taking into consideration the deepening constitutional crisis in Central Europe.

---

160 http://ec.europa.eu/justice/events/assises-justice-2013/discussion_papers_en.htm

161 http://ec.europa.eu/justice/events/assises-justice-2013/files/fundamental_rights_en.pdf

162 Nóra Chronowski: Enhancing the scope of the Charter of Fundamental Rights – problems of the limitations and advantages of directly applicable Charter rights with regard to the recent case law developments of the European Court of Justice and national courts, Discussion paper, http://ec.europa.eu/justice/events/assises-justice-2013/files/contributions/36.hungarianacademyofsciences__preliminary_contribution_assises_cfr_chronowski_en.pdf

163 http://ec.europa.eu/justice/events/assises-justice-2013/interventions_en.htm

164 For a federal approach see Csongor István Nagy: Est-ce que l'union européenne devrait avoir le pouvoir de forcer les états membres à respecter les droits de l'homme? Une analyse prospective relative à l'application de la charte des droits fondamentaux aux états membres, *Revue de droit international et de droit comparé* № 3, 2017, 505-522.

First I outline what I mean by the limited effect and scope of the Charter regarding its legislative effect and applicability. In the second part I argue for the removal of the legal limitations from the way of direct application, taking also its difficulties into account.

2.1 Limited effects and scope of the Charter

Despite its clear significance acknowledged by the jurisprudence, the Charter is not able to fulfil its task completely, unless it fully contributes to and serves as a basis for the harmonisation of common European standards of fundamental rights protection.

2.1.1 Limited legislative effect

Considering the limitations of the Article 6(1) second sentence of the TEU,[165] and Article 51(2) of the Charter[166] – which are in compliance with the liberal constitutional concept that fundamental rights norms do not attribute power, but merely limit the exercise of powers – the Union cannot directly influence the formation of the common standards, i.e. it has no legislative competences except of the treaty-based rights. In other words, the Commission can propose EU legislation that gives concrete effect to the rights and principles of the Charter only where the EU has competence to act under the TEU or the Treaty on the Functioning of the European Union (hereinafter: TFEU). This results that the Union content, effect and protection level of Treaty rights and Charter rights has been developed differently – in the former case by secondary legislation and by judicial way, in the latter only by case law.

---

165 Article 6(1) second sentence of the TEU: "The provisions of the Charter shall not extend in any way the competences of the Union as defined in the Treaties."

166 Article 51(2) of the Charter: "The Charter does not extend the field of application of Union law beyond the powers of the Union or establish any new power or task for the Union, or modify powers and tasks as defined in the Treaties."

The restrictive provisions contained in Article 6(1) of the TEU and Article 51(2) of the Charter give expression to the requirement that the Charter shall not extend the competences of the Union; in other words, Union legislation relating to fundamental rights shall continue to be based on specific legal grounds provided in the TEU or TFEU, the fundamental rights character of which is merely reinforced by the provisions of the Charter.

The second sentence of Article 6(1) confirms the conviction (or phobia in the case of some member states) that the restrictive interpretation of EU competences shall continue to be ensured. Regulation of such content may be found, for instance, in Article 4(1), Article 5(2), Article 6(2) second sentence of the TEU as well as in Protocol № 8[167] and the – legally non-binding – Declarations 1 and 2.[168] At the same time, the requirement of restrictive interpretation relating to Union competences and the exercise of these competences is unambiguously expressed and reinforced in the principle of transferred competences or subsidiarity (in particular Articles 4-5), therefore, it would not require further repetition. According to Pernice, the emphasis on restriction is surprising in the context of Article 6 also for the reason that fundamental rights, by their nature, are not of power-transferring but rather restrictive character, in other words, as regards their content, they appear as limiting the exercise of transferred competences (the power-restricting role of fundamental rights). This may also be formulated in the way that in so far as fundamental rights norms exclude the interference of public authorities with particular individual rights and freedoms,

167 Protocol (№ 8) annexed to the Treaty of Lisbon relating to Article 6(2) of the Treaty on European Union on the accession of the Union to the European Convention on the Protection of Human Rights and Fundamental Freedoms (OJ C 83, 30. 3. 2010, 273)

168 Declaration № 1 concerning the Charter of Fundamental Rights of the European Union and Declaration № 2 on Article 6(2) of the Treaty on European Union, annexed to the Treaty of Lisbon (OJ C 83, 30. 3. 2010, 337)

they constitute negative competences for the institutions concerned.[169]

2.1.2 *Uncertain and limited horizontal effect*

The limited effect of the Charter as a legal instrument has also led to differences in respect of vertical and horizontal effect of the Charter rights. The vertical effect of the fundamental rights stems from the historical function of the rights, which is to protect the individuals against the state organs and limit the public power. The horizontal effect of fundamental rights means that they prevail also between individuals; and influence or determine the legal relations of private actors. This horizontal or third party effect can be direct or indirect. According to the theory of indirect horizontal effect, the fundamental rights norm of the constitution is not applicable directly in private law relations; it is only used as an interpretative guide to determine private law relations among individuals inter se. The theory of direct horizontal effect represents that the fundamental rights enshrined in the constitution are applicable in the private relations of the individuals. This results that private or labour law contracts infringing fundamental rights are invalid. This idea would however transform the private law claims into human rights disputes, and the private law regulation would lose its function.[170]

Naturally it is true, that even in the member states' constitutional practice only the vertical effect of rights is inevitable and in the field of the horizontal effect the indirect version is accepted by most ju-

[169] I. Pernice: The Treaty of Lisbon and Fundamental Rights, in S. Griller and J. Ziller (eds.): *The Lisbon Treaty. EU Constitutionalism without a Constitutional Treaty?* Springer Verlag, Wien, 2008, 244.

[170] E. Engle 'Third Party Effect of Fundamental Rights' 165–166., Verica Trstenjak: General Report: The Influence of Human Rights and Basic Rights in Private Law, in Verica Trstenjak and Petra Weingerl (eds.): *The Influence of Human Rights and Basic Rights in Private Law,* Springer International, Heidelberg, New York, Dordrecht, London, 2016, 8–9.

risdictions. Only the Portuguese and Greek constitutions allow direct horizontal effect. The European constitutional case law seems to differentiate between rights in respect of their direct or indirect horizontal effect.[171] It is worth to mention that the courts, even the CJEU are very careful with the recognition of indirect horizontal effect. See e.g. *Viking, Laval* (on right to collective action, allowing indirect horizontal effect) and *Dominguez* (on right to paid annual leave, not granting clearly the horizontal effect) cases,[172] or the more recent *AMS* case (on worker's right to information).[173] Although certain rulings of the CJEU contain light indications of direct applicability of fundamental rights as general principles of EU law, and do not exclude the applicability of the rights "in all situations governed by EU law", the potential horizontal effect of Charter rights remains an open question.[174] Why would it be so important to give the chance to EU courts to clarify the horizontal effect of the Charter rights by making them fully binding? The EU has strongly committed[175] itself to promote the United Nations Framework Programme and Guiding Principles on Business and Human Rights,[176] but in the absence of a generally applicable bill of rights, the EU courts remain

171 L.F.M. Besselink 'General Report' 91–93.

172 See e.g. Viking, Laval and Dominguez cases (C-438/05 International Transport Workers' Federation and Finnish Seamen's Union v Viking Line ABP and OÜ Viking Line Eesti, Judgment of the Court of 11 December 2007; C-341/05 Laval un Partneri Ltd v Svenska Byggnadsarbetareförbundet, Svenska Byggnadsarbetareförbundets avdelning 1, Byggettan and Svenska Elektrikerförbundet, Judgment of the Court of 18 December 2007; C-282/10 Maribel Dominguez v Centre informatique du Centre Ouest Atlantique and Préfet de la région Centre, Judgment of the Court of 24 January 2012).

173 In AMS case concerned the question of potential horizontal effect of the workers' right to information and consultation enshrined in Article 27 of the Charter. Against the opinion by Advocate General Cruz Villalón, the Court did not grant Article 27 and such effect. C-176/12 Association de médiation sociale v Union locale des syndicats CGT and Others, Judgment of the Court (Grand Chamber) of 15 January 2014.

174 Trstenjak 'The Influence of Human Rights' 9.

175 http://ec.europa.eu/enterprise/policies/sustainable-business/corporate-social-responsibility/index_en.htm

176 Guiding Principles on Business and Human Rights: Implementing the United Nations "Protect, Respect and Remedy" Framework, Report of the Special Repre-

without means to contribute to the effective remedy system against the human rights violations of powerful private actors.

2.2 'Within the scope of' practice

The EU institutions are clearly bound by the Charter,[177] thus the CJEU has inevitable role in controlling the EU legislature's compliance with fundamental rights.[178]

The idea that member states are bound by the rights, freedoms and principles laid down by the Article 51(1) of the Charter[179] is implemented principally in the 'agency-situation' elaborated by the CJEU, at two levels: in a normative and administrative dimension. The normative level means the dimension when, during the transposition – or omitting the transposition – of Union law (directives) into the national law, the member state is bound by the fundamental rights during the adoption of normative decisions. The administrative level appears in the case of directly applicable Union law (regulations): in such a case the law of Union content is regarded formally as domestic law right away.[180] Furthermore, the respect of Charter rights has also been held by the CJEU to apply when a mem-

sentative of the Secretary-General on the issue of human rights and transnational corporations and other business enterprises, John Ruggie, 21 March 2011.

[177] Article 51(1) of the Charter: "The provisions of this Charter are addressed to the institutions, bodies, offices and agencies of the Union with due regard for the principle of subsidiarity (...)"

[178] E.g. C-92/09 and C-93/09. Volker joint cases, Judgment of the Court of 9 November 2010

[179] Article 51(1) of the Charter: "The provisions of this Charter are addressed (...) to the Member States only when they are implementing Union law. They shall therefore respect the rights, observe the principles and promote the application thereof in accordance with their respective powers and respecting the limits of the powers of the Union as conferred on it in the Treaties."

[180] M. Borowsky: Kapitel VII, Allgemeine Bestimmungen, in J. Meyer (ed.): *Kommentar zur Charta der Grundrechte der Europäischen Union*, Nomos, Baden-Baden, 2003, 567–572.

ber state derogates from a fundamental economic freedom guaranteed under EU law.[181]

Considering the CJEU case law related to Article 51(1) of the Charter, it is not clear, however, whether the phrase 'implementing Union law' has got a different meaning from 'acting within the scope of Union law' thus the margins of member states' obligation to apply the Charter rights remained ambiguous. In other words, the Charter binds the member states as well 'when implementing Union law', however, the CJEU understands this in a wider sense: member states have to respect the fundamental rights 'acting within the scope of' Union law.[182] Thus on the basis of the preliminary ruling of the CJEU (*Aziz Melki/Sélim Abdeli*), seemingly national courts of law may apply the Charter directly,[183] but only in those cases where any Union legal act is concerned. In purely domestic cases the national courts apply the bill of rights enshrined in the national constitution, and / or international human rights obligations of the given state. The extent and intensity of the latter activity is dependent on the monist or dualist approach of the national legal system. To date, the condition of the direct application of the Charter is the application of another Union legal norm.[184]

---

181 See, inter alia, C260/89 ERT, Elliniki Radiophonia Tiléorassi AE and Panellinia Omospondia Syllogon Prossopikou v Dimotiki Etairia Pliroforissis and Sotirios Kouvelas and Nicolaos Avdellas and others, Judgment of the Court of 18 June 1991, para. 42 et seq.; C112/00 Eugen Schmidberger, Internationale Transporte und Planzüge v Republik Österreich, Judgment of the Court of 12 June 2003, para 75.; and C36/02 Omega Spielhallen- und Automatenaufstellungs-GmbH v Oberbürgermeisterin der Bundesstadt Bonn, Judgment of the Court of 14 October 2004, paras. 30–31

182 K.L. Mathisen: The Impact of the Lisbon Treaty, in particular Article 6 TEU, on Member States' obligations with respect to the protection of fundamental rights, *University of Luxembourg Law Working Paper Series,* Paper № 2010-01, 29 July, 2010, 20.

183 C-188/10 and C-189/10. Aziz Melki (C-188/10) and Sélim Abdeli (C-189/10) joint cases, Judgment of the Court of 22 June 2010

184 As Rosas pointed out, "(…) the real problem is not so much the applicability of the Charter as such but rather the applicability of another norm of Union law." A. Rosas: When is the EU Charter of Fundamental Rights Applicable at National Level? *Jurisprudence* Vol. 19, № 4, 2012, 1269–1288.

In the *Åkerberg Fransson and Melloni cases*[185] the Court has even equated 'implementation' and 'acting within the scope of' Union law, and has gone far beyond the textual meaning of 'implementation', but still remained in the framework of the wide literal interpretation. However, according to Lavranos, in these judgments "the ECJ interprets the scope of application of the Charter of Fundamental Rights, in particular Articles 51 and 53 of the Charter in a very extensive way. The judgments establish the supremacy of the Charter of Fundamental Rights over national (constitutional) law and the ECHR, thereby positioning the ECJ as the «Supreme Court of Fundamental Rights» in Europe."[186] Anyway, according to the commentaries, these were "ground-braking" decisions,[187] triggering the academic debate on the scope of the Charter and the role of the EU in the framework of the European fundamental rights protection. As to the limitations set up in Article 51(1)-(2) of the Charter, the CJEU ruled,

> the fundamental rights guaranteed by the Charter must therefore be complied with where national legislation falls within the scope of European Union law, situations cannot exist which are covered in that way by European Union law without those fundamental rights being applicable. The applicability of European Union law entails applicability of the fundamental rights guaranteed by the Charter.[188]
>
> Where, on the other hand, a legal situation does not come within the scope of European Union law, the Court does not have jurisdiction to rule on it and any provisions of the Charter relied upon cannot, of themselves, form the basis for such jurisdiction (…).[189]
>
> Where a court of a Member State is called upon to review whether fundamental rights are complied with by a national provision or measure which, in a situation where action of the Member States is not entirely determined by

---

185 C-617/10 Åklagaren v Hans Åkerberg Fransson, Judgment of the Court of 26 February 2013; C-399/11 Stefano Melloni v Ministerio Fiscal, Judgment of the Court of 26 February 2013

186 N. Lavranos: The ECJ's Judgments in Melloni and Åkerberg Fransson: Une ménage à trois difficulté, *European Law Reporter* № 4, 2013, 133.

187 D. Sarmiento: Who's Afraid of the Charter? The Court of Justice, National Courts and the New Framework of Fundamental Rights Protection in Europe, *Common Market Law Review* Vol. 50, 2013, 1268.

188 C-617/10 Åkerberg Fransson, para. 21.

189 C-617/10 Åkerberg Fransson, para. 22.

> European Union law, implements the latter for the purposes of Article 51(1) of the Charter, national authorities and courts remain free to apply national standards of protection of fundamental rights, provided that the level of protection provided for by the Charter, as interpreted by the Court, and the primacy, unity and effectiveness of European Union law are not thereby compromised.[190]

In these judgments the Court declared the *effet utile* of the Charter, and limited the choices of national courts, because they shall compare the national fundamental rights standards with the Charter standard even in those situations where the links to the Union law are indirect and partial. After all, this judge-made basis created by the CJEU is still fragile and uncertain, furthermore, it triggers the debate on the borderlines of the application of EU fundamental rights and their relations with the national fundamental rights protection systems.[191] The case by case elaborated scope of the Charter vis-à-vis member states creates even tensions between the CJEU and national constitutional courts, for whom the interpretation of fundamental rights is a cherished area and some of them clearly indicated the willingness for scrutinizing EU law in the protection of domestic standards and constitutional identity. The German Constitutional Court almost immediately and unanimously ruled that the Åkerberg Fransson judgment of the CJEU neither changes the *status quo* in respect the scope of the Charter, nor expresses a general view.[192] The statements of the CJEU's decision shall be based on the distinctive features of the case, otherwise presumably it were considered *ultra vires* by the Constitutional Court.[193]

---

[190] C-399/11 Melloni, para. 60., Åkerberg Fransson, para. 29.

[191] S.I. Sánches: The Court and the Charter: The impact of the entry into force of the Lisbon Treaty on the ECJ's approach to fundamental rights, *Common Market Law Review* Vol. 49, № 5, 2012, 1582.

[192] I. Cs. Nagy also shares this view: "Although in the case of Åkerberg Fransson the CJEU interpreted the 'implementation of Union law' in an extensive sense, the principle fundamental constitutional architecture of the EU has not been challenged." Nagy 'Est-ce que l'union européenne devrait' 511.

[193] On the limits of the scope of application of EU fundamental rights see the judgment of the German Constitutional Court of 24 April 2013 on Counter-Terrorism Database Act (1 BvR 1215/07). See also Sarmiento 'Who's Afraid' 1268., Schima 'EU fundamental rights' 1106. and D. Thym: Separation versus Fusion – or:

The possibilities of the national courts are also limited under the present formulation of Article 51(1), although – considering the increasing number of references to the Charter in preliminary rulings[194] – they would be willing to apply the Charter rights in a broader scope.[195] It is worthwhile to add that not all of the constitutional courts are reticent with the application of the Charter.[196]

Against this background, about one year after Åkerberg Fransson the CJEU tightened its former interpretation by re-setting a number of criteria that should be examined to establish whether national legislation "involves the implementation of EU law for the purposes of Article 51 of the Charter" in *Siragusa* case.[197] By doing so, the Court became cautious again and showed due deference towards national courts and national fundamental rights protection. The CJEU ruled, that

> [i]n order to determine whether national legislation involves the implementation of EU law for the purposes of Article 51 of the Charter, some of the points to be determined are whether that legislation is intended to implement a pro-

How to Accommodate National Autonomy and the Charter? Diverging Visions of the German Constitutional Court and the European Court of Justice, *European Constitutional Law Review* Vol. 9, № 3, 2013, 395–398.

194 The Commission stated: "The important implications of the Charter are to be seen in the increasing number of requests for a preliminary ruling of national jurisdictions received by the Court." COM(2013) 271 final, 2012 Report on the Application of the EU Charter of Fundamental Rights, 7.

195 Besselink admitted that "... in some Member States the courts have referred to the Charter with such enthusiasm as to disregard whether the Charter could at all be considered applicable". Besselink 'General Report' 108.

196 The Austrian Constitutional Court "concluded that, based on the domestic legal situation, it follows from the equivalence principle that the rights guaranteed by the [Charter] may also be invoked as constitutionally guaranteed rights (...) and they constitute a standard of review in general judicial review proceedings in the scope of application of the Charter". Thus the alleged violation of the Charter may give rise to the competence of the Constitutional Court. U 466/11-18, U 1836/11-13, Austrian Constitutional Court Judgment of 14 March 2012, point 35. See to this Attila Vincze: Az osztrák Alkotmánybíróság döntése az Alapjogi Charta alkalmazandóságáról, *Alkotmánybírósági Szemle* Vol. 3, № 1, 2013, 126–132.

197 C-206/13. Cruciano Siragusa v Regione Sicilia – Soprintendenza Beni Culturali e Ambientali di Palermo, Judgment of the Court (Tenth Chamber) of 6 March 2014

> vision of EU law; the nature of that legislation and whether it pursues objectives other than those covered by EU law, even if it is capable of indirectly affecting EU law; and also whether there are specific rules of EU law on the matter or capable of affecting it.[198]

Regarding the EU fundamental rights protection, the CJEU clarified that it is not an objective in itself, but it has to serve the unity of EU law. In other words, the ground for fundamental rights protection is their basic value-character but to preserve the primacy of EU law.[199] Thus the Court refrained from connecting its rights protection activity with Article 2 TEU, and despite the clarifications the judgment clearly shows the fragility of the case law based scope of protection.

As to the way ahead, it is still worthwhile to consider Advocate General Sharpston's suggestion, which was formulated in his opinion to *Zambrano* case,

> Transparency and clarity require that one be able to identify with certainty what 'the scope of Union law' means for the purposes of EU fundamental rights protection. It seems to me that, in the long run, the clearest rule would be one that made the availability of EU fundamental rights protection dependent neither on whether a Treaty provision was directly applicable nor on whether secondary legislation had been enacted, but rather on *the existence and scope of a material EU competence.* To put the point another way: the rule would be that, provided that the EU had competence (whether exclusive or shared) in a particular area of law, EU fundamental rights should protect the citizen of the EU *even if such competence has not yet been exercised.*[200]

---

198 C-206/13. Siragusa, para 25

199 "It is also important to consider the objective of protecting fundamental rights in EU law, which is to ensure that those rights are not infringed in areas of EU activity, whether through action at EU level or through the implementation of EU law by the Member States. The reason for pursuing that objective is the need to avoid a situation in which the level of protection of fundamental rights varies according to the national law involved in such a way as to undermine the unity, primacy and effectiveness of EU law." C-206/13. Siragusa, paras 31–32.

200 C-34/09 Gerardo Ruiz Zambrano v Office national de l'emploi (ONEM), Opinion of Advocate General Sharpston, delivered on 30 September 2010, para 163.

2.3 Should the Charter bind the member states fully?

In this part, the difficulties and advantages of the direct applicability of the Charter shall be measured. Eliminating the limitations on the Union's competences and amending the scope of the Charter, the British and Polish 'opt-outs' from, and other member states concerns about the Charter – especially the fears for the constitutional identity and the level of national protection – must be considered. The respect of constitutional identity of the member states was implicitly confirmed by the CJEU,[201] but the member states may expect more explicit guaranties. However, clear advantages of these steps would be that (i) the Union could assume a more definite role in developing the common standards on fundamental rights,[202] (ii) renitent member states endangering these standards might be controlled more effectively even directly by their national courts,[203] and (iii) they could evolve the effect of Article 2 TEU, or moreover, it can contribute to the reform of Article 7 TEU, which remained a kind of political – and practically inapplicable – sanction of violating the Union values. The Charter with direct applicability beyond the scope of EU law – being the part of the primary sources of EU law – will

---

201 See to this e.g. the Omega-judgment (C-36/02. Omega Spielhallen- und Automatenaufstellungs-GmbH v Oberbürgermeisterin der Bundesstadt Bonn, Judgment of the Court of 14 October 2004) and the Sayn-Wittgenstein judgment (C-208/09. Ilonka Sayn-Wittgenstein v Landeshauptmann von Wien, Judgment of the Court of 22 December 2010)

202 As Bogdandy suggests, "the core idea of European law is no longer more and more integration (ever closer union) but to provide a common legal space that advances common aims under common values". (Armin von BOGDANDY: European Law Beyond 'Ever Closer Union' – Repositioning the Concept, its Thrust, and the ECJ's Comparative Methodology, *European Law Journal* Vol. 22, № 3, 2016, 519–538.) Still, the common standards of fundamental rights protection are exactly such aims and values that Union and member states laws shall equally protect.

203 See the actions taken by the Commission to ensure the respect of the Charter by Hungary, especially C-286/12 European Commission v Hungary, Judgment of the Court of 6 November 2012 (compulsory retirement of judges, prosecutors and notaries), where the national constitutional court avoided the application of the Charter.

have much stronger position than the European Convention on Human Rights (hereinafter: ECHR) whose applicability is dependent on the monist or dualist approach of the member states to international law. It could contribute to the creation of a European Fundamental Rights Area and guarantee the Union citizens an equal and calculable level of protection.[204]

2.3.1 *Difficulties - are they really significant?*

To make the Charter generally binding on member states and directly applicable by national courts, definitely an explicit amendment is necessary.[205] Viviane Reding, former Vice-President of the European Commission, EU Justice Commissioner also admitted,

> A very ambitious Treaty amendment – which I would personally favour for the next round of Treaty change – would be abolishing Article 51 of our Charter of Fundamental Rights, so as to make all fundamental rights directly applicable in the Member States, including the right to effective judicial review (Article 47 of the Charter). (...)This would open up the possibility for the Commission to bring infringement actions for violations of fundamental rights by Member States even if they are not acting in the implementation of EU law. I admit that this would be a very big federalising step. It took the United States more than 100 years until the first ten amendments started to be applied to the states by the Supreme Court.[206]

204 A. Jakab: Supremacy of the EU Charter in National Courts in Purely Domestic Cases, http://www.verfassungsblog.de/de/ungarn-was-tun-andras-jakab/#.Un652RAtb5R

205 It is worth to note that the Charter is not part of the treaty, thus the formal amendment procedure is open to discussion. Sándor-Szalay and Mohay suggests the convention method for the amendment, which is defined by Article 48 of TFEU. Á. Mohay and E. Sándor-Szalay: Hungary, in J. Laffranque (ed.): *The Protection of Fundamental Rights Post-Lisbon: The Interaction between the Charter of Fundamental Rights of the European Union, the European Convention on Human Rights and National Constitutions,* Tartu University Press, Tallinn, 2012, 520.

206 European Commission – SPEECH/13/67704/09/2013, The EU and the Rule of Law – What next? http://europa.eu/rapid/press-release_SPEECH-13-677_en.htm

At this point it cannot be suppressed that serious concerns were raised on the scope of the Charter during the debate of the Lisbon Treaty. Member states offering the most active resistance were the Czech Republic, Poland and the United Kingdom. Finally, in a Protocol annexed to the Lisbon Treaty (to simplify: the Opt-Out Protocol),[207] the UK and Poland were granted exemption from respect for certain rights and principles. The real opt-out nature of this exemption is, however, questionable both from the aspects of form and content. From a formal aspect its authenticity is doubtful because the Opt-Out Protocol, itself, declares: the Charter reaffirms the rights, freedoms and principles recognised in the Union and makes those rights more visible, but does not create new rights or principles. Therefore, there is no regulative content from which exemption could be granted, since in a legal sense the Charter does not add new rights to the range of earlier rights and obligations.[208] On this basis, the opt-out does not have a genuine legal effect; it rather has the character of a clarification.[209] From the aspect of content the most important question is in what situations national courts or the CJEU may establish that the national law is in conflict with the fundamental rights of the Union. For instance, shall the CJEU be entitled to question the validity of a piece of legislation of a member state with reference to conflict with the Charter and the violation of fundamental rights guaranteed by it? It is clear that the Court cannot annul laws of the member states; only national courts (constitutional courts) are competent to do so. At the same time, the CJEU may find – in proceedings for failure to fulfil an obligation or in the preliminary ruling procedure (Articles 258 and 267 TFEU) – that the national law is in conflict with Union law. The Czech

207 Protocol (№ 30) annexed to the Treaty of Lisbon on the Application of the Charter of Fundamental Rights of the European Union to Poland and to the United Kingdom (OJ C 83, 30. 3. 2010, 313)

208 Pernice 'The Treaty of Lisbon' 245.

209 C. Barnard: The 'Opt-out' for the UK and Poland from the Charter of Fundamental Rights: Triumph or Rhetoric over the Reality, in S. Griller – J. Ziller (eds.): *The Lisbon Treaty, EU Constitutionalism without a Constitutional Treaty?* Springer Verlag, 2008, 276.

Republic annexed a Declaration to the Treaties,[210] in which it emphasizes the limited binding force of the Charter on member states, the prohibition of extending the Union's competences and the importance of constitutional traditions common to the member states and that of international agreements. The similar declarations by Poland concern legislation relating to the sphere of family, public morality, family law, as well as the protection of human dignity and human integrity.[211] These declarations have no binding force, i.e., they do not grant exemption from the effect of the Charter in the way that the Opt-Out Protocol does. Altogether – even if the above reflected protocol and declarations are not completely convincing, they clearly indicate that – an amendment for enhancing the scope of the Charter is expected to be a harshly debated step by certain member states, thus cautious political preparation is necessary.

However, after the Brexit referendum in the UK – may decide its people either remain or leave – a treaty reform seems to be inevitable, which may reopen the debate on the scope of the Charter.

The constitutional identity of the member states is also a strong argument in the dispute on federal development of the EU. It might be a point of reference during the discussions that the extension of the scope of the Charter undermines the constitutional identity of the member states. However, besides affirming the shared values, the TEU also declares that the Union shall respect the national identities of its member states, as inherent part of their political and constitutional structures.[212] The definition emphasises the consti-

---

[210] Declaration № 53 by the Czech republic on the Charter of Fundamental Rights of the European Union.

[211] Declaration № 61 – Declaration by the Republic of Poland on the Charter of Fundamental Rights of the European Union; Declaration № 62 – Declaration by the Republic of Poland concerning the Protocol on the application of the Charter of Fundamental Rights of the European Union in relation to Poland and the United Kingdom.

[212] Article 4(2) of the TEU: "The Union shall respect the equality of member states before the Treaties as well as their national identities, inherent in their fundamental structures, political and constitutional, inclusive of regional and local self-government. It shall respect their essential state functions, including ensuring the

tutional, political and state aspects, thus in this context the national identity can be understood (much more) as constitutional (than as a cultural) identity. One of the legally relevant questions in this respect is who will decide on the content of the constitutional identity of a member state and on the acts or measures of Union affecting or infringing that constitutional identity. It is clear that a relationship of cooperation between the national (constitutional) courts and the CJEU is necessary in case of such conflicts, the first to determine the constitutional identity case by case, and the latter to decide on the meaning of the relevant EU law in dispute. As it is based on the case law, the margin of appreciation is given on both sides, but the CJEU has confirmed in the *Omega* judgment the respect of the constitutional identity, when it gave preference to the German concept of human dignity against the freedom of services.[213] The obligation to respect the constitutional identity of the member states may even mean the restriction of a certain fundamental right, as it happened in the *Sayn-Wittgenstein* case, in which the republican identity of Austria was considered stronger value than the free movement of citizens in respect of carrying the noble title.[214]

As a result of the multilevel European constitutional development, the constitutional traditions of the member states converged in their respective content and interpretation, while the single States managed to preserve their own constitutional identity. An EU member state is henceforth to a great extent free to decide on its own constitutional structure, which is the basis of its constitutional identity.

---

territorial integrity of the State, maintaining law and order and safeguarding national security. In particular, national security remains the sole responsibility of each member state."

213 See to the Omega-judgment of the CJEU (Case C-36/02 Omega Spielhallen- und Automatenaufstellungs-GmbH v Oberbürgermeisterin der Bundesstadt Bonn) and the Lisbon-judgment of the German Federal Constitutional Court (BVerfG, Urteil des Zweiten Senats vom 30. Juni 2009, 2 BvE 2/08), and BESSELINK 'General Report' 72.

214 See the Sayn-Wittgenstein judgment (C-208/09. Ilonka Sayn-Wittgenstein v Landeshauptmann von Wien, Judgment of the Court of 22 December 2010) and BESSELINK 'General Report' 72.

The introduction of the direct application of the Charter may reopen the debate on the relation of the Charter and the ECHR, the Strasbourg and Luxembourg courts. Analysing the existing text of the Charter, it can be stated that it provides for a satisfactory solution to this problem. The Charter takes the Convention as setting out the minimum level of protection, while making it clear that the Charter itself may provide for a more extensive level of protection. That solution is compatible with the Convention and reflects the principle of subsidiarity governing the relationship between the Convention and the national legal systems. It is furthermore intended to promote harmony between the two instruments and to avoid competition between them. The Charter expressly states that the meaning and scope of the Charter rights corresponding to the rights guaranteed by the Convention should be interpreted consistently with Convention rights.[215] Article 53 of the Charter contains a 'horizontal' clause on non-reversal,[216] which involves the recognition of the other legal mechanisms, in particular national constitutions and the international texts on the protection of human rights and fundamental freedoms, from the time that they are ratified by the member states. On the basis of this recognition, the principle used is that of the most favourable provision: the level of protection guaranteed by the Charter may not be lower than the level offered by the provisions of the texts cited, within their respective fields of application. These provisions of the Charter and the approximated case law of the two European Courts trigger the integration of the European human rights standard.

Although the CJEU in opinion 2/2013 rejected the draft agreement on the accession of the EU to the ECHR presuming that it

215 Costa 'The Relationship' 12.

216 Article 53 of the Charter: "Nothing in this Charter shall be interpreted as restricting or adversely affecting human rights and fundamental freedoms as recognised, in their respective fields of application, by Union law and international law and by international agreements to which the Union or all the Member States are party, including the European Convention for the Protection of Human Rights and Fundamental Freedoms, and by the Member States' constitutions."

would "upset the underlying balance of the EU and undermine the autonomy of EU law",[217] the Strasbourg court in 2016 proved its openness to dialogue again, and in *Avotiņš* judgment[218] for the first time applied the Bosphorus-presumption[219] to a case concerning obligations of mutual recognition under EU law. This suggests that the European Court of Human Rights (ECtHR) is still confident in the development of the European human rights area.

2.3.2 *Advantages*

The discussion paper suggests the direct applicability of the Charter by the national courts 'outside the scope' of the Union law. Thus the national courts can apply – and parties can refer to – the Charter even in purely domestic cases, independently from the application of another EU norm. There are two potential versions for the extension of the scope of the Charter. The modest version is – in accordance with Advocate General Sharpston's cited proposal – to prescribe that member states have to apply the Charter in all fields where the Union has competence to act, irrespectively to the fact whether the competence was exercised by the Union or not. Of course, this version might re-open the debate on the exact division of competences between the EU and the member states. A bolder step would be the removal of any limitation and creating the full

---

217 Opinion 2/13 of the Court (Full Court) of 18 December 2014 on the Accession of the European Union to the European Convention for the Protection of Human Rights and Fundamental Freedoms and Compatibility of the draft agreement with the EU and FEU Treaties.

218 Avotiņš v. Latvia (Application no. 17502/07) Judgment of 23 May 2016. See also Stian Øby Johansen: EU law and the ECHR: the Bosphorus presumption is still alive and kicking – the case of Avotiņš v. Latvia, http://eulawanalysis.blogspot.hu/2016/05/eu-law-and-echr-bosphorus-presumption.html

219 The presumption of equivalent protection of ECHR rights by the EU, even though the EU is not a party to the ECHR, in Bosphorus Hava Yollari Turizm ve Ticaret Anonim Şirketi v. Ireland (Application no. 45036/98) Judgment of 30 June 2005.

direct applicability of the Charter in any situations where Union citizens are concerned.

By the extension of its scope, the Charter norms will acquire inevitable and full primary law character, as it reads from Article 6(1) of the TEU. It does not mean that the individuals would get direct access to the CJEU in fundamental rights cases, i.e. the direct applicability of the Charter would neither create a rival human rights jurisdiction parallel to the ECtHR, nor allow this way a potential forum shopping. The amendment of the competences and procedure of the CJEU is not necessary. The elimination of the "only when they are implementing Union law" criterion simply means that the national courts have to apply beyond their domestic bill of rights the Charter as well, seek a harmonised interpretation and can ask for a preliminary ruling under the Article 267 of the TFEU. As it was mentioned above, the level of protection is provided for by the guarantees of Article 53 of the Charter, which refers – amongst other legal sources – in particular to the constitutions of the member states. As Sarmiento demonstrates, it is more than a simple minimum standard clause, because the CJEU has construed it as a kind of conflict of laws rule for those cases in which both EU and domestic fundamental rights can be applicable.[220]

The preliminary rulings on Charter rights may be useful on the one hand even to the ECtHR when it interprets the ECHR in comparison with the Charter. On the other hand these kind of judgments of the CJEU may serve as a legal evidence to the European Commission when it enters into a treaty infringement procedure or considers the application of Article 7 of the TEU. To date Article 7 is a harshly criticized as practically inapplicable norm, because it calls for the clear and present danger of the violence of the EU values for the initiation of the Council's procedure and decision. It can be presumed that in practice it would mean multitudinous or at least numerous proceedings and/or omissions leading to foreseeable and certain violation of Article 2 of TEU in a given member state.

[220] Sarmiento 'Who's Afraid' 1288–1289.

As Article 7 has never been applied, it also allows the presumption that the actors are very cautious and circumspect with initiating such procedure, because it cannot be legally supported sufficiently when exactly the violation happens, i.e. there is no due evidence procedure prescribed by the primary law. The number of preliminary ruling procedures, content of the questions put by the national courts and the decisions of the CJEU related to the Charter rights and the domestic law may clearly indicate if the respect of common EU values become doubtful in a certain member state. Hungarian and Polish constitutional crises point that despite a range of Venice Commission opinions and ECtHR judgments the EU is still not able and willing to intervene in the absence of legal basis.

* * *

This short proposal can of course be criticized for being utopian or fairly illusory, and can even be labelled as completely unrealistic to date. One must however bear in mind that the EU sometimes did not spare the efforts to enter into projects surrounded by scepticism. In the early 1990's no one thought that a decade later a convention would be called with the mandate of creating a constitution for Europe. The Treaty on the European Constitution failed, but several of its achievements has survived and has been introduced by the Lisbon Treaty in a more or less modest way. The Charter is definitely the part of the last decades of the evolution of EU law as it conceived in June 1999 by the decision of Cologne European Council,[221] lived its foetal life during the work of Fundamental Rights Convention and was born on 7 December 2000, when the Presidents of the Council, the Parliament and the Commission proclaimed it as an inter-institutional document. The European courts started to bring up the child, but it still lives its childhood. I do not think that by acquiring the legally binding force under the present

[221] 150/99 REV 1 Presidency Conclusions, Cologne European Council, 2-4 June 1999, point 44–45.

formulation the Charter's evolution came to an end. It is more like a beginning, and it is never in vain thinking ahead for Europe and on rendering the existing fundamental rights more effective for the benefit of individuals.

CONSTITUTIONAL CHALLENGES IN HUNGARY

Introduction - 2010/11 constitution making in Hungary

In Hungary a new constitution, the Fundamental Law (hereinafter FL) was promulgated on 25 April 2011 and came into force on 1 January 2012.[222] Its drafting rose to prominence in Europe and was severely criticized both by domestic experts[223] and Venice Commission. After the 2010 parliamentary elections, political forces forming a parliamentary majority – possessing two-thirds of the seats – have expressed their intention to create a new constitution. In the course of "replacing the old with new" the development of another constitutional regime and the writing of the FL came about in parallel with the devastation of the previous constitutional order with permanent amendments to the former Constitution.[224] In the background of this policy the unequal fight of the Constitutional Court and the governing majority took place which might be summarised in the question of 'who is the final arbiter in constitutional matters',[225] and ended in the partial incapacitating of the Constitutional Court by weakening it as a counterbalance of the executive and legislative powers.[226] Until the Fourth Amendment the Court made cautious efforts to strike

---

[222] For the official English translation of the Fundamental Law (consolidated version with six amendments), see http://www.kormany.hu/download/a/68/11000/The_Fundamental_Law_of_Hungary_01072016.pdf.

[223] A. VINCZE and M. VARJU: Hungary: the New Fundamental Law, *European Public Law* Vol. 18, № 3, 2012, 437–453.

[224] Act XX of 1949 on the Constitution of the Republic of Hungary as revised in 1989–90, in force until 31 December 2011; hereinafter former Constitution.

[225] Nóra CHRONOWSKI and Márton VARJU: Two Eras of Hungarian Constitutionalism: From the Rule of Law to Rule by Law, *Hague J Rule Law* Vol. 8, № 2, 2016, 281–282.

[226] See also Zoltán SZENTE: The Decline of Constitutional Review in Hungary – Towards a Partisan Constitutional Court? in *Challenges and Pitfalls in the Recent*

down the strivings of the supermajority government acting in the parliament.[227] Since then and especially after the failed Seventh Amendment – as the institutional and competence changes had their effect – the Court gives a helping hand to the constitution maker, and it is even ready to substitute the constituent will along the intents of the government.[228]

As to the antecedent circumstances of the Hungarian constitution making, the political situation was overloaded with the effects of the economic world crisis[229] and domestic tensions – „cold civil war", „prime minister lied 2006", „social" referendum 2008 (against health system reform and tuition fee), minority government, „expert" government for crisis management – thus after an 'altogether constitutional but unsuccessful governance' the society was deeply divided for the time of 2010 elections. The newly elected two-third majority government blamed the past for all the difficulties and the former Constitution became one of the scapegoats, which was not worth to respect any more.[230]

Before overviewing 'the replacement of the old with new', it is worthwhile to report about the constitutional background: how does the Hungarian constitutional law regulate the constitution making and amending process.

Hungarian Constitutional Development (eds. Zoltán SZENTE, Fanni MANDÁK and Zsuzsanna FEJES), L'Harmattan, Paris, 2015, 192–196.

[227] See to this Nóra CHRONOWSKI: The Fundamental Law Within the Network of Multilevel European Constitutionalism, in *Challenges and Pitfalls in the Recent Hungarian Constitutional Development* (eds. Zoltán SZENTE, Fanni MANDÁK and Zsuzsanna FEJES), L'Harmattan, Paris, 2015, 223–240.

[228] See below the story of the failed Seventh Amendment, and to the role of the Constitutional Court CHRONOWSKI Nóra and VINCZE Attila: Önazonosság és európai integráció – az Alkotmánybíróság az identitáskeresés útján, *Jogtudományi Közlöny* Vol. 72, № 3, 2017. 117–132.

[229] Zoltán SZENTE: Breaking and making constitutional rules, The constitutional effects of the world economic and financial crisis in Hungary, in Xenophon CONTIADES (ed.): Constitutions in the Global Financial Crisis: A Comparative Analysis, Farnham, Ashgate, 2013, 245–262.

[230] See also HALMAI 'Perspectives' 121–155.

Article S of the FL prescribes the rules of constitution making and amending. Paragraph (1) stipulates the initiation – in the same way as in case of legislative initiatives: "A proposal for the adoption of a new Fundamental Law or for the amendment of the Fundamental Law may be submitted by the President of the Republic, the Government, any parliamentary committee or any Member of the National Assembly." Paragraph (2) sets down the adoption, which does not differ from the majority required by the former Hungarian constitution (Act XX of 1949): "For the adoption of a new Fundamental Law or the amendment of the Fundamental Law, the votes of two-thirds of the Members of the National Assembly shall be required." This – together with Article 1 paragraph (2) point a) – expresses that the adoption and the amendment of the constitution is the exclusive competence of the National Assembly, the supreme organ of popular representation. It is worthwhile to add here, that Article 8 on national referendum in its paragraph (3) point a) stipulates: "[n]o national referendum may be held on any matter aimed at the amendment of the Fundamental Law", thus the electorate is not involved into constitutional matters. The people of Hungary may exercise its constitution making power stemming from popular sovereignty only indirectly, through the parliament.[231]

Paragraph (3) of Article S was revised by the Fourth Amendment of the FL in 2013, and now it clarifies that in the course of constitution making and constitution amending the head of state *(i)* cannot exercise political veto (i.e. he cannot send back the constitution or the amendment to the parliament for consideration), and *(ii)* his constitutional veto is limited to the initiation of the constitutional review of procedural requirements (validity)[232] thus the substantive constitutional review of the constitution or its amendment is excluded: "The Speaker of the National Assembly shall sign the adopted Fundamental Law or the adopted amend-

231 Petrétei József: *Magyarország alkotmányjoga I, Alapvetés, alkotmányos intézmények,* Kodifikátor Alapítvány, Pécs, 2013, 132.
232 Ibid.

ment of the Fundamental Law within five days and shall send it to the President of the Republic. The President of the Republic shall sign the Fundamental Law or the amendment of the Fundamental Law sent to him within five days of receipt and shall order its promulgation in the official gazette. If the President of the Republic finds that any procedural requirement laid down in the Fundamental Law with respect to adoption of the Fundamental Law or the amendment of the Fundamental Law has not been met, he or she shall request the Constitutional Court to examine the issue. Should the examination by the Constitutional Court not establish the violation of such requirements, the President of the Republic shall immediately sign the Fundamental Law or the amendment of the Fundamental Law, and shall order its promulgation in the official gazette." The formal constitutional review (regarding the procedural requirements of the adoption) of the FL or its amendment may take place subsequently as well – according to Article 24 paragraph (5) point b) – upon the request of the Government, one-fourth of the Members of the National Assembly, the President of the Curia [Supreme Court of Hungary], the Prosecutor General or the Commissioner for Fundamental Rights, but only within thirty days of promulgation.

Paragraph (4) of Article S provides for the special denotation of amendments, which is different from that of legislative acts of parliament as the FL and its amendments do not belong to the legal acts enumerated in Article T, instead they are special, independent and original[233] source of law: "The designation of the amendment of the FL in its promulgation shall include the title, the serial number of the amendment and the day of promulgation."

After the 2010 parliamentary elections, parallel with the declaration of creating a brand new constitution, the permanent amendments of the old Constitution also commenced. These amendments can be grouped into two types, one of them are 'normal' modifications and the others are 'demolishing' amendments. The 'normal'

---

233 Petrétei 'Magyarország alkotmányjoga' 131.

modifications are justified, because any new government is authorised to constitutional reforms on the basis of its electoral program and experiences of the constitutional practise. However, only the minority of the 2010-11 amendments belonged to this group:

1. seats in the parliament were reduced to 200 instead of 386,[234]
2. position of deputy prime minister was introduced,[235]
3. status of deputy major, other organs of local governments, and the transfer of state administration competencies were modified,[236]
4. clarifications on the legal system, legal acts, rules of ex ante norm control were set down,[237]
5. status of the prosecutor general was reformed to increase its independence,[238]
6. Supervisory Authority of Financial Organisations[239] and National Media Authority became constitutional organs.[240]

The subject matters of the 'demolishing' amendments were as follows:

1. nomination of *Constitutional Court* judges,[241]
2. freedom of press – creating constitutional basis for a new media legislation,[242]

---

[234] Act of 25 May 2010 (not exactly this solution was maintained in the FL).
[235] Act of 25 May 2010
[236] Act/1 of 6 July 2010
[237] Act CXIII of 2010 (published on 16 November 2010).
[238] Act CXIII of 2010 (published on 16 November 2010).
[239] Act CXIII of 2010 (published on 16 November 2010, it was not maintained in the FL).
[240] Act CLXIII of 2010 (it was not maintained in the FL).
[241] Act of 5 July 2010, authorised the governing majority in the parliament to nominate the judges unilaterally, without the consent of the opposition.
[242] Act/2 of 6 July 2010

3. *judiciary:* allowing court clerks to act as judge in certain cases,[243]
4. special tax on severance pay against *bona fides (morals)* in public service,[244]
5. limitations on right to be elected for officials of armed forces,[245]
6. limitation of the *Constitutional Court's competence* regarding the review of acts concerning public finances,[246]
7. special tax on severance pay – retroactive legislation back to five years,[247]
8. basis for changing pension system in order to get rid of early retirement benefits,[248]
9. nationalisation of local governments' property,[249]
10. *judiciary:* president of the *Kúria* (Supreme Court) shall be elected until 31. December 2011,[250]
11. *president of the Constitutional Court* shall be elected by the parliament instead of the court itself, and *15 instead of 11 judges* shall be elected.[251]

A pretty clear line of threatening (constitutional) judiciary and undermining rule of law can be observed in this group of amendments,

[243] Act/2 of 11 August 2010

[244] Act/2 of 11 August 2010

[245] Act/1 of 11 August 2010 (it was not maintained in the FL).

[246] Act CXIX of 2010 (published on 19 November 2010, it was announced as a temporary limitation, but the FL has maintained).

[247] Act CXIX of 2010 (published on 19 November 2010).

[248] Act LXI of 2011 (published on 14 June 2011).

[249] Act CXLVI of 2011 (published on 14 November 2011).

[250] Act CLIX of 2011 (published on 1 December 2011; with the intention to remove the acting president, András Baka; later the European Court of Human Rights stated the violation of the Convention, see Baka v. Hungary, Judgment of 27 May 2014, no. 20261/12.) See about the case Attila Vincze: Dismissal of the President of the Hungarian Supreme Court: ECtHR Judgment Baka v. Hungary, *European Public Law* Vol. 21, № 3, 2015, 445–456.

[251] Act LXI of 2011 (published on 14 June 2011).

while the supermajority strived to eliminate the constitutional impediments of economic governance and policy-making as well.[252]

In the meantime, after the announcement of constitution making intentions a parliamentary ad hoc committee responsible for preparing the constitution was set up in June, and started its work in September 2010. The composition of the committee reflected the parliamentary proportions of the party fractions. The preparatory activity was not intensive in 2010. During July and August some invited expert teams from universities and research institutes, as well as representative organizations of the civil society had the chance to share with the committee their recommendations to the constitution making. At this stage the expert and interest groups received no feedbacks from the parliamentary ad hoc committee, and their substantive participation was not provided for.

For a variety of reasons, the opposition left the preparatory committee, and then in December 2010 the concept of the new constitution was endorsed only by the representatives of the ruling coalition in the ad hoc committee. Finally on the basis of this concept no draft was elaborated, instead, the concept was put aside and all the parliamentary fractions were given the chance to submit their own draft constitutions.

In early March of 2011 two bills were lodged to the parliament, one of them by the governing party alliance and the other by an independent MP. They were parallel discussed from 21 March, and after 9 effective days of parliamentary debate on 18 April 2011 the bill of the governing parties was endorsed with the two-third majority of votes of the MPs. No opposition MPs voted for the bill. This short summary clearly shows that the actual and effective constitution-making was really quick but not transparent at all. The general public had only five weeks to evaluate the text, and the scope of the actors with effective influence on the formulation of the draft

---

252 Márton VARJU and Nóra CHRONOWSKI: Constitutional backsliding in Hungary, *TvCR* № 4, 2015, 298.

remained secret. Academic institutions, expert organizations, civilians, minorities and other groups of the society had no role in the process, and the preparatory committee in the parliament was also just the part of the scenery.

Assuming and accepting that the constitution making power is an original political will, which may adopt any kind of constitution, the process itself cannot be criticized. However, if one refuses this Schmittian approach,[253] and if the final goal is the creation of a democratic constitution integrating the society and meeting with the expectations of the international community, especially those of the European Union and the Council of Europe whom Hungary is a member state, then it is no wonder that the parallel methods of destruction and construction raised severe domestic and international criticism.

The Venice Commission issued two opinions during the narrow sense Hungarian constitution making, first upon the request of the

[253] Carl SCHMITT: *Constitutional Theory* (transl. and ed. Jeffrey SEITZER), Duke University Press, Durnham, London, 2008, 125. Dozens of essays challenge the Schmittian concept of constitution making power, trying to justify that under democratic developments this power cannot be formulated as an unlimited, pure political will. There are steady efforts in the academic discourse to distinguish the primary and secondary constitution making power, identify the limits of constituent power and constitution amending power. Georges BURDEAU: *Essai d'une théorie de la révision des lois constitutionnelles en droit français (Thèse pour le doctorat en droit, Faculté de droit de Paris)*, Macon, Paris, 1930; Antonio NEGRI: *Le pouvoir constituent: essai sur les alternatives de la modernité*, Presses Universitaires de France, Paris, 1997; Giovanni BIANCO: Brevi note su potere costituente e storia, in *Studi in onore di Pietro Rescigno*, Giuffrè, Milan, 1999; Kemal GÖZLER: *Pouvoir constituant*, Editions Ekin Kitabevi, Bursa [Turquie], 1999; H.P. SCHNEIDER: Die verfassunggebende Gewalt, in *Handbuch des Staatsrechts der Bundesrepublik Deutschland*, Band VII (hrsg. J. ISENSEE and P. KIRCHHOF), C. F. Müller Verlag, Heidelberg, 1992; E.W. BÖCKENFÖRDE: Die verfassungsgebende Gewalt des Volkes – Ein Grenzbegriff des Verfassungsrechts, in E.W. BÖCKENFÖRDE: *Staat, Verfassung, Demokratie – Studien zur Verfassungstheorie und zum Verfassungsrecht*, Suhrkamp Verlag, Frankfurt am Main, 1991; Yaniv ROZNAI: *Unconstitutional Constitutional Amendments, The Limits of Amendment Powers*, Oxford University Press, Oxford, 2017; PETRÉTEI 'Az alkotmányos demokrácia' 67–80.; CSINK Lóránt: *Mozaikok a hatalommegosztáshoz*, Pázmány Press, Budapest, 2014., KUKORELLI István: Hány éves az Alaptörvény? A régi-új kérdése az Alaptörvényben, *Iustum Aequum Salutare* № 4, 2016, 47–49.

Hungarian government[254] (March 2011),[255] and second upon the request of the Monitoring Committee of the Parliamentary Assembly CE (June 2011).

It must be noted that the draft of the new constitution was not sent to the Venice Commission on time, thus the first opinion of 28 March 2011 contained general comments and not evaluated any particular provisions of the draft constitutional text.

The Venice Commission in its second opinion, which was published on 20 June 2011, examining the final text revealed several criticalities that should be eliminated by utilising the common European values during the interpretation.[256] Although the commission welcomed the youngest European constitution, it also formulated important concerns and critics regarding the (i) procedure of drafting, deliberating and adopting without the opposition and the wider public, (ii) the high number of cardinal (organic) laws, especially

[254] The Venice Commission was addressed three legal questions by the Deputy Prime-Minister and Minister of Public Administration and Justice of Hungary. The three questions: (i) 'To what extent may the incorporation in the new Constitution of provisions of the Charter of Fundamental Rights enhance the protection of fundamental rights in Hungary and thereby also contribute to strengthening the common European protection of these rights?', (ii) The role and significance of the preliminary (ex ante) review among the competences of the Constitutional Court. In particular, two questions should be addressed: Who is entitled to submit a request for preliminary review? What is the effect of a decision passed by the Constitutional Court in a preliminary review procedure on the legislative competence of the Parliament? (iii) The role and significance of the actio popularis in ex post constitutional review. What is the state of play in Europe as regards the availability of actio popularis in matters of constitutionality? Could it be considered as an infringement of the European constitutional heritage (acquis) if the main focus of the Constitutional Court's activity was to shift from the posterior review, carried out on the basis of an actio popularis, to the examination of specific constitutional complaints?

[255] European Commission for Democracy Through Law (Venice Commission) Opinion № 614/2011, Strasbourg 28 March 2011, Opinion on Three Legal Questions Arising in the Process of Drafting the New Constitution of Hungary, Available at tasz.hu/files/tasz/imce/2011/opinion_on_hungarian_constitutional_questions_enhu_0.pdf.

[256] Venice Commission, Opinion № 621/2011, Strasbourg 20 June 2011, Opinion on the New Constitution of Hungary, www.venice.coe.int/webforms/documents/CDL-AD%282011%29016-E.aspx.

in the fields of family legislation, social and taxation policy, which are typically simple majority decisions of any government, (iii) the concept of 'historical constitution' as rule of interpretation, (iv) the wording of preamble, (v) the provisions related to Hungarians living beyond the borders, (vi) the constitutional obligations with uncertain content, (vii) the lack of explicit reference to abolition of death penalty, (viii) the limitation of the Constitutional Court's competence.

However, the Hungarian constituent power circumvented the recommended way of interpretation and insisted on the challenged solutions. Parliament has modified the FL six times (not considering the transitional provisions of unique status and history) since its entry into force, and has, *inter alia*, cemented the model of limited constitutional judicature, attempted to break constitutional continuity, to restrict the exercise of the right to vote and freedom of expression and perpetuated the practice of overruling the decisions of the Constitutional Court.[257]

1 To what extent does the Hungarian Fundamental Law defy EU values after its amendments?

This chapter analyses the relationship between the FL and the normative values of the European Union with special regard to the legally binding Charter of Fundamental Rights that articulates the general values into individual rights.

To ground this comparison and evaluation, the notion of EU values will be clarified and their impact on member states' constitution making will be outlined.

---

[257] See also Pál SONNEVEND, András JAKAB and Lóránt CSINK: The Constitution as an Instrument of Everyday Party Politics: The Basic Law of Hungary, in *Constitutional Crisis in the European Constitutional Area, Theory, Law and Politics in Hungary and Romania* (eds. Armin von BOGDANDY – Pál SONNEVEND), C.H. Beck, Hart, Nomos, Oxford, Portland, Oregon, 2015, 52–63.

After this short introduction, the chapter focuses on the question, to what extent the new FL is compatible with the shared values of the European Union, with special regard to its fundamental rights standard.

The ensuing analysis is twofold: on the one hand it compares the provisions of the FL with the norms of the former Constitution and tries to evaluate the changes. On the other hand, it also considers the relevant rules of the FL in the light of the Charter of Fundamental Rights and other Union values such as rule of law, democracy and loyal cooperation. Because of its frequent amendments, the FL is time to time in the centre of international and European attention, and raises concerns of EU institutions and other human rights watchdogs,[258] thus this part tries to explain the process

[258] On 8 February 2013, members of the governing coalition, having two thirds of the seats in the Hungarian Parliament, submitted a proposal to amend the FL. The Parliament adopted the amendment on 11 March 2013. It was published in the official journal on 1 April 2013. In March 2013, in the course of the Fourth Amendment to the FL, the Council of Europe, the UN High Commissioner, the President of the European Commission, Hungarian human rights associations and scholars voiced concerns over the changes. See e.g. <http://www.bbc.co.uk/news/world-europe-21740743>,<http://livewire.amnesty.org/2013/03/12/hungarys-constitutional-undermining-of-internationally-protected-human-rights/>, <http://www.un.org/apps/news/story.asp?NewsID=44389&Cr=judiciary&Cr1#.UUOI7jdMcY6>, <http://www.politics.hu/20130311/ex-president-solyom-urges-successor-to-veto-constitutional-changes-slams-fidesz-use-of-basic-law-for-daily-political-goals/>, <http://krugman.blogs.nytimes.com/2013/03/12/guest-post-the-fog-of-amendment/>

For joint expert opinion of Hungarian Helsinki Committee, Eötvös Károly Policy Institute and Hungarian Civil Liberties Union on Fourth Amendment, see: <http://helsinki.hu/wp-content/uploads/Appendix_1_Main_concerns_regarding_the_4th_Amendment_to_the_Fundamental_Law_of_Hungary.pdf>. Unofficial translation of the Fourth Amendment is available at <http://helsinki.hu/wp-content/uploads/Appendix_2_Fourth_Amendment_to_the_Fundamental_Law_Unofficial_translation.pdf>. The amendment was firmly criticised by the Venice Commission, see Opinion № 720/2013 of the Venice Commission on the Fourth Amendment of the Fundamental Law of Hungary, Strasbourg 17 June 2013, http://www.venice.coe.int/webforms/documents/?pdf=CDL-AD%282013%29012-e.

For academic evaluation, see Judit ZELLER: Nichts ist so beständig… Die jüngsten Novellen des Grundgesetzes Ungarns im Kontext der Entscheidungen des Verfassungsgerichts, *Osteuropa Recht* Vol. 59, № 3, 2013, 307–320.

of dismantling of rule of law and legal certainty that seems to deepen the gap between EU values and Hungarian constitutional architecture.

1.1 EU normative constraints and national constitution-making

The multilevel constitutional system of the Union is based on the national constitutional traditions in the field of fundamental rights and basic constitutional principles. It is important, however, that its basis is the common constitutional traditions as a whole, not any single tradition of a certain State.[259] These common traditions are recognised by Article 2 of the Treaty on the European Union (hereinafter: TEU) as amended by the Lisbon Treaty (hereinafter: TL), which establishes the common values as legitimating source of the polities forming a union: 'The Union is founded on the values of respect for human dignity, freedom, democracy, equality, the rule of law and respect for human rights, including the rights of persons belonging to minorities. These values are common to the member states in a society in which pluralism, non-discrimination, tolerance, justice, solidarity and equality between women and men prevail.' Although Article 2 formulates values, these can be considered as basic principles[260] of the Union, because they produce legal conse-

---

[259] See John Erik FOSSUM and Agustín José MENÉNDEZ: The Constitution's Gift? A Deliberative Democratic Analysis of Constitution Making in the European Union, *European Law Journal* Vol. 11, № 4, 2005, 380, 390–391.

[260] Principles command, values recommend. Principles are legal norms that regulate substantive components of the legal order. Values have moral character, and they can be conceptualised as normative objectives. See more in Jürgen HABERMAS: *Between Facts and Norms.* Polity Press, Cambridge, 1996. 255., and Armin von BOGDANDY: Doctrine of Principles, *Jean Monnet Working Paper Series* 9/03, 2003, 10., available at <http://www.jeanmonnetprogram.org/archive/papers/03/030901-01.pdf>

quences.[261] Thus, they influence the objectives of the Union,[262] their infringement is sanctioned,[263] and their respect is one of the conditions for EU membership.[264] As Bogdandy stated, the values of Article 2 are to be understood as legal norms, and since they are overarching and constitutive, they are founding principles.[265] The Court of Justice of the European Union (hereinafter: CJEU) for the first time referred to these values – enshrined at that time in Article 6(1) of the TEU pre-Lisbon – in its famous decision in Kadi, as principles that cannot be derogated by any acts of the Union even by those based on international law.[266] Besselink pointed out, that

---

261 See e.g. Articles 3(1), 7 and 49 of the TEU.

262 Article 3(1) of the TEU: The Union's aim is to promote peace, its values and the well-being of its peoples.

263 Article 7(1)-(3) of the TEU: 'On a reasoned proposal by one third of the member states, by the European Parliament or by the European Commission, the Council, acting by a majority of four fifths of its members after obtaining the consent of the European Parliament, may determine that there is a clear risk of a serious breach by a member state of the values referred to in Article 2. ... The European Council, acting by unanimity on a proposal by one third of the member states or by the Commission and after obtaining the consent of the European Parliament, may determine the existence of a serious and persistent breach by a member state of the values referred to in Article 2, after inviting the member state in question to submit its observations. ... [T]he Council, acting by a qualified majority, may decide to suspend certain of the rights deriving from the application of the Treaties to the member state in question, including the voting rights of the representative of the government of that member state in the Council.'

264 Article 49 of the TEU: 'Any European State which respects the values referred to in Article 2 and is committed to promoting them may apply to become a member of the Union.'

265 Armin von Bogdandy: Founding Principles of EU Law: A Theoretical and Doctrinal Sketch, *European Law Journal* Vol. 16, № 2, 2010, 95, 106.

266 Joined Cases C-402/05 and C-415/05 Kadi and Al Barakaat International Foundation v Council and Commission [2008] ECR I-06351, §303: 'Th[e EC Treaty] provisions [on the direct effect and priority of international law, in particular the obligations member states have accepted for the purpose of maintaining international peace and security] cannot, however, be understood to authorise any derogation from the principles of liberty, democracy and respect for human rights and fundamental freedoms enshrined in Art. 6(1) EU as a foundation of the Union.'

this judgment was the full recognition of the values shared by the Union and the member states.[267]

Besides affirming the shared values, the TEU also declares that the Union shall respect the national identities of its member states, defined by the TL as inherent part of their political and constitutional structures.[268] The definition emphasises the constitutional, political and state aspects, thus in this context the national identity can be understood (much more) as constitutional (than as a cultural) identity. One of the legally relevant questions in this respect is who will decide on the content of the constitutional identity of a member state and on the acts or measures of Union affecting or infringing that constitutional identity. It can be supposed that a relationship of cooperation between the national (constitutional) Courts and the CJEU is necessary in case of such conflicts, the first to determine the constitutional identity case by case, and the latter to decide on the meaning of the relevant EU law in dispute.[269]

As a result of the multilevel European constitutional development, the constitutional traditions of the member states converged in their respective content and interpretation, while the single States

---

267 Leonard F.M. Besselink: National and constitutional identity before and after Lisbon, *Utrecht Law Review* Vol. 6, № 3, 2010, 36, 41.

268 Article 4(2) TEU: 'The Union shall respect the equality of member states before the Treaties as well as their national identities, inherent in their fundamental structures, political and constitutional, inclusive of regional and local self-government. It shall respect their essential state functions, including ensuring the territorial integrity of the State, maintaining law and order and safeguarding national security. In particular, national security remains the sole responsibility of each member state.' According to Besselink, the plural in the first sentence of Article 4(2) may refer to the fact that the national identity does not mean merely state identity, instead, the TEU acknowledges the potential multinational character of member states, where the – national, ethnic, cultural etc – diversity is part of the constitutional structure. See Besselink 'National and constitutional identity' 43–44.

269 Besselink 'National and constitutional identity' 45. See to this e.g. the Omega-judgment of the CJEU (Case C-36/02 Omega Spielhallen- und Automatenaufstellungs-GmbH v Oberbürgermeisterin der Bundesstadt Bonn [2004] ECR I-9609]) and the Lisbon-judgment of the German Federal Constitutional Court (BVerfG, Urteil des Zweiten Senats vom 30. Juni 2009 [2 BvE 2/08]).

managed to preserve their own constitutional identity. An EU member state is henceforth to a great extent free to decide on its own constitutional structure, which is the basis of its constitutional identity. It is clear, however, that the functions of the constitution (integration of society, division of public power, ensuring human rights etc.) shall be taken into account during the constitution making, and formally the international obligations – unless the state intends to abrogate them – limit this freedom.[270] In other words, some manifestations of this "constituent freedom" may lead to break with the community of states, and result in withdrawal or exclusion. Taking into consideration the global tendencies of constitutionalism as well, it is worth to mention that the national constitutional development of democratic States converge since the 1950's in three features: (i) supremacy of the legislation is refused and judicial (constitutional) review is emerging,[271] (ii) States are committed to the protection of fundamental rights and basic freedoms prescribing explicit – sometimes implicit – limitation clauses with respect to the principle of proportionality, (iii) States are committed to the respect of guarantees of the rule of law.[272]

If a state wishes to remain the member of the Union, it cannot disregard membership criteria, and must not deny the primacy of the Union law in its national constitution. The first hypothesis

---

270 Constitution-making power is original as it is not bound by the former Constitution and determines the procedural frameworks itself. However, it does not mean, that this power would be unlimited. Constitution-making takes place in a particular political community and in a particular situation. If it aims at creating a democratic constitution, this objective limits the scope, content and procedure of the constitution-making. International obligations of the State and respected international and European standards are viewed also as external legal limits during constitution-making. See PETRÉTEI 'Az alkotmányos demokrácia' 75–78.

271 As Klug pointed out, while before 1989, in about 10 countries was an effective method for constitutional review applied, a decade later in 70 countries continued the (constitutional) Courts substantive norm control. Heinz KLUG: Constitutional Transformations: Universal Values and the Politics of Constitutional Understanding, in Charles SAMPFORD and Tom ROUND (eds): *Beyond the Republic, Meeting the Global Challenges to Constitutionalism,* Leichhardt, NSW, The Federation Press, 2001, 192.

272 TUSHNET 'The Inevitable Globalization' 985, 985–986.

arises if a member state tries to abolish democracy, or gives up the essential elements of the rule of law. Different forms of democracy or the rule of law, however, are still possible. The second hypothesis occurs if a state declares in its constitution that the domestic law and national legislation overrides EU law. In any other cases – that is, if the government is committed to membership in the EU – the freedom of constitution making is not complete, since the implementation of EU law is the duty of domestic public administrations and national Courts in the first place. Therefore, the system and functioning of national Courts and public administration is not indifferent to the EU. EU membership sets certain requirements for state organisation and the national legal system, in particular to ensure the uniform and effective application of EU law. If the relevant rules of organisation, responsibility and procedure are laid down by the national constitution, then to that extent it also shall correspond to the EU requirements.[273]

1.2 Compatibility of the new Hungarian Constitution with the Charter of Fundamental Rights

In Pernice's opinion, the Charter in particular explains and specifies what the common values referred to in Article 2 of the TEU as the foundation of the Union may really mean. The Charter rights may be invoked both in political processes (i.e. against adopted legislation) and as individual actions for judicial review.[274] The respect of the Charter as legally binding instrument creates a direct legal relationship between the citizens and those who exercise the power for and on behalf of them in the EU. Thus the Charter makes it clear that the Union is different from any other international organisation, since it is the Union of citizens, not simply that of member

[273] Dieter GRIMM: Zur Bedeutung nationaler Verfassungen in einem vereinten Europa in Detlef MERTEN and Hans-Jürgen PAPIER (eds), *Handbuch der Grundrechte in Deutschland und Europa,* Vol. VI/2 § 168 RN 59, C.F. Müller, 2009, 26.
[274] PERNICE 'The Treaty of Lisbon' 252.

states.[275] The Charter fully respects the implementation of subsidiarity, as it contains many references to national law and practice, and as primarily the EU institutions are bound by it – the member states only when implementing Union law. However, it is worth mentioning that the Charter has codified the CJEU case law, which is based on the constitutional traditions of the member states.[276] As it was already explained, the Charter contains a "horizontal" clause on non-reversal,[277] which involves the recognition of other legal mechanisms, in particular national constitutions and the international texts on the protection of human rights and fundamental freedoms, from the time that they are ratified by the member states. On the basis of this recognition, the principle used is that of the most favourable provision: the level of protection guaranteed by the Charter may not be lower than the level offered by the provisions of the texts cited, within their respective fields of application.[278] The Charter binds the member states as well 'when implementing Union law', however, the CJEU understands this in a wider sense: member states have to respect the fundamental rights 'acting within the scope of' Union law.[279] Thus on the basis of the preliminary ruling of the CJEU, national Courts of law may apply the Charter directly.[280]

---

[275] Pernice stated: 'The new reference in Article 6, para. 1 TEU-L underlines that the Treaty establishes a direct relationship between the citizens and those who are exercising power on their behalf and upon them. I am not aware of any other treaty or international instrument with this specific feature. It does constitute, I submit, the basis of what we call in French terms the contrat social.' PERNICE 'The Treaty of Lisbon' 236.

[276] László BLUTMAN: Az alkotmányos és európai alapjogok viszonya, in László BODNÁR (ed.): *EU-csatlakozás és alkotmányozás*, SZTE ÁJK Nemzetközi Jogi Tanszék, Szeged, 2001, 38., and Nóra CHRONOWSKI: *"Integrálódó" alkotmányjog*, Dialóg Campus, Budapest-Pécs, 2005, 66.

[277] Article 53 of the Charter.

[278] See Nóra CHRONOWSKI: Integration of European Human Rights Standard – the Accession of EU to the ECHR, in Jerzy JASKIERNIA (ed.): *Efektywność europejskiego systemu ochrony praw człowieka*, Adam Marszałek, 2012, 974–975.

[279] MATHISEN 'The Impact of the Lisbon Treaty' 20.

[280] Joined Cases C-188/10 Aziz Melki and C-189/10 Sélim Abdeli [2010] I-05667.

During the Hungarian constitution making in 2011 it occurred – and the Hungarian Government inquired from the Venice Commission[281] – whether and to what extent it was necessary to incorporate the Charter rights into the national constitution. The Venice Commission emphasised 'that up-dating the scope of human rights protection and seeking to adequately reflect, in the new Constitution, the most recent developments in the field of human rights protection, as articulated in the EU Charter, is a legitimate aim and a signal of loyalty towards European values.' However, the Commission also underlined that the incorporation of the Charter as a whole or of some parts of it could lead to legal complications. Thus, as the Commission suggested, it should be taken into account that the interpretation of the EU Charter by the CJEU might deviate from the one provided by the Constitutional Court of Hungary; the interpretation of the substantive provisions of the EU Charter is dependent on the ECHR and the case-law of the ECtHR; in the case law of the ordinary domestic Courts it might lead to problems that they should distinguish between the application of the Charter within and outside the scope of Union law. All these may lead to the erosion of constitutional autonomy of the member state. The Venice Commission recommended 'that it would be more advisable (...) to consider the EU Charter as a starting point or a point of reference and source of inspiration in drafting the human rights and fundamental freedoms chapter of the new Constitution.'[282]

---

[281] The Venice Commission was addressed three legal questions by the Deputy Prime-Minister and Minister of Public Administration and Justice of Hungary. One of the questions was the following: 'To what extent may the incorporation in the new Constitution of provisions of the Charter of Fundamental Rights enhance the protection of fundamental rights in Hungary and thereby also contribute to strengthening the common European protection of these rights?' See also above, note 254.

[282] European Commission For Democracy Through Law (Venice Commission) Opinion № 614/2011, Strasbourg 28 March 2011, Opinion on Three Legal Questions Arising in the Process of Drafting the New Constitution of Hungary, points 21., 25-28., 32. Available at <http://tasz.hu/files/tasz/imce/2011/opinion_on_hungarian_constitutional_questions_enhu_0.pdf>.

It must be noted that the draft of the new Constitution was not sent to the Venice Commission on time, thus the Opinion of 28 March 2011 contained general comments and not evaluated any particular provisions of the draft constitutional text. Meanwhile the governing party alliance published (on 7 March 2011) and submitted to the Parliament (on 15 March) a draft, which originally did not follow precisely the spirit and the content of the Charter. After a short – approximately one month – parliamentary debate, the adopted FL contains 'almost' the same rights as the Charter in its relevant Chapter ("Freedom and Responsibility"), and some sentences of the Charter were finally incorporated, but – compared to the Charter – the content of the rights enumerated by the FL is less detailed and the text raises the possibility of wider limitation of rights. The Venice Commission in its second opinion, which was given upon the request of the Parliamentary Assembly of the Council of Europe and was published on 20 June 2011, examining the final text revealed several criticalities that should be eliminated by utilising the common European values during the interpretation.[283]

1.2.1 General remarks

The FL under the title 'Freedom and Responsibility' lists in 28 articles the catalogue of fundamental rights (Articles II-XXIX). These articles contain partly constitutional rights (amongst which compared to the former Constitution new ones are the right to good administration,[284] some social rights of the employees,[285] right to self defence[286]), partly prohibitions (new ones are the *ne bis in idem*,[287] the non-

283 European Commission For Democracy Through Law (Venice Commission) Opinion № 621/2011, Strasbourg 20 June 2011, Opinion on the New Constitution of Hungary, <http://www.venice.coe.int/webforms/documents/CDL-AD%282011%29016-E.aspx>.

284 Article XXIV of the FL.

285 Article XVII of the FL.

286 Article V of the FL.

287 Article XXVIII of the FL.

refoulement,[288] the biomedicine prohibitions[289]), principles (new ones are equality before the law[290] or the social responsibility for property[291]), and in the field of social rights constitutional objectives (the protection of elderly and persons living with disabilities,[292] striving to provide decent housing,[293] the use of technological solutions and scientific achievements[294]). Some of the new rights were definitely inspired by the Charter and are in line with the global development.[295] Several provisions of the FL, however, regulate moral duties, the legal content of which has not been clarified yet, and the interpretation of which may influence also the content of certain fundamental rights. Of course it is not useless to write into the constitution some basic duties, and with regard to the consequences of globalisation, and common safety, environmental, health risks of the mankind the scope of the duties can be widened in the course of constitution making.[296] The former Constitution also declared as a basic duty to obey the constitution and legal provisions, the lawful action against the effort to obtain power with violent means or hold possession of power exclusively, contribution to rates and taxes in accordance to income and wealth, general and free compulsory

[288] Article XIV of the FL.

[289] Article III of the FL.

[290] Article XV of the FL.

[291] Article XIII of the FL.

[292] Article XV of the FL.

[293] Article XXII of the FL.

[294] Article XXVI of the FL.

[295] The number of the fundamental rights, prohibitions and principles is in line with the 'global average', which might be the effect of the European human rights regime. According to Law's and Versteeg's rights index the most popular rights and principles are the freedom of religion, the freedom of expression and/or press, equality rights, the right to private property, the right to private life, the habeas corpus, the right to assembly, the right to association, women's rights, freedom of movement, right of access to Court, prohibition of torture, right to vote, right to work, positive right to education at state expense, judicial review, prohibition of ex post facto laws. See more in LAW and VERSTEEG 'The Evolution and Ideology' 1163, 1190, 1200–1201.

[296] Antal ÁDÁM: On novel goals and tasks of the public power, in Bogusław BANASZAK (ed.): *Festschrift für Professor Kazimierz Działocha,* University of Wroczlaw, Wroczlaw, 2012.

school attendance, military defence obligation, and parents and guardians have the obligation of seeing to the education of minor children.[297] However, it is not accidental that there is no international convention on the basic human duties yet, as such an international obligation presumably would cause more damage than advantage to human rights law, providing governments with excuses to limit the exercise of human rights.[298] Unfortunately, several of the basic duties in the FL are of indefinite content, they have not been adequately defined (for example, contribution to the "community's enrichment" with work; or the method and extent of contribution to state and community tasks; connections between the contribution to satisfying community needs and contribution capabilities etc.). All this leaves wide scope for action of legislature in specifying these communitarian obligations, and the directions are unpredictable yet.

It is worth referring also to the preamble of the FL, according to which 'individual freedom can only be complete in cooperation with others.' The Charter applies a completely different approach, and emphasises in its preamble that the Union 'places the individual at the heart of its activities.' It raises the individuals' respon-

---

[297] As opposed to the six explicit basic duties contained in the former Constitution, the FL lays down twelve: action against arbitrary power [Article C(2)], contribution to the performance of state and community tasks [Article O], the protection, sustenance and preservation of the environment – in particular natural resources, biodiversity, cultural assets – for future generations [Article P], the obligations relating to law-abidance and interpretation [Article R(2)-(3)], respect for fundamental rights [Article I(1)], obligation to work [Article XII(1)], parents' obligation to look after and provide schooling for their children [Article XVI(3)], adult children's obligation toward their parents [Article XVI(4)], employers' and employees' obligation to cooperate with each other [Article XVII], contribution to satisfying community needs [Article XXX], obligation to defend the country [Article XXXI], obligation to appear before a parliamentary committee (regulated by a cardinal Act) [Article 7(3)].

[298] In 2003, the United Nations Commission on Human Rights received a draft declaration on human social responsibilities, but the Human Rights Council has not considered them. See John H. Knox: Horizontal Human Rights Law, *The American Journal of International Law* Vol. 102, № 1, 2008, 1–3.

sibility only in connection with the enjoyment of rights.[299] While the approach of the FL – taking also into consideration the numerous basic obligations – is communitarian, the Charter focuses on the philosophy of individual freedom.[300]

1.2.2 *Dignity*

The following points set out some ambiguities by comparing the Charter rights with FL regulation in the fields of dignity, freedom and solidarity. However, it is worth to note that the level of protection of the specific rights will depend on the interpretation given to the text.

Although the value of human dignity is recognized in the preamble[301] and in Article II of FL,[302] the rights connected with the right to life and human dignity might be interpreted restrictively. Just a few examples to highlight, that protection of foetal life from the moment of conception allows in principle the restriction of the right

[299] Charter Preamble: 'Enjoyment of these rights entails responsibilities and duties with regard to other persons, to the human community and to future generations.'

[300] Also refers to this the Opinion no. 621/2011 of the Venice Commission, point 57.

[301] 'We hold that human existence is based on human dignity.' This sentence more or less expresses that human life and human dignity indivisible values creating a unity. Thus also in the future the monist approach based on the unity of body and soul prevails, which was elaborated by the Constitutional Court in 1990. 'Human life and human dignity form an inseparable unity and have a greater value than anything else. The rights to human life and human dignity form an indivisible and unrestrainable fundamental right which is the source of and the condition for several additional fundamental rights. The constitutional state shall regulate fundamental rights stemming from the unity of human life and dignity with a view to the relevant international treaties and fundamental legal principles in the service of public and private interests defined by the constitution. The rights to human life and dignity as an absolute value create a limitation upon the criminal jurisdiction of the State.' HCC Decision 23/1990. (X. 31.) AB, point V.2.

[302] Article II of the FL: 'Human dignity shall be inviolable. Every human being shall have the right to life and human dignity; embryonic and foetal life shall be subject to protection from the moment of conception.'

to abortion and the women's right to self-determination.[303] Article IV(2) of the FL – uniquely in international comparison – allows the life sentence; however, without proper guaranties for judicial review it may risk to violate human dignity and to contradict the prohibition of torture and inhuman or degrading treatment or punishment.[304] Article XIX(3) also gives reason for concern from the viewpoint of equal dignity, as it contains the new measure of 'usefulness of activity to the community', which may be taken into account in deciding on the nature and extent of social aids. It is also regrettable that Article II does not contain explicitly the complete abolition of death penalty.[305] It would have been reasonable to mention, because the Republic of Hungary committed itself internationally to that prohibition,[306] and the Charter also reaffirms the abolition.

A new rule is contradicting the principle of dignity after the Fourth Amendment: it is the issue of criminalizing homelessness. Article XXII(3) of the FL reeds as follow: 'In order to protect public order, public security, public health and cultural values, an Act of Parliament or a local ordinance may declare illegal staying in a public area as a permanent abode with respect to a specific part of such

303 However, the FL does not declare the positive right to life of the foetus, just declares the protection of foetal life by the State. It does not necessarily imply an obligation for the State to penalise abortion. See also Opinion № 621/2011 of the Venice Commission, points 66–67.

304 Article IV(2) of the FL: 'No person shall be deprived of his or her liberty except for statutory reasons or as a result of a statutory procedure. Life imprisonment without parole shall only be imposed in relation to the commission of wilful and violent offences.' See also the concerns of the Venice Commission: 'By admitting the life imprisonment without parole, be it only in relation to the commission of wilful and violent offences, Article IV of the new Hungarian Constitution fails to comply with the European human rights standards if it is understood as excluding the possibility to reduce, de facto and de jure, a life sentence.' The Venice Commission also reminded of the case law of the ECtHR (Kafkaris v Cyprus, App. № 21906/04, 12 February 2008). Opinion № 621/2011 of the Venice Commission, points 69–70.

305 Similarly, see the Opinion № 621/2011 of the Venice Commission, point 68.

306 See the 6th and the 13th Protocols of the ECHR – promulgated by Acts XXXI of 1993 and III of 2004.

public area.' The amendment was a reaction to the former decision of the Constitutional Court on the Petty Offence Act,[307] in which the Court stated that the punishment of unavoidable living in a public area fails to meet the requirement of the protection of human dignity. The Venice Commission criticized the constitutional rank of the regulation, because it aims to prevent the review by the Constitutional Court.

1.2.3 Freedom

As to the rights related to freedom, the regulation in the FL also raises some problems. The habeas corpus provision which is part of the right to personal freedom and security was not developed during constitution-making, thus it is formulated also in the future as the duty of authorities, not as an individual right to the judicial review of an arrest.[308] The term 'as soon as possible' was not specified in connection with the bringing before a judge either.[309] By

---

[307] HCC Decision 38/2012. (XI. 14.) AB, see the press release, http://hunconcourt.hu/sajto/news/provisions-of-the-act-on-contraventions-criminalizing-people-living-at-public-areas-permanently-are-against-fundamental-law.

[308] Article IV(3) of the FL: 'Any person suspected of and arrested for committing any offence shall either be released or brought before a Court as soon as possible. The Court shall be obliged to give such person a hearing and to immediately make a decision with a written justification on his or her acquittal or conviction.' See Article 5(4) of the ECHR: 'Everyone who is deprived of his liberty by arrest or detention shall be entitled to take proceedings by which the lawfulness of his detention shall be decided speedily by a Court and his release ordered if the detention is not lawful.'

[309] This is particularly problematic, because Act LXXXIX of 2011 amending Act XIX of 1998 on Criminal Procedure allowed in criminal cases of special significance 120 hours (5 days) of arrestment. It conflicts with the requirement of 'reasonable time' and with the case law of the ECHR. See McKay v the United Kingdom, App. № 543/03, 3 October 2006, §47 (in the given case the ECHR has held 4 days at the longest as reasonable). See also Bence Mészáros: Kiemelt jelentőségű ügyek, alkotmányos aggályok – új különeljárás a büntetőeljárási törvényben, *Közjogi Szemle* № 3, 2011, 59, 62–63. The Constitutional Court found this provision on 120 hours of arrestment unconstitutional in December 2011, see HCC Decision 166/2011. (XII. 20.) AB.

introducing the right to self-defence in the constitutional provisions, the boundaries of the individual and state responsibility become uncertain. The relationship between the new right and the monopoly of the State to enforce the constitution and the legislation as outlined in Article C(3) of FL remains an open question.[310] It can be presupposed that the former is an exception to the latter rule, however, this solution is rather unfortunate in case of a constitutional provision, because the constitutional text should be unambiguous, without exception rules. Furthermore, it is also open to debate, what the relationship between the right to self-defence and the norm on justified defence in the Criminal Code is.

The formulation of the individual freedom of conscience and religion[311] is in line with the text of the Charter and the former Constitution. What changed, however, is that on the basis of conscience the military service cannot be renounced, only unarmed military service can be chosen as an alternative,[312] thus there is no possibility to choose civilian service outside the armed forces. Article 10(2) of the Charter explicitly recognises conscience objection. The Venice Commission also emphasised: 'The exception for conscientious objectors may raise a specific problem. While it is true that the ECHR leaves it to the member states to decide whether to establish any obligation to perform armed services, the obligation to perform unarmed service in Article XXXI has to be interpreted using a systematic approach. Unarmed services should be performed outside the army in order to avoid potential conflicts with Article 9 ECHR (the right to freedom of thought, conscience and religion). This would resemble regulations in other European States and their handling of armed and unarmed services.'[313] Unfortunately the new

310 Article V of the FL: 'Every person shall have the right to repel any unlawful attack against his or her person or property, or one that poses a direct threat to the same.' Article C(3) of FL: 'The State shall have the exclusive right to use coercion in order to enforce the Fundamental Law and legislation.'

311 Article VII of the FL.

312 See Article XXXI of the FL.

313 Article 10(2) of the Charter: 'The right to conscientious objection is recognised, in accordance with the national laws governing the exercise of this right.' See also

law of 2011 on national defence does not follow the mentioned case law and the recommendation of Venice Commission.[314]

An additional new constitutional rule is that under the FL the State and the churches shall cooperate for community goals, while they remain separate. Under the former constitutional regulation the independent Courts of law registered the churches and decided whether a religious community asking for the church status fulfilled the legal conditions. According to the Transitional Provisions of the FL[315] (hereinafter TPFL) and the new cardinal act[316] on churches, the Parliament decides on church status of applicant religious communities. This procedure makes the separation of State and churches relative, and infringes the principle of division of powers.[317] The Constitutional Court annulled the regulation of the TPFL and some provisions of the act on churches;[318] however, the Fourth Amend-

---

Opinion № 621/2011 of the Venice Commission, point 84.

314 See Sections 4 and 9-10 of Act CXIII of 2011.

315 The Transitional Provisions were adopted by the Parliament on 30 December 2011, published on 31 December 2011, and it came into force on 1 January 2012. The TPFL served the coming into force of the new Constitution. However, regarding its content the TPFL was more like an amendment, as about half of its rules were not transitory at all. For a more detailed evaluation, see point 1.3.1 below. An unofficial translation of the TPFL by Miklós Bánkuti, Gábor Halmai and Kim Lane Scheppele is available at <http://lapa.princeton.edu/hosteddocs/hungary/The%20Act%20on%20the%20Transitional%20Provisions%20of%20the%20Fundamental%20Law.pdf>.

316 Cardinal act means organic law. The adoption requires two-third majority of the MPs present. See also Boldizsár Szentgáli-Tóth: The Scope of Qualified Law: Comparative Analysis, 22nd International Academic Conference, Proceedings, ISBN 978-80-87927-21-2, IISES, Lisbon, 22 March 2016, 271–273.

317 See Act CCVI of 2011 on right to freedom of conscience and religion, and on status of churches, religious denominations and communities. The relevant article of the TPFL was annulled by the Constitutional Court as non-transitional rule. See also Antal Ádám: Vallás, vallásszabadság és egyház Magyarország Alaptörvényének, továbbá „A lelkiismereti- és vallásszabadság jogáról, valamint az egyházak, vallásfelekezetek és vallási közösségek jogállásáról" szóló 2011. évi C. törvény figyelembe vételével, *JURA* Vol. 17, № 2, 2011, 7, 21–22. <http://jura.ajk.pte.hu/JURA_2011_2.pdf>. See also the Amicus Brief by Halmai, Scheppele (eds.), cit. 25–29.

318 HCC Decision 6/2013. (III. 1.) AB, press release: 'The Constitutional Court, during the examination of the regulations of Act on Churches, has declared that

ment[319] of the FL incorporated the repealed TPFL rules into the text of the constitution. Under the modified regulation, all religious communities (churches) may operate freely, but those of them seeking further cooperation with the State must be voted for by the Parliament, thus receiving "established" or "accepted" church status. This solution also erodes secularism and leaves room for political considerations in the recognition of churches.

Among the rights guaranteeing free communication, the freedom to express one's opinion originally was formulated in the FL similarly to the former Constitution, but the Fourth Amendment of the FL introduced serious bans on speeches violating human dignity, the dignity of the Hungarian nation or minority groups.[320] Even the Venice Commission found it contradicting European standards, because 'the provisions on the dignity of communities are too vague and the specific protection of the "dignity of the Hungarian nation" creates the risk that freedom of speech in Hungary could, in the future, be curtailed in order to protect Hungarian institutions and office holders.'[321]

---

the Act does not contain any obligation for detailed reasoning regarding the proposal or the decision which refuses the acknowledgement as a Church. The rejected religious communities do not get any official, written explanation which contains the reason why they could not get religious status or why they could not keep it. Furthermore, the Act does not contain any deadline for the Parliamentary Committee to make a proposal or for the Parliament to make the decision and does not ensure possibility for legal remedy in case of the rejecting decision or the lack of the decision. The acknowledgement of religious status by the voting of the Parliament, the fact that it is the Parliament who decides on the status of churches, might result in decisions based on political aspects. The decision-making in these individual cases, which should be assessed by legal discretion and which have fundamental legal aspects as well, should be dealt by the independent Courts and not transferred to the Parliament's competence, which basically has political character, and so it is incompatible with the Fundamental Law.' http://hunconcourt.hu/sajto/news/press-release-regarding-the-constitutional-review-of-the-act-on-churches.

319 See Art. 4 of the Fourth Amendment.

320 See Art. 5 of the Fourth Amendment.

321 Opinion № 720/2013 of the Venice Commission, point 141.

The State also recognises and defends the freedom and diversity of the press (see Article IX). The FL does not contain the prohibition of censorship, and does not formulate such guarantees as the Charter or the ECHR for precluding any interference by public authorities.

1.2.4 Solidarity

Solidarity rights were codified by the EU Fundamental Rights Convention in 2000 with regard to their close connection to the value of dignity. The principle of social solidarity also appeared in the case law of the CJEU as the foundation of social welfare system.[322] Solidarity in the European Union is a common value recognised also by the preamble of the Charter and Articles 2-3 of the TEU, which can be considered as an identity-forming feature and socially it may serve the supranational community-building.[323]

Article XVII of the FL regulates solidarity in more details in the world of employment than the former Constitution did, and for that purpose the Charter was taken as a basis. The FL ensures fair and just working conditions for the employees, and guarantees a right to employees, employers and their representatives 'to bargain and to conclude collective agreements, and to take any joint actions.' The employees have the right to hold strikes in defence of their interests.

Article XVII(1) prescribes the obligation of employees and employers to cooperate, and the purpose of this cooperation (ensuring jobs, making the national economy sustainable and other community goals), but does not mention either the social dialogue, or the

---

[322] Alexander SOMEK: Solidarity Decomposed, Being and time in European citizenship, University of Iowa Legal Studies Research Paper 07-13, 2007, 4. Available at ssrn.com/abstract=987346.

[323] Juliane OTTMANN: The Concept of Solidarity in National and European Law: The Welfare State and the European Social Model, *Vienna Journal on International Constitutional Law* – www.icl-journal.com Vol. 1, 2008, 36, 43–44.

system of social and economic interest reconciliation, or the workers right to information and consultation within the undertaking (cf. the latter with Article 27 of the Charter). The FL does not contain either the protection in the event of unjustified dismissal[324] (cf. with Article 30 of the Charter), or any guarantees to reconcile family and professional life (cf. with Article 33 of the Charter, containing the right to protection from dismissal for a reason connected with maternity and the right to paid maternity leave and to parental leave following the birth or adoption of a child). Article XVII(2) of the FL although refers to the protection of parents in the workplace, but the level of this protection depends on the measures adopted by the State, thus it is not a fundamental right.

Social security does not appear as a fundamental right in the FL, but merely as something the State "shall strive" for, thus it only appears to be a state goal, which can be evaluated as a step backward in comparison with the former Constitution. In Article XIX(1) of FL among the titles to statutory subsidies (within the group of people in need) old age is not listed; it appears alone, separately from the categories of neediness, in paragraph (4). Social insurance does not appear as a constitutional institution, instead, in Article XIX(2) the expression 'a system of social institutions and measures' is used as the means of achieving the defined state goal. The above already referred paragraph (3) of Article XIX raises serious concerns as it refers to uncertain measures: 'The nature and extent of social measures may be determined by law in accordance with the usefulness to the community of the beneficiary's activity.' What is useful to the community and who decides on the usefulness in certain cases? Might the social support be withhold in the absence of "useful activity" on this constitutional bases, even if the person concerned is needy and the cause of the situation falls outside his or her own fault? The principle of "self-responsibility" is also weakened by the

[324] It is no surprise. Until 31 May 2011 the government officers and until 7 April 2011 the public servants were dismissed without reasoning, by this time annulled the Constitutional Court the challenged laws. See HCC Decisions 8/2011. (II. 18.) AB and 29/2011. (IV. 7.) AB, in *Magyar Közlöny*, 2011/14, 2011/37.

regulation of the FL relating to social security, especially by the obligation of the State to maintain a general state pension system based on social solidarity. As a basis for the state pension system (as a constitutional institution) the FL specifies exclusively social solidarity, although the system is based on individual financial contribution, thus the right to property,[325] and the principle of individual responsibility should also be guaranteed. The member states has a wide margin of appreciation regarding their social security system, thus the new constitutional regulation does not breach the EU law directly, but it is worth to mention that the new Hungarian constitutional regulation on social security does not properly guarantee the equal dignity and the property protection.

1.3 Rule of law, democracy, international and EU obligations

1.3.1 Rule of law – "Rechtsstaat"

Rule of law principle has a rich content in constitutional theory, but at this point the aspects of legal security and division of powers doctrine will be highlighted by focusing on the characteristics of Hungarian constitution amending process and limitation of the Constitutional Court's powers.

The rule of law enjoyed a paramount position among the norms which constituted the constitutional order of post-1989 Hungary. It was modelled almost exclusively on the German *Rechtsstaat* concept.[326]

---

[325] Cf. the first sentence of Article XIII(1) of the FL: 'Every person shall have the right to property and inheritance.'

[326] As László Sólyom, the first president of the Constitutional Court outlined 'Even the traditional difference between the formal and the substantial concepts of the Rechtsstaat (...) was revived and had to be reinterpreted. (...) The Court made both the politicians and the population conscious of the secure protection constitutional rights (...) and aware of one of the most important characteristic of the rule of law: political intentions can only be implemented lawfully and within the framework of the Constitution – not vice versa, as before, when the law was conceived as merely a political tool. (...) The Court, moreover, developed a moral explanation of its position. It introduced the paradoxical phrase "revolu-

There is scholarly consensus[327] that the incorporation of the substantive, structural and procedural components of the *Rechtsstaat* principle led to the anchoring in Hungarian constitutionalism of foundational ideas, such as the protection of fundamental rights, the separation of powers and limited government, the legality of public administration, legal certainty, the independence of the judiciary and the right of access to justice. The influence of the *Rechtstaat* principle also meant that in Hungary the written constitution enjoys the highest rank in the hierarchy of legal norms superseding other pieces of legislation, which primacy is manifested primarily through the process of constitutional review exercised by the Constitutional Court. The jurisprudence developed by the Constitutional Court in a long chain of constitutional review cases emphasized primarily the formal dimensions of the rule of law, especially the principle of legal certainty, and left the substantive aspects of the principle somewhat underdeveloped.[328]

The prominence of the rule of law among the principles of the constitution, which was matched only by the human dignity principle, and the emphasis on its formal dimensions were thought to provide an essential guarantee for the successful completion of the post-1989 transition process.[329] The rule of law offered that formal guarantee which was able to establish a boundary between the constitutional arrangements which had been in place before the regime change and the new constitutional order where public powers are subjected to genuine legal constraints. The position held on the rule of law by the Constitutional Court, the central architect

tion under the rule of law".' László Sólyom: Introduction to the Decisions of the Constitutional Court of the Republic of Hungary, in L. Sólyom and G. Brunner (eds.): *Constitutional Judiciary in a New Democracy, The Hungarian Constitutional Court,* University of Michigan Press, Ann Arbor, 2000, 1 et sqq., 38.

327 Petrétei 'Az alkotmányos demokrácia' 139–159.

328 Tamás Győrfi, András Jakab: Jogállamiság, in A. Jakab (ed.): *Az Alkotmány kommentárja,* Századvég, Budapest, 2009, 155 et sqq., 174.

329 László Sólyom: The Rise and Decline of Constitutional Culture in Hungary, in A. von Bogdandy and P. Sonnevend (eds.): *Constitutional Crisis in the European Constitutional Area,* Hart Publishing, Oxford, 2015, 5 et sqq., 6–7.

of the novel constitutional order and a key actor in the process of political and legal transition, was simple, but effective: "the rule of law cannot be achieved against the rule of law".[330] This meant foremost that the Court systematically enforced the principle of legal certainty and applied the rule of law, which it aimed to interpret and develop as a neutral concept,[331] as the fundamental benchmark of its constitutional control powers.[332] It was interpreted as having a normative content independent from concrete constitutional provision the violation of which could give rise to protection before the Constitutional Court. The rule of law was also available to support as their conceptual basis more specific constitutional norms, and it provided a philosophical umbrella for the entire constitutional order, the individual norms of which were in turn available to give effect in individual instances to the rule of law as a general principle.

In the jurisprudence of the Constitutional Court under the 1989 Constitution,[333] the rule of law emerged as a self-standing normative principle, and it was used to provide the basis of other, more specific constitutional norms, such as legal certainty and the separation of powers.

The new FL accorded a position in Hungarian constitutionalism to the rule of law similar to that in the 1989 Constitution. Its Article B) recognised the rule of law and democracy as the foundational principles of the Hungarian republic. Article C) contains the now self-standing principle of the separation of powers, which principle continues to be expressed in the detailed constitutional provisions on the organisation and the functioning of the state. Beyond the constitutional text, there are, however, a number of systemic devel-

330 HCC Decision 11/1992. (III. 5.) AB.

331 Gábor Attila Tóth: *Túl a szövegen, Értekezés a magyar alkotmányról,* Osiris, Budapest, 2009, 147.

332 For example, the Constitutional Court never paid much attention to the concept of democracy and to its relevance in constitutional interpretation, see minority opinion of Judge Kiss in HCC Decision 39/1999. (XII. 21.) AB.

333 Act XX of 1949 on the Constitution of the Republic of Hungary as revised in 1989–90, in force until 31 December 2011.

opments which raise doubts as to the commitment of the new constitutional order, and of the political order which developed the new constitutional framework, to sustaining and building upon the legacy of post-1989 Hungarian constitutionalism which had placed the rule of law at the heart of the functions performed by the constitution in the Hungarian political, economic and social order. These developments include the instability of the constitution which followed from its frequent, politically-driven modifications, the imposition of serious limitations on the constitutional review exercised by the Constitutional Court, and the open struggle between the Constitutional Court and the government acting in parliament for the supreme constitutional authority in the country. The events of constitution-making after 2010 seem to contradict the iconic statement in the early jurisprudence offering the foundations of a culture of the rule of law in Hungary that "the rule of law cannot be achieved against the rule of law".[334]

Article B of the FL also supports the most important principles of the former Constitution – these are rule of law and democracy – and, although not in the official name of the country, but at least regarding the form of State, Hungary remains a republic,[335] thus the republican traditions and guarantees may prevail. Article C(1) of the FL explicitly provides the principle of division of powers, which is welcomed considering the fact that until now this significant principle appeared only in the preamble of the former act on Constitutional Court[336] and of course in the Constitutional Court's case law. It is worth to mention, however, that the division of powers should also be reflected in the rules on state organs in the FL and in constitutional practice – the declaration of the principle in itself does not add anything to the more detailed provisions on the constitutional architecture. At most it may serve as a point of reference for the constitutional court.

334 HCC Decision 11/1992 (III. 5.) AB.

335 Article B(1)-(2) of the FL.

336 Act XXXII of 1989, in force until 1 January 2012.

In addition, it was an extremely alarming issue concerning the basic principles of the FL that the TPFL has constructed an unusual constitutional liability for the "communist past", furthermore it has overruled some important statements of the constitutional court e.g. on the right to the lawful and impartial judge[337] and undermined some rules of the FL itself.[338] According to the Commissioner for Fundamental Rights of Hungary, the TPFL 'severely harms the principle of the rule of law, which may cause problems of interpretation and may endanger the unity and operation of the legal system. The Ombudsman is concerned because the Transitional Provisions contain many rules obviously having not transitional character.'[339] Thus the Ombudsman requested the Constitutional Court to examine whether the Transitional Provisions comply with the requirements of the rule of law laid down in the FL. After the Ombudsman's initiative, the Parliament adopted the First Amendment to the FL clarifying that the Transitional Provisions are part of the FL. By this amendment the governing majority intended to avoid the constitutional review of the TPFL, confirming its constitutional rank.[340] Despite this, the Constitutional Court ruled on the

337 HCC Decision 166/2011 (XII. 20.) AB.

338 On the TPFL and other cardinal acts read more in Gábor Halmai, Kim Lane Scheppele (eds.): Amicus Brief for the Venice Commission on the Transitional Provisions of the Fundamental Law and the Key Cardinal Laws, February 2012, available at <http://halmaigabor.hu/dok/426_Amicus_Cardinal_Laws_final.pdf>.

339 On the petition of the Ombudsman lodged in March, 2012 to the Constitutional Court concerning the TPFL see http://www.ajbh.hu/en/web/ajbh-en/press-releases/-/content/ujPUErMfB9lw/petition-of-the-ombudsman-to-the-constitutional-court-concerning-the-transitional-provisions-of-the-fundamental-law.

340 In April 2012 the Government of Hungary lodged a bill to the Parliament as the First Amendment of the FL of Hungary so as to clarify that the Transitional Provisions are the part of the FL. The First Amendment was adopted in June 2012. It added a new 5th point to the Closing Provisions of the FL: '5. The transitional provisions related to this Fundamental Law adopted according to point 3 (31 December 2011) are part of the Fundamental Law.' Other relevant points of the Closing provisions: '2. Parliament shall adopt this Fundamental Law according to point a) of subsection (3) of Section 19 and subsection (3) of Section 24 of Act XX of 1949. 3. The transitional provisions related to this Fundamental Act shall be adopted separately by Parliament according to the procedure referred to in point

Ombudsman's petition declaring that all the provisions of the TPFL lacking transitory character are invalid.[341] As a response, the governing majority adopted the Fourth Amendment of the FL, which incorporated into the Constitution most of the abolished articles, and overrode several former Constitutional Court decisions. The Venice Commission expressed its serious concerns about the systematic shielding ordinary law from the constitutional review. The reduction (budgetary matters) and in some cases complete removal (constitutionalised matters) of the competence of the Court to review ordinary legislation undermines on the one hand the rule of law – as the constitutional protection of the standards of the FL became limited; on the other hand, infringes the democratic system of checks and balances – as the Constitutional Court lost its influence and is not able to provide effective control.[342]

Regarding the mechanism for safeguarding the constitution, one of the weaknesses is that the FL – similarly to the former Constitution – can be amended relatively easily, only two-third majority of

2 above.' (The FL was not in force yet when the Parliament adopted the Transitional Provisions – that is the reason of the reference to the former Constitution).

341 The Constitutional Court annulled approximately half of the articles of the TPFL in its decision of 28 December 2012 (HCC Decision 45/2012. (XII. 29.) AB). Press release: 'The Constitutional Court has declared that the Hungarian Parliament exceeded its legislative authority, when enacted such regulations into the "Transitional Provisions of the Fundamental Law" that did not have transitional character. The Hungarian Parliament shall comply with the procedural requirements also when acting as constitution-maker, because the regulations that violate these requirements are invalid. Therefore, the Constitutional Court annulled the concerned regulations due to formal deficiencies. The Constitutional Court, regarding its consistent practice, did not examine the constitutionality of the content of the Fundamental Law and the Transitional Provisions', available at http://hunconcourt.hu/sajto/news/certain-parts-of-the-transitional-provisions-of-the-fundametal-law-held-contrary-to-the-fundamental-law. It is worth to mention the governing party's response, in which the faction leader immediately declared that the annulled provisions will be inserted into the FL.

See also Zoltán SZENTE: Az Alkotmánybíróság döntése Magyarország Alaptörvényének Átmeneti rendelkezései alkotmányosságáról: az Alaptörvény integritása és az alkotmányozó hatalom korlátai, *Jogesetek Magyarázata* Vol. 4, № 1, 2013, 11–21.

342 Opinion № 720/2013 of the Venice Commission, point 87.

all MPs is needed. The constitution amending process that started in 2010 and led to the constant amendments of the former Constitution based on *ad hoc* political interests, made it clear that more guarantees are necessary – e.g. unchangeable provisions (eternity clause), referendum on certain amendments, approval of two sequential parliaments – for a stable constitution. The overwhelming practice of amending the constitution is going on with the FL as well, because the governing majority adopts modifications again and again with the purpose of punishing the Constitutional Court for unfavourable decisions, overrule the Court's judgments or to prevent constitutional review.

The other key institution in safeguarding the constitution is the Constitutional Court. In parliamentary governmental systems, if the government is supported by a wide parliamentary majority, constitutional jurisdiction counterbalancing the unity of action of parliament and government constitutes the guarantee for the separation of powers and the sovereignty of the law (constitution). The greater the unity of action between the parliament and government, the wider competence is needed for constitutional jurisdiction to maintain the balance. In respect of the principle of rule of law it is very harmful that the FL upholds for an indefinite time the restriction of the supervision and annulment rights of the Constitutional Court that was introduced in November 2010.[343] More specifically, Article 37(4) of the Chapter on Public Finances of the FL lays down that with regard to *ex post* norm control and constitutional complaint procedures, the Constitutional Court is prevented from reviewing

[343] Because of a constitutional amendment in November 2010, a serious limitation of the competences of the Constitutional Court was introduced. According to this amendment, the Constitutional Court may assess the constitutionality of Acts related to the state budget, central taxes, duties and contributions, custom duties and central conditions for local taxes exclusively relating to the rights to life and human dignity, the protection of personal data, the freedom of thought, conscience and religion or with rights related to the Hungarian citizenship. Also, the Court may only annul these Acts in case of violation of the abovementioned rights. The restriction of the Constitutional Court's competences was the answer of the alliance of the governing parties to a Court decision, which annulled a law on a certain tax imposed with retroactive effect.

the content of or annulling acts on public finances, with the exception of four "protected fundamental rights", as long as state debt exceeds half of the Gross Domestic Product.[344] Thus, the power of annulment is curtailed by Article 37(4) of the FL, because it excludes the constitutional review and annulment of Acts relating to public finances from the side of content, apart from four exceptions. This is not rectified even by the fact that Acts relating to this subject-matter may be annulled in case the requirements of the legislative process were not met (for formal reasons). Paradoxically, this way the FL also excludes the protection by the Constitutional Court of its own provisions relating to public finances, because the violation of rules relating to public finances contained in the FL is most likely to occur by way of Acts relating to the state budget, taxes, customs duties etc., which are subject to ex post review by the Constitutional Court only from the aspect of the four protected fields of fundamental rights. The TPFL upheld and extended the effect of the disputed limitation on constitutional review,[345] and the Fourth Amendment incorporated it into the FL.[346]

The restriction of the Constitutional Court's rights of review and annulment is not in conformity either with the principles of European constitutional achievements or the traditions of Hungarian constitutionalism and democratic political culture developed since

[344] 'As long as state debt exceeds half of the Gross Domestic Product, the Constitutional Court may, within its competence set out in Article 24(2)b-e), only review the Acts on the State Budget and its implementation, the central tax type, duties, pension and healthcare contributions, customs and the central conditions for local taxes for conformity with the Fundamental Law or annul the preceding Acts due to violation of the right to life and human dignity, the right to the protection of personal data, freedom of thought, conscience and religion, and with the rights related to Hungarian citizenship. The Constitutional Court shall have the unrestricted right to annul the related Acts for non-compliance with the Fundamental Law's procedural requirements for the drafting and publication of such legislation.'

[345] Article 27 of the TPFL: 'Article 37(4) of the Fundamental Law shall remain in force for Acts that were promulgated when the state debt to the Gross Domestic Product ratio exceeded 50% even if the ration no longer exceeds 50%.' This Article was also annulled by the Constitutional Court in its HCC Decision 45/2012. (XII. 29.) AB.

[346] See Art. 17 of the Fourth Amendment.

1989-90. It violates the constitutional principles of the rule of law, legal security and separation of powers. Because of the restriction of the procedure of the Constitutional Court, numerous fundamental rights (especially, for example, the right to property, social rights, the freedom of enterprise, the right to a profession) become "defenceless".[347]

The TPFL introduced further indirect constraints on the right to effective judicial protection. If the ruling of Constitutional Court or the CJEU results a debt obligation of the State, under certain circumstances a general contribution covering the common needs – i.e. extra tax – shall be adopted. It can be understood as an intention to sanction – at least indirectly – the lawsuits and complaints in cases of great economic significance.[348] The Constitutional Court annulled this regulation; however, the Fourth Amendment[349] of the FL incorporated it into the text of the Constitution. As the European Commission expressed its serious concerns about the conformity with EU law of the new article on CJEU judgments entailing payment obligations, the Fifth Amendment[350] repealed this rule.

---

347 See also Opinion № 621/2011 of the Venice Commission, points 91–101, 120–127.

348 See Article 29 of TPFL: 'As long as the public debt exceeds 50% of the GDP, if the Constitutional Court, the CJEU, other Court or other law applying that body's decision requires the State to pay a fine, and the Act on the central budget does not contain necessary reserves to pay the fine, and the amount of the fine cannot be allocated from the budget without undermining a balanced management of the budget or no other item from the budget may be eliminated to provide for the fine, a general contribution covering the common needs must be specified that relates in its name and content exclusively and explicitly to the above fine.' This Article was annulled by the Constitutional Court in HCC Decision 45/2012. (XII. 29.) AB.

349 See Art. 17 of the Fourth Amendment.

350 The Fifth Amendment of the FL was adopted by the governing majority in September 2013 with the intention of 'closing international debates', however not all of the challenged articles were modified. It entered into force on 1 October 2013.

1.3.2 Democracy

The democracy principle is undermined in the FL on the one hand by defining ambiguously the political community, and on the other hand by reducing the significance of future elections through the instrument and high number of cardinal acts in the field of simple majority policies.

It is problematic, from the perspective of the principle of democracy, that the FL does not clearly identify the political community to which it shall be applied, because the use of the concepts of political nation and cultural nation is inconsistent and controversial in the constitutional text. Article B of FL refers to the 'people' as the source of public power, and the preamble is written on behalf of citizens – both sentences are the proofs of the political nation approach. At the same time, Article D of FL uses the expression of 'one single Hungarian nation' and the preamble also refers to the 'intellectual and spiritual unity of our nation torn apart.' This wording seems to support the cultural nation concept.[351] These controversies are further outlined in the chapter on ethnicity.

The creation of democratic will is restricted by the fact that the FL stipulates that in many fields of public policy – from family and tax policy to pension policy – the detailed regulation shall be enacted in form of cardinal acts, the adoption and amendment of which requires a two-thirds majority of the votes of members of Parliament present. Thus the voters who are dissatisfied with the present government policy will hardly be able to achieve a change in the direction of governance, because future governments cannot shape in a more flexible manner, on the basis of a simple majority, their social and taxation policy. At this point it is worth to quote the criticism of the Venice Commission: 'a too wide use of cardinal laws is problem-

351 See PETRÉTEI 'Az alkotmányos demokrácia' 186–187, Georg BRUNNER: *Nationality problems and minority conflicts in Eastern Europe: strategies for Europe,* Gutersloh Bertelsmann Foundation Publishers, 1996, 9–10, András JAKAB and Pál SONNEVEND: Continuity with Deficiencies: The New Basic Law of Hungary, *European Constitutional Law Review* Vol. 9, № 1, 2013, 109–112.

atic with regard to both the constitution and ordinary laws. In [the Commission's] view, there are issues on which the Constitution should arguably be more specific. These include for example the judiciary. On the other hand, there are issues which should/could have been left to ordinary legislation and majoritarian politics, such as family legislation or social and taxation policy. The Venice Commission considers that parliaments should be able to act in a flexible manner in order to adapt to new framework conditions and face new challenges within society. Functionality of a democratic system is rooted in its permanent ability to change. The more policy issues are transferred beyond the powers of simple majority, the less significance will future elections have and the more possibilities does a two-third majority have of cementing its political preferences and the country's legal order. Elections, which, according to Article 3 of the First Protocol to the ECHR, should guarantee the "expression of the opinion of the people in the choice of the legislator", would become meaningless if the legislator would not be able to change important aspects of the legislation that should have been enacted with a simple majority. When not only the fundamental principles but also very specific and "detailed rules" on certain issues will be enacted in cardinal laws, the principle of democracy itself is at risk.'[352]

The open regulation of right to vote also related to the problems of defining democratic principle. A strongly debated issue connected to the right to vote was the introduction of the periodical electoral registration. In the past decades the electoral rolls were created by the authorities on the basis of the personal data and residence register and all the adult citizens with voting right and having residence in Hungary were enrolled automatically. While Article 2 of the FL declares universal and equal suffrage, the TPFL and the new act on electoral procedure adopted in November 2012 prescribed the registration upon request as precondition of voting on any elections.[353] The constitutionality of the new act on elec-

[352] Opinion № 621/2011 of the Venice Commission, point 24.

[353] The related provisions of the TPFL were annulled by the Constitutional Court in HCC Decision 45/2012. (XII. 29.) AB.

toral procedure was judged in January 2013 by the Constitutional Court upon the request of the Head of State. The Court declared that certain provisions of the new act – on electoral registration and political campaign – are contrary to the FL.[354] This Constitutional Court decision was partly successful because the governing majority gave up the idea of the introduction of voters' registration, but the bans on media campaign[355] were inserted into the FL with the Fourth Amendment, overriding this way the Constitutional Court's ruling. Finally the Fifth Amendment modified this ban, and at the moment the Constitution allows publishing political ads in all types of media, not just on public service broadcasts, but exclusively free of charge and with equal air time, or alternatively not at all. It is rather hypocritical solution, because if the commercial media is

---

354 HCC Decision 1/2013. (I. 7.) AB. Press release: 'The Constitutional Court has declared that in the Act additional conditions are defined: in order to practice the right to vote, a previous registration should be done. Regarding these provisions, the Constitutional Court has examined whether there is any constitutional reason for the previous registration. Taking the practice of the European Court of Human Rights into consideration, the Constitutional Court has declared that in case of citizens domiciled in Hungary, the mandatory registration disproportionately restricted the right to vote without any reason, thus this is contrary to the Fundamental Law. (...) In connection with the rules of election campaign, the Constitutional Court has declared that the freedom of expression and the freedom of press are disproportionally limited, because according to the Act during the electoral campaign the publication of political advertisements is allowed only in the public media service, thus these rules are contrary to the Fundamental Law. The rules that ban the publication of public opinion polls regarding the elections within six days before the elections has also been found contrary to the Fundamental Law.' Available at http://hunconcourt.hu/sajto/news/certain-provisions-of-the-act-on-election-procedure-held-contrary-to-the-fundamental-law.

355 Article IX(3) of the FL shall be replaced by the following provision: 'For the dissemination of appropriate information required for the formation of democratic public opinion and to ensure the equality of opportunity, political advertisements shall be published in media services, exclusively free of charge.' In the campaign period prior to the election of members of Parliament and of Members of the European Parliament, political advertisements published by and in the interest of nominating organisations setting up country-wide candidacy lists for the general election of members of Parliament or candidacy lists for the election of Members of the European Parliament shall exclusively be published by way of public media services and under equal conditions, as determined by cardinal Act.

prohibited to charge for political advertisements and has to guarantee equal air time for all qualified parties during the campaign, the more economic choice may be to refrain from this activity.

1.3.3 International and Union requirements

Loyal cooperation is one of the fundamental principles in the EU that ensures the functioning of its supranational architecture.[356] The FL expresses the commitment to the international community and law (Article Q) and contains also a European clause mandating the cooperation in the EU (Article E). The function and the purpose of these articles are similar to the corresponding rules of the former Constitution.[357]

---

[356] See Article 4(3) of the TEU.

[357] FL Article Q(1) In order to create and maintain peace and security, and to achieve the sustainable development of humanity, Hungary shall strive for cooperation with every nation and country of the world. (2) Hungary shall ensure harmony between international law and Hungarian law in order to fulfil its obligations under international law. (3) Hungary shall accept the generally recognised rules of international law. Other sources of international law shall become part of the Hungarian legal system by publication in the form of legislation.

FL Article E(1) In order to enhance the liberty, prosperity and security of European nations, Hungary shall contribute to the creation of European unity. (2) With a view to participating in the European Union as a member state, Hungary may exercise some of its competences arising from the Fundamental Law jointly with other member states through the institutions of the European Union under an international agreement, to the extent required for the exercise of the rights and the fulfilment of the obligations arising from the Founding Treaties. (3) The law of the European Union may stipulate a generally binding rule of conduct subject to the conditions set out in Paragraph (2). (4) The authorisation to recognise the binding nature of an international agreement referred to in Paragraph (2) shall require a two-thirds majority of the votes of the members of Parliament.

Former Constitution art. 6 (1) The Republic of Hungary renounces war as a means of solving disputes between nations and shall refrain from the use of force and the threat thereof against the independence or territorial integrity of other states. (2) The Republic of Hungary shall endeavour to co-operate with all peoples and countries of the world. (4) The Republic of Hungary shall take an active part in establishing a European unity in order to achieve freedom, well-being and security for the peoples of Europe. Art. 7 (1) The legal system of the

Article Q(1) FL differs from the former Constitution in as much as it does not contain the renouncement of war and the prohibition of the use of force based on Article 2(4) of United Nations Charter.[358] Instead, it positively formulates the aims of peace, security and sustainable development in international cooperation. Thus it incorporates the minimised version of one of the Union objectives in Article 3(5) of the TEU;[359] however, the latter covers more aspects of participation in international community. Unfortunately, the FL reduces the scope of cooperation to nations and countries and does not refer to other actors of the international community (e.g. international and transnational organisations). Article Q(2)-(3) of the FL regulates the relation between international and domestic law. It maintains the principle of harmony, and in respect of the 'generally recognised rules of international law' it retains the monist concept with adoption theory. In case of other sources then 'generally recognised rules' of

---

Republic of Hungary accepts the generally recognized principles of international law, and shall harmonize the country's domestic law with the obligations assumed under international law. Art. 2/A (1) By virtue of treaty, the Republic of Hungary, in its capacity as a member state of the European Union, may exercise certain constitutional powers jointly with other member states to the extent necessary in connection with the rights and obligations conferred by the treaties on the foundation of the European Union and the European Communities (hereinafter referred to as 'European Union'); these powers may be exercised independently and by way of the institutions of the European Union. (2) The ratification and promulgation of the treaty referred to in Subsection (1) shall be subject to a two-thirds majority vote of the Parliament.

358 Gábor SULYOK: 6. § [Nemzetközi kapcsolatok], in András JAKAB (ed.): *Az Alkotmány kommentárja,* Századvég, 2009, mn. 16, 23. and Gábor SULYOK: A nemzetközi jog és a belső jog viszonyának alaptörvényi szabályozása, *Jog Állam Politika* № 1, 2012, 17. For the detailed analysis of FL Article Q(2)-(3) see Gábor SULYOK: Incorporation of International Law into Domestic Law under the Fundamental Law of Hungary, in Péter SMUK (ed.): *The Transformation of the Hungarian Legal System 2010–2013,* CompLex, 2013, 31–50.

359 Article 3(5) of the TEU: 'In its relations with the wider world, the Union shall uphold and promote its values and interests and contribute to the protection of its citizens. It shall contribute to peace, security, the sustainable development of the Earth, solidarity and mutual respect among peoples, free and fair trade, eradication of poverty and the protection of human rights, in particular the rights of the child, as well as to the strict observance and the development of international law, including respect for the principles of the United Nations Charter.'

international law (i.e., treaties and case law of international Courts) it supports the dualist model with transformation. It still does not express the priority of international law over domestic law.

To ensure 'harmony', the Constitutional Court under Article 24(2) point f) of the FL continues to review the conflict between domestic legislation and international treaties in the future, but the FL does neither regulates who may initiate this procedure, nor refers to the possibility of *ex officio* revision. This is defined in the cardinal act on the Constitutional Court.[360] It is not clear either, how 'harmony' shall be ensured, if a domestic legal act violates one of the 'generally recognised rules of international law', thus – as hitherto – it can be answered by constitutional interpretation. The annulment of the domestic legislation breaching an international treaty is optional under Article 24(3) point c) of FL, which weakens the effectiveness of the constitutional requirement of harmony. It would have been preferable to oblige the Constitutional Court in the FL to annul those domestic legislative acts that are at the same rank as, or lower rank than the act transposing the international treaty.[361]

---

[360] According to the Act CLI of 2011 on the Constitutional Court the revision either takes place ex officio, or upon the initiation of one-fourth of the MPs, the Government, the President of the Supreme Court, the Supreme Prosecutor, the Commissioner for Fundamental Rights, or the judge of any Court of law if in a given case s/he shall apply a domestic legislative act conflicting with an international treaty.

[361] Cf. with the former Act XXXII of 1989 on the Constitutional Court. Under articles 44-47 the annulment was obligatory in such cases. The new Act CLI of 2011 on the Constitutional Court is ambiguous at this point. Under art. 42(1) the Constitutional Court shall annul the domestic legal act conflicting with an international treaty, if the given domestic legal act may not conflict with the act promulgating the given international treaty according to the FL. I.e., if an international treaty is promulgated by an act of parliament, and the challenged domestic legal act is e.g. a government decree then the latter shall be annulled. Under art. 42(2) the Constitutional Court shall call the Government or the lawmaker to eliminate the conflict, if a domestic legal act conflicts with an international treaty, and the act promulgating the given international treaty may not conflict with the concerned domestic legal act according to the FL. That is the case when an international treaty is promulgated by a government decree, and the domestic legal act conflicting with it is an act of parliament. The new regulation does not answer the question of the same rank collisions, i.e. if the interna-

The domestic legislation conflicting with TEU or TFEU should have been an exception to this rule. The breach of TEU or TFEU shall be established by the CJEU, thus it is an external limitation for the Constitutional Court's competence.[362]

Article E(1) as the basis of the European and Union cooperation essentially follows word by word the §6(4) of former Constitution.[363] Thus the frame of interpretation remains unchanged;[364] this objective expresses the commitment to each kind of European (international or supranational) cooperation. The most intensive form of cooperation is within the framework of the European Union.[365] Article E paragraphs (2) and (4), with some simplification, adopts the rules of §2/A of the former Constitution; however, the formulation differs at one point. The difference is that the two distinct clauses of §2/A(1) ['exercise certain constitutional powers jointly with other member states (...); these powers may be exercised independently and by way of the institutions of the European Union'] have been merged in Article E(4) ['jointly with other member states through the institutions of the European Union']. However, in legal understanding, in the course of Union legislative processes the member states do not exercise the competences "jointly", but those are exercised by the institutions.[366] §2/A – which also uses inadequate terminology – defined the 'way of institutions' as one of the forms of joint exercising powers in the EU. In Article E of the FL,

---

tional treaty is promulgated by the act of parliament, and the domestic legal act conflicting with it is also the act of parliament.

362 Tamás MOLNÁR: Az új Alaptörvény rendelkezései a nemzetközi jog és a belső jog viszonyáról, in Tímea DRINÓCZI and András JAKAB (eds.): *Alkotmányozás Magyarországon 2010–2011,* PPKE JÁK, PTE ÁJK, 2013.

363 See also András BRAGYOVA: No New(s), Good News? The Fundamental Law and the European law, in Gábor Attila TÓTH (ed.): *Constitution for a disunited nation,* CEU Press, 2012, 335–338.

364 See also László BLUTMAN and Nóra CHRONOWSKI: Hungarian Constitutional Court: Keeping Aloof from European Union Law, *International Constitutional Law* Vol. 5, № 3, 2011, 329.

365 László BLUTMAN and Nóra CHRONOWSKI: Az Alkotmánybíróság és a közösségi jog: alkotmányjogi paradoxon csapdájában I, *Európai Jog* № 2, 2007, 8–9.

366 BLUTMAN 'Az Európai Unió joga' 94.

yet, the exercise of powers 'through the institutions' is referred to as joint exercise. While the Lisbon Treaty abolished the so-called pillar system, and created a single institutional system, the supranational (i.e., Community) method has not became automatically dominant. The Lisbon Treaty intended to integrate the perspectives of supranational and intergovernmental methods e.g. by respecting the constitutional identity of member states, the effective involvement of national parliaments, the consolidation of member states' initiative in respect of some competences.[367] Strictly speaking the joint exercise of powers is not the same as the exercise through the institutions.[368] All these would have been surmounted, if in the text of FL the 'conferral' of certain constitutional powers appeared in accordance with Article 5 of the TEU.

Article E contains only one new rule compared to §2/A of the former Constitution, in its paragraph (3) it states that '[t]he law of the European Union may stipulate a generally binding rule of conduct.' From the domestic legal viewpoint, the ground for constitutional validity of Union law becomes clearer than it used to be; however this paragraph still does not solve the problem of primacy, i.e. that the domestic legal act conflicting with an EU legal act is not applicable. The duty of the Courts of law to ensure the consistency of domestic and Union law still stems from EU Treaties (i.e., asking for preliminary ruling) and not from the constitution itself. Thus the position of international law in the domestic legal system is still better defined under Article Q of the FL by the harmony-requirement than the constitutional rank of Union law.

With respect to Articles Q and E of the FL, international agreements continue to oblige Hungary to respect, protect and uphold the rule of law, democracy and fundamental rights. These obligations thus stem from the constitution itself. The above-mentioned provisions – since they relate to the effect that the international and su-

367 BESSELINK 'National and constitutional identity' 38–41.

368 The Constitutional Court has also respected the relevance of the difference of exercising powers jointly and by the way of institutions. See the HCC Decision 143/2010. (VII. 14.) AB on the Act promulgating the Lisbon Treaty.

pranational laws governing nations have on Hungarian law – are valid in respect of the constitution (as prevailing at any time), and set requirements that broach no exceptions. The European national constitutions also contain similar provisions with the same functions, reaffirming the existence of multilevel and parallel constitutionalism in the European legal area. Thus these kinds of constitutional provisions preliminary commit and restrain national governments for and by the international and common European values.[369]

Several provisions of the FL, however, can also be interpreted as permitting exceptions to the aforementioned European requirements – pertaining to democracy, the rule of law and the protection of fundamental rights – and as such they could come into conflict with international commitments.

1.4 Conclusion

It cannot be denied that the FL is an ideological constitution with nationalist-ethnocentric and communitarian features that diverges from the liberal trends of West European constitutional evolution.[370] It is also true that the amendments of the FL – especially the fourth one – raise criticalities again concerning the principle of rule of law, independence of Constitutional Court and judiciary, freedom of expression, freedom of religion, free movement of work, etc. Ultimately, the direction of interpretation of these problematic provisions depends on the Parliament,[371] the Constitutional Court and the courts of law.

---

369 Tom GINSBURG, Svitlana CHERNYKH and Zachary ELKINS: Commitment and Diffusion: Why Constitutions Incorporate International Law, *University of Illinois Law Review*, 2008, 101. Available at <http://works.bepress.com/zachary_elkins/1>.

370 VINCZE and VARJU 'Hungary: the New Fundamental Law' 437-453.

371 It is worth to mention that the Hungarian Parliament – i.e. the two-third governing majority – in the First Amendment of the FL in June 2012 gave up its intention to change the constitutional status of the Central Bank by merging it with the authority supervising financial bodies. Thus it repealed Article 30 of the TPFL, which originally stated: 'A cardinal act (…) may specify that a new organisa-

The constitutional practice based on the FL could have been developed nevertheless in line with the Union values; at the most some provisions of the FL would have not been effective or remained empty declaration – and belonging to Europe is worth this price. It is the responsibility of the Hungarian State authorities interpreting the FL, but first of all the duty of the Constitutional Court to take into consideration the international and especially EU obligations, if other state organs neglect them.[372] Only a member state

---

tion assume the tasks and jurisdiction of the organisation charged with Financial Supervisory Authority and the Hungarian National Bank.' The rationale of this amendment can be found in the pressure from EU institutions, especially from ECB. Ironically – and contrary to the First Amendment – the Fifth Amendment reintroduced the constitutional basis for merging the authority supervising financial bodies and the National Bank. Later it led to transparency problems that the Constitutional Court partly resolved. See to this Emese SZILÁGYI: Hungarian Constitutional Court: Transparency and Business Activities of the State, *Vienna Journal on International Constitutional Law* Vol. 10, № 3, 2016, 339–351.

The Parliament was also forced to change the regulation on early retirement of judges in 2012 after the decision of the Constitutional Court and CJEU. The Hungarian Constitutional Court declared the violation of the independence of judges in its HCC Decision 33/2012. (VII. 17.) AB. On the request of the European Commission the CJEU ruled in November 2012 that the abrupt and radical lowering of the retirement age for judges, prosecutors and notaries in Hungary violates EU equal treatment rules (Directive 2000/78/EC). According to the Court's judgment (case C-286/12), the forced early retirement of hundreds of judges and prosecutors in the course of 2012 as well the notaries in 2014 under a new Hungarian law constitutes unjustified age discrimination. In fact, the court decisions were not able to reinstate the dismissed judges into their original position. See to this Attila VINCZE: Der EuGH als Hüter der ungarischen Verfassung – Anmerkung zum Urteil des EuGH v. 6.11.2012, Rs. C-286/12 (Kommission/Ungarn), *Europarecht* Vol. 48, № 3, 2013, 323–333.

372 As it will be discussed below in this part at point 2.1., the Constitutional Court originally seemed to be open to this. In its landmark decision on the unconstitutionality of TPFL the Court emphasised that the constitutional criteria of a democratic state governed by the rule of law are respected by the international community. They are reaffirmed by international treaties as values, principles and fundamental freedoms and some of them are part of the international ius cogens. These criteria must not be eroded or endangered. The Constitutional Court may keep under control whether the substantive guaranties and requirements of the democracy and rule of law prevail, and how they are incorporated into the constitution. The Court criticized and condemned the constitutional practice of the Parliament that infringed the principle of rule of law by enacting the TPFL with

that sets aside constitutional fetishism and insists on its voluntary commitment to European integration and legal values can vindicate the 'constitutional tolerance'[373] implicitly enshrined among the Union values and principles.[374]

As the time goes by, however, fewer and fewer are the hopes that the EU values are enforceable in Hungary internally by the judiciary as the system of checks and balances was weakened over the past years, and the governing majority listened to the European critics selectively without changing the status quo. Hungary has instituted sweeping and controversial changes, prompting the European Commission and Council of Europe jointly to express concern regarding the rule of law in Hungary. If political pressure has no effect, and Article 7 of the TEU is not applicable, there are still some financial and budgetary instruments for compelling a disobedient member state in order to act in compliance with EU criteria system. It is clear however, that a more effective course of action – comprising political, legal and financial instruments – is necessary at EU level, because the respect of common European constitutional traditions remains fragile in some countries of transition.

2 The Constitutional Court and the network of multilevel European constitutionalism

To continue the former line of thoughts, this chapter analyses how effectively did – or did not – the Constitutional Court use international and European values in its reasoning to protect the pre-2010 constitutional traditions.

its controversial and non-transitional rules. The Court underpinned that TPFL is a slippery-act or chute-act, which is suitable to deprive the Court itself from its jurisdiction and to establish controversial provisions with constitutional rank outside the text of the FL. (HCC Decision 45/2012. (XII. 29.) AB, points IV.7-8).

373 Joseph H.H. Weiler: In defence of the status quo: Europe's constitutional Sonderweg, in Joseph H.H. Weiler and Marlene Wind (eds.): *European Constitutionalism Beyond the State,* Cambridge University Press, 2003, 21.

374 See Article 4(2) of the TEU.

The Constitutional Court tried, sometimes with greater, sometimes with less vehemence, to protect the FL, with more or less success. European bodies followed the process with great interest: the Venice Commission of the Council of Europe kept providing its opinions on the significant amendments to the FL and on the cardinal laws and the European Parliament adopted several resolutions as well. The sharpest criticism was induced by the Fourth Amendment to the FL, in which amendment *lex specialis* rules (e. g. Article U) were introduced in comparison to the fundamental principles of the rule of law, democracy and the protection of fundamental rights; regulations (e.g. student contracts, acknowledgement of churches, concept of family) evading or bypassing Constitutional Court rulings were enacted substantially reducing the space for constitutional protection, a specific review- and a new interpretation-limit was raised in the way of constitutional judicature (excluding substantial review of the amendments to the constitution, repealing of Constitutional Court decisions adopted before the FL), open infringement of EU law (limitation of election campaigns, possibility of special taxation as an indirect result of court rulings) was also risked. The European Commission initiated several infringement procedures as well, on the basis of which the Court of Justice of the European Union (hereinafter referred to as CJEU) adopted two judgments: in the subject of radical lowering of the retirement age of judges and in the subject of bringing to an end the term served by the Data Protection Supervisor. Hungary infringed EU law in both cases.[375]

The European Court of Human Rights (hereinafter referred to as ECtHR) also received Hungarian cases which had arisen from the elimination of the previous constitutionalism and from the arrangements based on the new FL – such as the recognition of churches, layoff without reasoning, lifetime imprisonment without compulsory review, premature termination of the mandate of the President

---

[375] Case C-286/12, Commission v Hungary, judgment of 6 November 2012; Case C-286/12, Commission v Hungary, judgment of 8 April 2014.

of the Supreme Court, and ban on parliamentary right to expression.[376] The State of Hungary infringed the European Convention on Human Rights (hereinafter referred to as ECHR) in every case.

There is no room herein to provide a comprehensive analysis of all of the issues arisen and debated at European forums.[377] I undertake in this chapter to examine in terms of some European constitutional values how much did the Constitutional Court of Hungary endeavour to enforce European standards in the course of interpreting the FL and how much did it try to contribute in the European Network of (Constitutional) Courts.[378]

The reason for the chosen approach is that no European constitutional system may be regarded as isolated within the multilevel constitutional area. Constituents of this area, the European judicial forums, may provide a legally binding decision on the harmony between the system based on the FL and the values and standards of European constitutionalism, but the opinion of a body holding

[376] Magyar Keresztény Mennonita Egyház and others v. Hungary, Judgment of 8 April 2014; K.M.C. v. Hungary, Judgment of 10 July 2012; László Magyar v. Hungary, Judgment of 20 May 2014, no. 73593/10; Baka v. Hungary, Judgment of 27 May 2014, no. 20261/12., Karácsony and others v. Hungary, Judgment of 16 September 2014, no. 42461/13.

[377] See for example Imre VÖRÖS: The constitutional landscape after the fourth and fifth amendments of Hungarian Fundamental Law, *Acta Juridica Hungarica* № 1, 2014, 1–20.; ZELLER 'Nichts ist so beständig' 307–325., Attila VINCZE: Wrestling with Constitutionalism: the supermajority and the Hungarian Constitutional Court, *International Constitutional Law* № 4, 2013, 86–97.

[378] Voßkuhle characterises the system of European courts and constitutional courts as follows: "The European constitutional courts are parts of a system that provides room for coordination: they constitute a, as it is called in German, 'Verbund', a network, the cooperating network of European constitutional courts. There is not any supreme guard of fundamental rights in Europe. The whole European construction of human rights is not based on a single foundation stone, but on columns: and these columns are the European constitutional courts. As for their functions, the European Court of Human Rights and the Court of Justice of the European Union may be regarded today, in my opinion, as the 'European constitutional court'." Andreas VOßKUHLE: Az emberi jogok védelme a bíróságok európai együttműködésében [Protection of human rights in the European cooperation of courts], *Alkotmánybírósági Szemle* № 1, 2013, 69.

great professional authority, such as the Venice Commission, may also be governing and influence their decisions.

2.1 The Fundamental Law and the requirements of European constitutionalism

2.1.1 *Declarations of intent of the Constitutional Court within the framework of relevant interpretation*

It is without any doubt that the FL expresses commitment towards the international community and law (Article Q) and contains the Europe Clause (Article E) providing basis for cooperation with the EU. Having regard to these provisions – confirming Article B(1) and Article I –, the international treaties in force still oblige Hungary to maintain the rule of law, democracy, to respect and protect and enforce fundamental rights. Consistency between international law and Hungarian law must be assured, and part must be taken in the creation of European unity under the rules in, *inter alia,* the treaties on which the European Union is founded and in the ECHR. The relationship between the domestic law and the EU law has not changed, and the Constitutional Court emphasised its commitment to the European constitutional evolution, sometimes in a demonstrative manner only, sometimes in a way affecting the case in question as well.

Even when it was searching for standards in its Decision 61/2011. (VII. 13.) AB for the review of the unconstitutional amendment, but did not find any, provided however *obiter dictum* two important and forward thoughts, still (or already) before the entry into force of the FL. One of them suggested a potential standard for review, the other one promised a level of protection of fundamental rights. The first one had an overall negative career and brought harmful consequences for the Constitutional Court and is actually a floating one without having concretised itself in practice. The second one has however expanded itself, and played a role in specific cases as well.

2.1.2 *International and European Union constraint with uncertain boundaries?*

The first quotation: "The standards, fundamental principles and fundamental values of *ius cogens* provide altogether a standard that must be met by every subsequent constitutional amendments and Constitutions. A larger part of these principles and values has been incorporated into the Constitution and into the case-law of the Constitutional Court or has become part of laws of the branches of law (e.g. formulation of the prohibition of retroactive effect in terms of criminal law, the *nullum crimen sine lege* principle, the *nulla poena sine lege* principle or the principle of exercise of rights of good faith, the principle of fair trial, etc. in other branches of law). The principles, guarantees of *ius cogens* appear in the form of values in the laws of the branches of law and in other legislation as well."[379] This part seems to suggest that the Constitutional Court would in general, but not in specific cases, attribute in principle a certain level of "supraconstitutionality" to the international *ius cogens* standards, i.e. would consider them as holding an interpretative priority in the course of constitutional judicature.[380] The quoted thought is however not so convincing: the only positive and in terms of law interpretable argument of the body as regards the (potential) call for the *ius cogens* may be its incorporation into domestic law, i. e. its transformation from supra-constitutional into intra-constitutional.

The above-mentioned standards appear again, although in a much more wrapped and an even more blurred form, in the Decision on the TPFL, as adopted about a year after the entry into force of the new constitution. The Constitutional Court established in its Decision 45/2012. (XII. 29.) AB that it has the power to review the TPFL, whereas it had become a regulation substituting the constitution

---

379 HCC Decision 61/2011. (II. 13.) AB, ABH [Decisions of the Constitutional Court] 2011, 696, 711.

380 BLUTMAN László: Az Alkotmánybíróság és az alkotmány feletti normák: könnyű liaison elkötelezettség nélkül? [Constitutional Court and Supraconstitutional Norms: An Airy Liaison Without Commitments?], *Közjogi Szemle* № 4, 2011, 1–11.

and disrupting the unity and structure thereof and taking away the scope of competence of the Constitutional Court. The body provided an extremely faint reference in this decision to the possibility of eventual substantial review of future amendments to the FL in comparison with international standards. „Constitutional legality has not only procedural, formal and public law validity requirements, but also substantial ones. The constitutional criteria of a democratic State under the rule of law are at the same time constitutional values, principles and fundamental democratic freedoms enshrined in international treaties and accepted and acknowledged by communities of democratic States under the rule of law, as well as the *ius cogens,* which is partly the same as the foregoing. As appropriate, the Constitutional Court may even examine the free enforcement and the constitutionalization of the substantial requirements, guarantees and values of democratic States under the rule of law."[381] International standards are transformed here into a requirement to a democratic state governed by rule of law, and are internalised – without precise reference to their source, origin or scope.

Parliament exercising the power to amend the constitution found this indirect reference however more than enough – the fourth amendment closed the ways to substantial review of future amendments. Upon the motion of the Commissioner of Fundamental Rights, the Constitutional Court undertook to review this amendment, but no invalidity was found by Decision 12/2013. (V. 24.) AB. Getting out of the embarrassing situation, or in order that the previous searching for international standards does not appear as vain or as a kind of "fleeing ahead" from the expectable international criticism, the following admonishment was given *obiter dicta* in the closing remarks:

"The Constitutional Court emphasises that the limitations implied by the interrelated system of fundamental rights, and implied in Articles E and Q of the Fundamental Law and applicable to the prevailing legislative and constitution making powers as well, which

381 HCC Decision 45/2012. (II. 29.) AB, ABH 2012, 347, 403. para [118]

limitations result from the obligations of Member State of the EU and from ensuring the harmony between the international law and Hungarian law in order to fulfill the obligations of Hungary under international law and from acceptance of the rules generally acknowledged by international law may not be ignored either in these acts [i. e. the ones specifying the Fourth Amendment to the Fundamental Law] or in other ones. (...) [Besides the coherence of the Fundamental Law, the Constitutional Court], in the course of assessing the given constitutional issue, acting according to the governing rules, shall also consider the obligations undertaken by Hungary in international treaties and those accompanying its EU membership, and the rules generally acknowledged by international law and the fundamental principles and values therein. All these rules, having special regard to their values being enshrined in the Fundamental Law as well, form such a single system (system of values) which may not be ignored either in the constitutional or the legislative process or in the course of constitutionality review by the Constitutional Court."[382] The encoded message is more specific than the previous one: inherent constraints are implied by the European Union membership and international obligations, i.e. from Articles E and Q, for the constitution making and legislative power. In light of the foregoing it is however highly improbable that the Constitutional Court would confront the constitution making power with these constraints.

2.1.3 Equivalences and the lack of conflicts

In Decision 61/2011. (VII. 13.) AB, as direct continuation of the thoughts firstly quoted, the body adjusts the level domestic constitutional protection of fundamental rights to the international level, not on hierarchic basis but as a conclusion from the *pacta sunt servanda* principle: "In case of certain fundamental rights, the Consti-

382 HCC Decision 12/2013. (II. 24.) AB, ABH 2013, 542, 547. paras [46] and [48]

tution defines the substance of the fundamental right in the same way as it is in some international treaty (for example the Covenant of Civil and Political Rights and the European Convention of Human Rights). In these cases, the level of protection of fundamental rights provided by the Constitutional Court may in no case be lower than the level of international protection of rights (typically elaborated by the Strasbourg Court of Human Rights). As resulting from the *pacta sur servanda* principle [Section 7(1) of the Constitution, Article Q(2)-(3) of the FL], the Constitutional Court is required to follow the Strasbourg jurisprudence and the level of protection of fundamental rights defined therein, even if it did not necessarily arise from its own previous case-law decisions."[383]

Later it extends the international determination of the level of protection of fundamental rights with the stipulations of EU law, moreover, it considers the above quoted conclusion as being "even more true" for the law of the European Union, having regard to Article E(2)-(3) of the FL (compared to the rules of the Constitution however it did not elaborate in detail the meaning of the new Article E(3)).[384] Therefore, without any particular dogmatic argument or foundation, Decision 32/2012. (VII. 4.) AB on student contracts did indeed refer to the jurisprudence of the CJEU and mentioned the necessity to consider fundamental freedoms of the EU, but did not profoundly investigate the connections between "binding down" and EU citizenship. With these decisions, the Constitutional Court basically defined the requirement for the equivalence of internal protection of fundamental rights.

In the decision on the concept of family, which decision had a big effect (because it resulted in an amendment to the constitution), the body confirmed maintaining the practice preceding the FL with that the case-law of the ECtHR is the starting point for interpreting the ECHR: "It takes, in line with its practice so far, the jurisprudence of the Court empowered by the states parties to the Convention to

383 HCC Decision 61/2011. (VII. 13.) AB, ABH 2011, 696, 711.

384 HCC Decision 32/2012. (VII. 4.) AB, ABH 2012, 228, 233.

provide authentic (authoritative) interpretation of the Convention for interpreting and clarifying the content of the relevant provisions of the Convention. This taking as a basis is done on the basis of those *dictums* ('case-law', in a figurative sense) of the Court when the Court interprets the Convention itself, its certain expressions, when it points out what is compatible with the requirements of the Convention and what is not".[385] It is important to underline that taking as basis does not mean the recognition of the ECtHR decisions as binding or as automatic interpretative priority[386] concerning the text of the FL.

Logically, the body adjusts itself when interpreting other conventions concluded in the framework of the Council of Europe: "The interpretation by the Constitutional Court as regards the content of international treaties should of course coincide with the official interpretation by the Council of Europe as regards these treaties."[387]

The body acknowledged in Decision 4/2013. (II. 21.) AB, in the case of the red star, that the ECtHR decision establishing infringement of the convention by Hungary may eliminate the *res iudicata*,[388] moreover upon the effect of the Strasbourg jurisprudence, but not expressly because of a specific decision, the Constitutional Court may depart from its previous case-law. The body confirmed at the same time that the Strasbourg ruling itself does not overwrite the

---

385 HCC Decision 43/2012. (XII. 20.) AB, ABH 2012, 788, 800–801., referring back to HCC Decision 166/2011. (XII. 20.) AB, ABH 2011, 557.

386 For the concepts of interpretative, applicative and abrogative priorities and primacies see BLUTMAN László: A nemzetközi jog érvényesülése a magyar belső jogban: két előkérdés [The functioning of international law in Hungarian internal law: two preliminary questions], in BLUTMAN László, CSATLÓS Erzsébet and SCHIFFNER Imola: *A nemzetközi jog hatása a magyar joggyakorlatra* [The effect of international law on Hungarian legal practice], HVG-ORAC, Budapest, 2014, 107–108.

387 HCC Decision 41/2012. (XII. 6.) AB, ABH 2012, 742, 745. [17]. Interpretation by the Constitutional Court of the conventions of the Council of Europe on the protection of minorities became necessary in this case.

388 HCC Decision 4/2013. (II. 21.) AB, ABH 2013, 188, 191. [20]: "Considering all that, the Constitutional Court established that the ruling of the ECtHR in the case Vajnai v Hungary, which ruling contains conclusions as regards Section 269/B of the Criminal Code (...), is such a new condition and aspect significant in terms of law, that makes the repeated constitutional review necessary."

jurisprudence of the Constitutional Court and established the requirement for reverse equivalence, i.e. the fact that the protection system of the ECHR is only a minimum standard which may not erode any higher level protection at member state level. With this declaration the Hungarian body did not say anything new, wherefore this is clearly stated in Article 53 of the Convention, in the clause on non-reversal.[389] According to the Constitutional Court therefore, "The ruling of the ECtHR is of declarative nature, i.e. it does not mean direct alteration of the points of law, its jurisprudence may however provide assistance in the interpretation of constitutional fundamental rights, as set out in the Fundamental Law and in international conventions, and in the determination of their content and extent. The meaning of rights ensured by the European Convention of Human Rights (hereinafter referred to as 'the Convention') is embodied in the decisions adopted by the ECtHR in specific cases facilitating uniform perception of the interpretation of human rights. The Convention and consideration of the jurisprudence of the ECtHR may not lead to the limitation of the protection of fundamental rights under the Fundamental Law or to setting a lower level of protection. The Strasbourg jurisprudence and the Convention set the minimum level for protection of fundamental rights that must be ensured by every state party thereto, the international law may however develop a different and higher system of requirements for the protection of human rights."[390] In the case of the red star the situation was however on the contrary: the Constitutional Court adjusted the national level of protection of the freedom of expression to the level of Strasbourg.[391]

Decision 36/2013. (XII. 5.) AB declaring transfer of cases to be (*ex post facto*) unconstitutional and in conflict with the Convention

---

389 Article 53 of the ECHR: Nothing in this Convention shall be construed as limiting or derogating from any of the human rights and fundamental freedoms which may be ensured under the laws of any High Contracting Party or under any other convention to which it is a party.

390 HCC Decision 4/2013. (II. 21.) AB, ABH 2013, 188, 191. para [19].

391 See also Erzsébet Csatlós: The Red Star Story and the ECtHR in the Hungarian Legal Practice, *Jogelméleti Szemle* Vol. 15, № 4, 2014, 2–11.

goes even beyond and expressly acknowledges that interpretative primacy may be attributed to the decisions of the ECtHR in certain situations. "In case the national legislation has the same content as the law in the Convention or in any of its Additional Protocols or it serves the fulfilment of the obligation to ensure this right, then Article Q of the Fundamental Law implies that the Constitutional Court should refrain from interpreting the particular legislation (or legislative provision) in a way that would inevitably result in the infringement of obligations undertaken under international law and in repeated condemnation of Hungary in front of the Court."[392] The other significant result of the decision is that the Constitutional Court confirmed the followings as derived from the constitution: no reference may be made to the FL in order to become exempt from the obligations undertaken under international law. The constitution making power, according to the reading of the body, acknowledges to respect this fundamental rule of international law.[393]

---

[392] HCC Decision 36/2013. (XII. 5.) AB, ABH 2013, 1268, 1273. para [28].

[393] HCC Decision 36/2013. (XII. 5.) AB, ABH 2013, 1268, 1276. paras [46]–[47]: "The Constitutional Court reminds that the Fourth Amendment to the Fundamental Law, regardless of the fact that Article Q of the Fundamental Law has already ascertained the fundamental rules of the relationship between Hungarian Law and international law taking the text of Section 7(1) of the Constitution as basis, but with the conscious readjustment thereof, devoted a separate point in the closing provisions again for the importance of the continuity of and respecting the obligations under international law. Therefore, by virtue of the Closing and miscellaneous provisions of the Fundamental Law: '8. The entry into force of the Fundamental Law shall not affect the legal force of legal regulations adopted, normative acts governing public organisations, and other legal instruments of state control issued, specific decisions taken and international legal commitments undertaken before its entry into force.' The Constitutional Court established that the constitution making power expressed in this point its attachment to one of the fundamental rules of international law which had been declared by the Permanent Court of International Justice when it did not accept that Germany would become exempt from its obligations under the Peace of Versailles on the basis of its internal legal act (declaration of neutrality). (CPJI: A Wimbledon steamship case, 17 August 1923. Série A n° 1., pp 29–30). The Permanent Court of International Justice stated in the case of Polish citizens of Danzig, and so setting the standards even higher, that 'no state may refer to its own constitution against another state in order to become exempt from its obligations under international law or treaties in force'. (CPJI: Advisory Opinion to the case on Treatment

This argument may be called as the requirement for conflict-free coexistence, which argument the Constitutional Court may use as a corollary of this decision to prevent eventual conflicts between the international law and the new Hungarian constitution.

Decision 6/2014. (II. 26.) AB is the last step that is worth mentioning in the process of adjustment to the European standard of fundamental rights. The body granted direct enforcement (applicative) priority to the ECtHR decision establishing that the 98 percent special tax infringes the Convention,[394] resulting in a certain level of supra-constitutionality regarding the specific limitation to review in the FL.[395] The stakes were however not high because the 98 percent tax rate is not in force any more (it is 75 percent due to the modification), the Constitutional Court ordered therefore a prohibition of application in cases where the previous tax rate should be applied.[396] The body took the opportunity however to "save" another element of the practice preceding the FL for "the period fol-

of Polish Nationals in the Danzig Territory; 4 February 1932, Série A/B n° 44, pp 24). These sentences have been of determinative nature since their statement: they provide the basis for conflict-free coexistence of international law and national constitutions, and are already reflected in the Fundamental Law."

394 HCC Decision 6/2014. (II. 26.) AB, ABH 2014, 202, 204. paras [22] and [24]: "The Chamber of the Strasbourg European Court of Human Rights established in its Decision № 41838/11. (R. Sz. v Hungary) of 2 July 2013 (Para. (62)), Decision № 66529/11. (N. K. M. v Hungary) of 14 May 2013 (Para. 76) and Decision № 49570/11. (Gáll v Hungary) of 25 June 2013 (Para. 75) that the tax rate of 98 percent under the law for lawful severance pays is in conflict with Article I (property protection) of the Additional Protocol I" (...) "The Constitutional Court did not see any reason in this case to depart from the content that was attributed by the decisions of the Court through interpretation to Article I of the Additional Protocol I in connection with the extent of the special tax. The Constitutional Court therefore establishes that Section 10 of the Act is in conflict with Article I (protection of property) of Additional Protocol I."

395 The Constitutional Court made it clear that the review limitation does not cover investigation of conflict with international treaties: "The rule limiting the competences under Article 37(4) of the Fundamental Law is not applicable, either as regards the aspects of investigation or the establishment of legal consequence, to the investigation of conflict between legislation and international treaties." HCC Decision 6/2014. (II. 26.) AB, ABH 2014, 202, 204. para [21].

396 The enforcement/applicative priority of would have become abrogative primacy only if there had been any standard that could have been repealed. (The

lowing the Fourth Amendment". It reinforced that any infringement to international obligations does not only violates the requirement of harmony between Hungarian and international law (Article Q(2)) but the principle of rule of law (Article B(1)) as well.[397]

2.2 Judicial independence, fair trial, rule of law

Assurance of the effective enforcement of EU law is significant in terms of EU membership, therefore the integration organisation generally pays a special interest to the functioning of the guarantees of justice at member state level. It is a special coincidence, obviously implied by the content of motions and the practice of their acceptance, that the Constitutional Court has dealt relatively much with the requirement of judicial independence and fair trial since the entry into force of the FL.

After the adaption of the new constitution, the two-third majority also challenged the judicial branch of power in many ways. First, the legislator lowered the retirement age of judges from 70 to 62 years. Since 1869, Hungarian judges could remain in office beyond the retirement age, thus they could freely choose their day of retirement between the age of 62 and 70.[398] However, the FL and Act 162 of 2011 on the legal status of judges unexpectedly obliged them to retire at the general retirement age from the beginning of 2012.[399] It has led to a mass removal of over 270 judges in the first half of 2012.

---

body did not investigate of course whether the new tax rate of 75 percent complies with the ECHR.)

397 HCC Decision 6/2014. (II. 26.) AB, ABH 2014, 202, 205. para [30], with reference to HCC Decision 7/2005. (III. 31.) AB.

398 See also Balázs Fekete: How to Become a Judge in Hungary? From the Professionalism of the Judiciary to the Political Ties of the Constitutional Court, in Sophie Turenne (ed.): *Fair Reflection of the Society in Judicial Systems: a Comparative Analysis*, Springer, Heidelberg/London/New York, 2015, 169–186.

399 Tamás Gyulavári and Nikolett Hős: Retirement of Hungarian Judges, Age Discrimination and Judicial Independence: A Tale of Two Courts, *Industrial Law Journal* Vol. 42, № 3, 2013, 289.

Second, in the course of the constitutional and judicial reform, the Supreme Court was renamed to Curia (in Hungarian Kúria, it is the historical name of the highest judicial body), without any significant changes regarding its competences, however, the TPFL terminated the mandate of the President of the Supreme Court, who was elected by the Parliament in 2009 for a 6 year term.[400] The President of the Supreme Court earlier criticized the premature retirement of judges and other supermajority actions concerning the independence of judiciary.

Third, before the FL, the administration of justice based on autonomy and judicial independence. In 2011 the reforms aiming to improve the efficacy placed the administrative powers held by the National Council of Justice and its president (the President of the Supreme Court) into the hands of two new bodies – the National Judicial Office and the National Judicial Council. While the Council serves mostly control and consultative functions, the latter exercises the effective administrative competences over the judiciary. The President of the NJO had originally a vast array of competences relating to judicial appointments, case allocation, administration, management and supervision, and thus this extensive power over the judiciary belonged to a politically-appointed individual. However, following the widespread alarm of the national and international community regarding these powers and their impact on the independence of the judiciary, in 2012 the parliament restricted certain of the competences of the President of the NJO and increased those of the NJC.

Fourth, the so called Nullity act, Act XVI of 2011 on the redress of the court judgments in connection with the crowd controls in the autumn of 2006, nullified certain judgments relating to the civil unrest of autumn 2006,[401] on the basis that the law interfered with

---

400 Attila Vincze: Judicial independence and its guarantees beyond the nation state – some recent Hungarian experience, *Journal of the Indian Law Institute* Vol. 56, № 2, 2014, 204.

401 On 18 September 2006 a massive demonstration was held near the Hungarian Parliament. The protests, allegedly attended by 40,000 people, concerned the

the right of judges (rather than the legislature) to assess evidence and decide on individual cases. The act suggested that the police gave false evidence in each case when exclusively their evidence confirmed the commitment of the act, in these cases the prosecutors brought charges wrongly, and that the judgments of the first and second instance were wrong.

These issues raised international criticism and ended in procedures before the Constitutional Court. In most cases the Court argued solely upon domestic constitutional basis and did not refer to the European values of rule of law.

The radical lowering of the retirement age of judges in 2012 was the subject of the constitutional appeal leading to the declaration of the first unconstitutionality.[402] The main argument of the body in this matter was the irremovability implied by judicial independence, which means that the retirement age may be lowered gradually, with a necessary transition period only. The decision was dominated by internal argumentation on basis of domestic constitutional law, and only one of the relevant recommendations of the Council of Europe[403] appeared to provide suitable support, though it was known that the CJEU was also dealing with the case as initiated by the European Commission. The Constitutional Court did however avoid involving the issue of age discrimination into the review, seeking assistance in the law of the EU to interpret the amendments of the new constitution in the TPFL, or seeking direct contact to the Luxembourg court through initiating a preliminary ruling procedure. Impropriety of the ostrich policy and the insufficiency of the *pro futuro* nullification was even more highlighted by

---

audio recording, which surfaced on 17 September 2006, on which the then Prime Minister Gyurcsány admitted to lying to the public for a couple of years, including lying about budget deficit. Police violence during the crowd control ended in criminal or offence procedures.

402 HCC Decision 33/2012. (VII. 17.) AB, ABH 2012, 242.

403 Recommendation CM/Rec(2010)12 of the Committee of Ministers to member states on judges: independence, efficiency and responsibilities. Quoted by HCC Decision 33/2012. (VII. 17.) AB, ABH 2012, 242, 248.

the decision of the CJEU[404] a few months later.[405] Although the Hungarian Constitutional Court stated the unconstitutionality, failed to repair the infringement of the affected judges' fundamental rights.

Premature termination of the mandate of the President and Vice President of the Supreme Court is also related to the transformation of the judicial organisation. Whereas the mandate of the President of the Supreme Court was terminated by the TPFL,[406] only the Vice President could lodge a constitutional appeal, his term was terminated pursuant to the Act on the organisation and administration of courts. The Constitutional Court found, with the narrow majority of 8 to 7, that the transformation of the organisation of courts and the significant modification of the scope of responsibilities of the Kúria (Curia), its president and vice president provide sufficient constitutional justification for the shortening of their mandates and did not deal with reviewing the relevant Strasbourg jurisprudence.[407] According to the judges of the Constitutional Court providing a dissenting opinion, prejudice to the rule of law and violation of the right to remedies of the petitioner should have been established. Comparatively, the ECtHR stated on the basis of the complaint of the President of the Supreme Court that the State of Hungary had infringed the right to fair trial, whereas it had not ensured any judicial revision in the case, moreover the right of the President of the Supreme Court to free expression had also been infringed, whereas his removal may be related to his criticism concerning the transformation of the organisation of courts, which had not been his right only but as a court leader his obligation as well.[408]

In the decision on case allocation that belonged to the competences of the President of the National Judicial Office the Constitu-

---

404 Case C-286/12, Commission v Hungary, judgment of 6 November 2012.

405 Vincze Attila calls attention on the same: Vincze 'Der EuGH als Hüter' 324–325.

406 Presently in Point 14(2) of the Closing and miscellaneous provisions of the FL: The mandate of the President of the Supreme Court and of the President and members of the National Council of Justice shall terminate upon the entry into force of the Fundamental Law.

407 HCC Decision 3076/2013. (III. 27.) AB, ABH 2013, 434, 439.

408 Baka v. Hungary, Judgment of 27 May 2014, no. 20261/12, § 79, 100, 103.

tional Court held the right to an appointed judge and the prohibition of being removed from an appointed judge to be basic requirements for a fair trial, and concluded that the appointment of the members of the proceeding court at the sole discretion of the President of the National Judicial Office does infringe these rights, and that the legal regulation does not meet the so-called objective test of an impartial judiciary.[409] The Court heroically declared the rules to be not in force any more, but still having an effect on the cases of the petitioners causing them, to be unconstitutional and in conflict with international treaties, and provided subjective protection of fundamental rights as befits the function of a constitutional appeal. The Court's reasoning provided extensive references to the relevant jurisprudence of the ECtHR, and it also took into consideration the relevant, and sharply critical, positions of the Venice Commission.

More of the decisions rejecting the petitions for appeal dealt with fundamental procedural rights. In the scope of the requirements for fair trial enshrined in Article XXVIII of the FL, the body considered the jurisprudence of the ECtHR established on the right to reasoned judicial decision.[410] To the interpretation of the right to protection, the Constitutional Court used the "understanding" of the ECtHR as well, moreover, it referred in order to support its argument, obviously interestingly, to the resolution of the Council of the EU on full enforcement and uniform application of fundamental procedural rights and to the draft directive of the Commission outlining alternatives for regulating the issues of the right to employ legal counsel in criminal prosecution.[411] It did not delay in recalling the Observation № CCPR/C/ HUN/CO/5 of United Nations Human Rights Committee of 16 November 2010 to Hungary.[412] Such inter-

[409] HCC Decision 36/2013. (XII. 5.) AB, upon normative appeal, with eight dissenting opinions.

[410] HCC Decision 7/2013. (III. 1.) AB, ABH 2013, 382, 387–388. paras [30]–[32].

[411] HCC Decision 8/2013. (III. 1.) AB, ABH 2013, 391, 402. para [50]. Recommendation of the European Commission COM(2011) 326 final; 2011/0154 (COD)

[412] HCC Decision 8/2013. (III. 1.) AB, ABH 2013, 391, 402. para [49]. According to the recommendation, it would be necessary to establish the conditions warranting effective legal aid for every person deprived of his freedom.

national, "meta-legal" reference of EU origin is rather of symbolic significance and is aimed at presenting the awareness of the Constitutional Court. The body stated in cases connected to the principle of impartiality, in harmony with the interpretation of the ECtHR, that it is necessary to enforce that strict standard by virtue of which the ruling court may not cease to appear impartial beyond impartial consideration of the cases. The ECtHR acknowledges two aspects of impartiality: impartiality in terms of subjectivity and impartiality in terms of objectivity. The subjective side of impartiality defines the need that no member of a court may be prejudiced or biased in a particular case. Comparatively, the objective side of impartiality means whether any right doubt may arise regarding the impartiality of the judge beyond his behaviour in the course of the particular case.[413]

The picture would not be complete without mentioning the fact that the independence of judicial branch and the principle of rule of law suffered a severe defeat from the rather obscure argument about justice in the Constitutional Court decision on the Nullity Act, in which the reasoning considered foreign solutions only, and European standards did not appear included in the reasoning.[414] The Court found the act of Parliament on annulling the judgments of the courts of law justifiable and constitutional in the given historical circumstances, which is clearly an argument beyond constitutional law.

Reference to the principle of rule of law seems to become more and more relegated to the background in these decisions, and in other constitutional judicial review cases as well. The Court protects the principle of rule of law to a very narrow extent only, as far as the lack of required preparation time and the prohibition of adverse retroactive effect are concerned, but still not as far as the course of

---

413 HCC Decision 25/2013. (X. 4.) AB, ABH 2013, 960, 964–965, 967–968. paras [27]–[28]; [38]; HCC Decision 34/2013. (XI. 22.) AB, ABH 2013, 1212, 1218–1221. paras [32]–[38]

414 HCC Decision Decision 24/2013 (X. 4.) AB.

constitutional complaint procedures are concerned.[415] Protection of acquired rights or protection of legitimate expectations (*Vertrauensschutz*) are completely disappearing.[416]

2.3 Democracy – right to vote and political participation

The principle of democracy has a central value in the legal order of the Council of Europe and of the European Union. It is an extremely complex principle, its conceptual items include pluralism, the majority principle together with respecting minority rights and human dignity, and the principle of representation complemented with direct exercise of power, legitimacy of the political institutional system, fundamental rights, especially the enforcement of political participation rights, transparency of public authority, publicity and freedom of the civil sector. Democracy formally presumes at the same time that the people (such as the population, the constituent population, conscious political community) requires democratic functioning of power and active participation in the assurance thereof. It is much more an issue of social need, practice and political culture than of a legal construction. In another way, while the rule of law may be controlled with legal instruments and may ideally be judicially enforceable, democracy may much less be. Due to the multitude of its components it may become deficient in several ways and may turn into post-democracy and then drift towards autocracy.

415 Originally: HCC Order 1140/D/2006 AB, but at the time when the Constitution was in force, this did not mean any problem due to the actio popularis subsequent constitutional review.

416 See early retirement – HCC Decision 23/2013. (IX. 25.) AB; gambling monopoly – HCC Decision 26/2013. (X. 4.) AB. It is to be mentioned that when investigating the rules limiting the operation of slot machines, the Constitutional Court considered the legislative efforts of the EU and the decisions of the CJEU supporting free discretion of national authorities and the exceptions of public interest from the freedom of service provision as regards organising gambling.

The Venice Commission emphasised in its comprehensive opinion assessing the FL: "Elections (...) would lose their meaning if the legislative power would not be able to achieve changes in such important fields of legislation which should have been regulated with simple majority. If, as regards certain issues, not only fundamental principles but very specific and detailed rules are adopted in cardinal laws as well, then the principle of democracy itself shall become threatened as well."[417] In its position assessing the Fourth Amendment to the Fundamental Law, it recalled the followings while condemning the instrumental treatment of the constitution: "Democracy may not be reduced to the rule of majority; exercise of power of the majority is limited by the constitution and by law, primarily in order to protect minority interests."[418]

It is without any doubt that the right to vote and political participation rights are of outstanding significance in terms of democracy. Within the limits of its possibilities, namely depending on petitioning and acceptance, the Hungarian Constitutional Court dealt with these substantial elements of democracy in some of its decisions.

In Decision 1/2013. (I. 7.) AB it investigated the justification of registration, namely the necessity of limiting fundamental rights, as a preliminary question to the proportionality of the regulation of registration upon request. For this, it scrutinised the relevant jurisprudence of the ECtHR, from which it concluded that setting the condition of active registration for exercising the right to vote may limit the right to vote freely with a reason of relevant gravity only, and such legitimate reason may not be found besides the already established and functioning voting list.[419] As a result of the nature of the procedure, establishment of being in conflict with international treaty, within preliminary constitutional review, was not possible but the body adjusted its internal arguments in constitutional law to the starting point synthetized from the Strasbourg jurispru-

[417] See Point 24 of Opinion 618/2011. of the Venice Commission.

[418] See Point 136 of Opinion 720/2013. of the Venice Commission.

[419] HCC Decision 1/2013. (I. 7.) AB, ABH 2013, 50–87.

dence. The propriety of declaring the rules limiting media campaigns as unconstitutional was confirmed by international criticism and the official objections of the European Commission that followed the incorporation of these limitations into the FL. (Perhaps these mutually strengthening effects had lead to the transformation of the limiting rule into a presentable one by the Fifth Amendment.)

In the case of the so called winner-compensation (or winner-premium), the Constitutional Court, in order to get out of the delicate situation, tried to support the thesis of freedom of the legislative power concerning the election system as much as possible, and called upon assistance from two of the decisions of the ECtHR.[420]

The body contributes to the protection of the freedom of expression with having changed its previous restrictive jurisprudence concerning the wearing of totalitarian symbols with regard to the decision of the ECtHR in the Vajnai case.[421] This step forward was followed by a step back: the new and restrictive interpretation of

---

[420] HCC Decision 3141/2014. (V. 9.) AB, ABH 2014, 654, 659.: "The rules of the election system which effect the relative weight of votes as a result of the precisely non-predictable expression of will of the citizens, are not in connection with the equality in terms of procedure but with the so-called 'effective equality'. Such typical rules are requirements defining the order of acquiring mandates, which requirements themselves are 'neutral', i.e. do not put groups of voters into a disadvantaged position. These result advantages or disadvantages implied by the improprotionality of the acquisition of mandates exclusively on the basis of the decision of the voters and subsequently establishable. This is not an issue of the discriminatory nature of the rule any more but of the proportionality of the voting system. The jurisprudence of the Constitutional Court in this matter is in harmony with the jurisprudence of the European Court of Human Rights as related to the right to free vote enshrined in Article 3 of the First Additional Protocol of the European Convention on Human Rights. 'The Court has already established that Article 3 of Protocol 1 ensures individual rights including the right to vote and the right to be voted for. No matter how important these rights are, they are not absolute. Whereas Article 3 recognises them as not mentioning and defining them expressis verbis, 'implicit limitations' are possible and the states parties to the convention have a wide margin of manoeuvre in this respect. They may stipulate conditions for the right to vote and to be voted for in their own internal legal order whereas this is not excluded in principle by Article 3.' (ECtHR, Orujov v Azerbaijan (4508/06), 26 July 2011, Para (40)"

[421] HCC Decision 4/2013. (II. 21.) AB, ABH 2013, 188–211.

the freedom of expression appeared, already after the Fourth Amendment to the FL, with recognising the denial of the sins committed by the totalitarian systems as constitutional.[422] The Constitutional Court relied on the decisions of the ECtHR related to Holocaust denial and abuse of rights as well although these decisions are only partly conclusive as compared to the Hungarian criminal facts of the case, which should have been assessed more sophisticated in the light of the relevant EU law and Strasbourg jurisprudence as according to the dissenting opinions. Criticism of public persons did however win: the body maintained its former practice and tried to develop standards that may be used in the application of law as well and that are necessary for the harmony between the criminal judgment of public statements regarding the discussion of public affairs and the requirements implied by the freedom of expression as ensured in Article 10 of the Convention and in the FL.[423] The Constitutional Court provided an implicit answer by this to one of the reservations of the Venice Commission to the Fourth Amendment.[424]

2.4 Conclusions

Constitutional evolution and constitutional practice has drifted away in many fields from European standards during the five years that have passed since the adoption of the FL.

The Constitutional Court however, at least in the first two years tried to counterbalance the excesses of the constitution-amending and legislative power but did not exhaust the possibilities provided by the European standards. Questioning or complete rejection of

422 HCC Decision 16/2013. (VI. 20.) AB, ABH 2013, 688.

423 HCC Decision 7/2014. (III. 7.) AB, ABH 2014, 230. and HCC Decision 13/2014. (VI. 18.) AB, ABH 2014, 588.

424 See Point 141 of Opinion 720/2013 of the Venice Commission: the wording of the provisions on the dignity of communities is too general and the separate protection of the "dignity of the Hungarian nation" creates the risk that freedom of expression in Hungary may be restricted in order to protect Hungarian institutions and officials in the future.

the necessity to refer to the European and international standards and jurisprudence appears in the minority opinions within the body itself.[425] For the time being, the majority does not share this understanding and does rely on the jurisprudence of the ECtHR in its reasonings at least as an interpretation tool. Because of the Strasbourg ruling establishing infringement of the Convention by Hungary, the body was ready to change its practice and to establish unconstitutionality in the case of the communist red star. In the

[425] Dissenting opinion of Dienes-Oehm Egon Judge of the Constitutional Court, HCC Decision 36/2013. (XII. 5.) AB, ABH 2013, 1268, 1282.: "Ad hoc decisions of the European Court of Human Rights established for the rectification of infringements to fundamental rights enshrined in the Convention and for ruling in individual cases only are not binding either for Hungarian legislation or for the Hungarian Constitutional Court. Following the jurisprudence of the Court is justified in several aspects, moreover it is a question meaning budgetary burden, in pure legal terms however it may not be of such gravity as to determine the decisions of the Constitutional Court and may not have more power than the own set of arguments and decisions, based on the Fundamental Law, of the Constitutional Court."

Concurring reasoning of Béla Pokol Judge of the Constitutional Court, HCC Decision 3025/2014. (II. 17.) AB, ABH 2014, 172, 168.: "The relevant decisions of the ECtHR may play a useful role in our draft decisions as information in the decision process of the Constitutional Court and pro domo for internal use; but my opinion is that they may not appear in the final decision, maximum as further arguments of the positions of individual Judges of the Constitutional Court in their concurring and dissenting opinions opposing it. Such a reference in the Decision of the Constitutional Court would mean that we attribute, beyond the Fundamental Law, a normative and for us binding power not only to the Convention but to the judicial practice interpreting it as well, and by this we acknowledge that the ECtHR may continue establishing international standards binding for the states parties to the Convention without their contribution." ... "In their so-called Lisbon Ruling of 2009, the judges of the German Constitutional Court elaborated a theoretical construction enabling a country to act against the interpretation of any convention as delivered by the court of any multilateral international convention, with reference to the integrity of constitutional identity and further to prohibit a decision made with such understanding to be applied within the country. Although the German constitutional judges formulated this doctrine of constitutional judicature against legal acts of the European Union affecting the Member States, but its significant findings stand for every multilateral convention if the particular country waives its prerogative concerning its sovereignty therein and the court of the international organisation maintains a jurisprudence concerning the standards of the constitution of that country."

subject of the application of the, not in force any more, rules on special taxation, the body granted applicative (almost abrogative) priority to the decisions of the ECtHR upon judicial initiation, ordered general prohibition of application, wherefore it was able to ensure the protection of fundamental rights (namely property protection) against the Tax Act and the restrictive rule in Article 37(4) of the FL.

At the same time, there is no change in terms of the fact that the Constitutional Court still selects precedents from the jurisprudence of the ECtHR and the CJEU[426] in order to support its arguments as adjusted to its own preconception; and it bases its decisions rather on internal arguments of constitutional law, i.e. it uses the option of interpretative primacy to a limited extent only when using international and EU law and grants applicative priority to these standards exceptionally only.[427] It did not clarify its position on the relationship between EU law and constitutional protection which had been controversially developed in the previous jurisprudence[428] and does not seek formal contact, manifesting in a request for preliminary ruling, with the CJEU, for which it would have had the possibility not only in the case of the retirement of judges but in the review of the Hungarian regulation on the implementation of the European arrest warrant as well, where in the latter case it could have inquire about the harmony with the Charter and so contributing to the development in the protection of fundamental rights at

---

[426] Zoltán SZENTE: The interpretive practice of the Hungarian Constitutional Court – A critical view, *German Law Journal* № 8, 2013, 1591–1614., 1602. http://www.germanlawjournal.com/pdfs/Vol14-No8/14.8.30.pdf

[427] As it relatively rarely uses the option of establishing conflict with an international treaty, and in general the option of investigating ex officio the conflict with an international treaty.

[428] Attila VINCZE, Odahull az eszme és a valóság közé az árnyék: a szuverenitás-átruházás az alkotmánybíróság esetjogában [The shadow falls between the idea and the reality: transfer of sovereignty in the case-law of the Constitutional Court], *MTA Law Working Papers* № 2014/23, 13–15. http://jog.tk.mta.hu/uploads/files/mtalwp/2014_23_Vincze.pdf.

EU level.[429] The Constitutional Court did also not undertake to involve the procedural bond between ordinary courts and the CJEU, the procedure of preliminary ruling with constitutional emphasis into the interpretation of the right to a legitimate judge in case the EU legal conditions are met.[430] According to the permanent jurisprudence of the German Federal Constitutional Court, the CJEU may also be a "legitimate judge" by virtue of Sentence 2 of Article 101(1) of the German Basic Law, namely if the German judge fails to request a preliminary ruling although the EU conditions are met, then reference may be made to the infringement of right to a legitimate judge within a constitutional appeal procedure.[431] According to the Hungarian Constitutional Court, this is not a constitutional issue but a technical legal issue falling within the scope of the judge of the proceedings.

> "The Constitutional Court, acting within its powers regulated by Section 27 of the CCA, ensures the harmony between the judicial ruling and the Fundamental Law. Consequently, the Constitutional Court shall refrain from taking a position on technical legal issues or issues exclusively about interpreting the law that belong to the revisory power of courts while investigating the unconstitutionality of the judicial ruling. {first see: Order № 3003/2012 (VI. 21.) AB, Reasoning [4]; (...)]}, {Order № 3028/2014. (II. 17.) AB, Reasoning [12]}. According to its jurisprudence, the Constitutional Court interprets the essence of the fundamental right to a fair trial in the enforcement of procedural rules of constitutional significance, wherefore it does not consider elements of court

[429] HCC Decision 3025/2014. (II. 17.) AB, ABH 2014, 172, 189. In this decision by the way, the Constitutional Court used ECtHR decisions when interpreting the right to freedom and personal security, but did so only at one occasion, indicating a reference to the CJEU decision. It appears from the dissenting opinion of Miklós Lévay that other decisions from the case-law of the CJEU may have been used for the argument and it would have been worth requesting the interpretation of the EU law for the sake of clarity at all.

[430] HCC Order 3110/2014. (VI. 17.) AB, ABH 2014, 559.; reinforced by: HCC Order 3165/2014. (VI. 23.) AB, ABH 2014, 764. Petitioners argued in both cases that the court had not fulfilled the request to initiate a preliminary ruling in the base case and Article XXVIII(1) of the FL had been therefore infringed.

[431] BVerfGE 73, 339, 366 ff. (Solange II); 75, 223, 233 ff. (Kloppenburg); 126, 286, 315 ff. (Honeywell), latest in 2010 Urheberrechtsabgabe: 1 BvR 1631/08. www.bundesverfassungsgericht.de/entscheidungen/rk20100830_1bvr163108.html.

> proceedings beyond that, especially the manner of deciding, with the application of legislation and exercising the discretional right of the court, in the particular legal disputes as a constitutional issue. In the present case, with the interpretation of applicable legislation and having regard to the issues of fact, the court, the legitimate judge under national law, i.e. a judge acting at a competent court and appointed pursuant to the order of distribution of cases defined in advance, of the proceedings had to decide whether it falls under the obligation to initiate a preliminary ruling or is exempt from it; wherefore the Constitutional Court does not have the competence to review that as according to Section 29 of the CCA."[432]

Although the Constitutional Court does not refuse but also does not endeavour to actively participate in the network of cooperative constitutionalism, however it could emphasise the Europe-friendly interpretation of the new constitution in a political context for which rejection by otherwise constructive European criticism, questioning of the decisions of Strasbourg and Luxembourg and a generally anti-EU rhetoric is typical. It appears that the political circumstances do not favour an extensive and activist constitutional judicature,[433] reciprocity is however the essence of cooperative constitutionalism and the Hungarian Constitutional Court also received confirmation for example from the CJEU in the case of radical lowering of the retirement age of judges and from the ECtHR in the case of recognition of churches.[434]

---

432 HCC Order 3110/2014. (IV. 17.) AB, ABH 559, 562. See also Georgina NASZLADI: The Hungarian Constitutional Court's judgement concerning the preliminary ruling procedure – comments on a rejection order, *Pécs Journal of International and European Law* Vol. 1, № 1, 2015, 37–43.

433 See to this B. POKOL: *A jurisztokratikus állam [The juristocracy]*, Dialóg Campus, Budapest, 2017, 38–42.

434 See also R. UITZ: Collective Constitutional Learning in Europe: European Courts Talk to Hungary (Again), *VerfBlog*, 2014/4/10, http://verfassungsblog.de/collective-constitutional-learning-in-europe-european-courts-talk-to-hungary-again/

3 Solidarity in and beyond the constitution

3.1 The topicality of solidarity and its relevance to constitutional law

In the era of the financial-economic crisis, terror threats, racism and segregation, impoverishment and famines, world-wide pandemics, climate change, environmental dangers and natural disasters, the *question* arises as to whether the motivation behind the *measures* planned, formulated and implemented with reference to combating the above-mentioned phenomena constitutes an effort merely to reduce, fight and eliminate the undesirable phenomenon or mitigate its consequences, or, underlying this *primary* motivation – as a *secondary* one – there is some common driving force.[435]

My starting point is that such secondary motivation could be *solidarity*. In the case of such hypothesis, the question presents itself *to what extent law* as a means and the *constitution* as a system of values *can be used to serve the purpose of solidarity*. For such an inquiry one may need to answer the following questions. What constitutes solidarity based on the general and normative approach? Is it defined by the constitution, in other words, can it be considered a legal or constitutional value in a democratic state governed by the rule of law? If it has relevance from the aspect of (constitutional) law, is it expressed in the norm content? When and how does it appear as reality, to what extent does it have an effect on law-making as a motivating factor or impulse? In the present essay, out of the enumerated ramifying questions, I will concentrate only on the quality of solidarity as a legal and constitutional value; at the same time, I consider that the exploration and evaluation of solidarity norms to be found in the legal system would be worth further research.

---

[435] The characteristic features of the era are comprehensively analysed in Antal ÁDÁM: *Alkotmányi értékek és alkotmánybíráskodás [Constitutional Values and the Practice of the Constitutional Court]*, Osiris, Budapest, 1998, 10–11; Antal ÁDÁM: Biztonság, felelősség, kötelesség [Security, Responsibility, Duty], *Jogtudományi Közlöny* № 7-8, 2005, 307–315.

Before the interpretation of solidarity as a constitutional value, it is worth giving a brief overview of the conclusions of Hungarian dogmatics concerning constitutional values and how they permeate the practice of the Constitutional Court. Antal Ádám distinguishes between three layers of constitutional values. "Among the components of the *first layer* of constitutional values, one may find values *having existed already before constitutional regulation or existing independently of it*, values that are generally considered necessary, useful or advantageous. [...] A large, wide-ranging group and, at the same time, also the *second layer* of constitutional values is made up of objectives, tasks, basic principles, basic requirements, basic rights, basic duties, essential prohibitions, qualities, responsibilities, executive and other organizations, organs, institutions *defined or established by the constitution-making power.* [...] As the *third layer* of constitutional values one may consider the *provisions* of the basic law pertaining to the values of the former two layers. Professor István *Losonczy* from Pécs qualified basic provisions and other legal regulations grounded on them as *legal instrumental values* in his excellent work on values written in 1948. "[436]

By comparison, the *Constitutional Court* made an attempt at outlining the content elements of the *"scale of constitutional values"* in its decision on the conferment of honours.[437] "The scale of constitutional values of the Republic of Hungary comprises primary (fundamental) values defined in a normative way by the Constitution, constitutional principles and values deduced through construction from the normative provisions of the Constitution (derived values), as well as further values contained in the codes (statutes and other regulations) of the individual branches of law [...] – which give expression to (i.e., mediate) the primary and derived scale of values

[436] See earlier, Ádám 'Alkotmányi értékek' 39.; and for the quoted text, Antal Ádám: A rendőrség az alkotmányi értékek között [The Police and Constitutional Values], in Gy. Gaál and Z. Hautzinger (eds.): *Pécsi Határőr Tudományos Közlemények IX. Tanulmányok a „Rendészet és rendvédelem – kihívások a XXI. században" című tudományos konferenciáról,* Magyar Hadtudományi Társaság Határőr Szakosztály Pécsi Szakcsoportja, Pécs, 2008, 10.

[437] HCC Decision 47/2007. (VII. 3.) AB, ABH 2007-I. 620.

of the Constitution. These values are present in the interpretations (decisions) of the Constitutional Court and, in the final analysis, in the whole constitutional culture."[438] The Court considers "the scale of constitutional values" as a scale of values defined by the existing social, economic and political system, fixed in space and time, the basic elements of which are laid down in the basic law during constitution-making by Parliament.[439] The values *expressed in the Constitution* are called *terminal values* by the Constitutional Court; while *legal regulations* detailing constitutional provisions and *implementing* those ends are considered *instrumental values*.[440]

Solidarity – from the aspect of constitutional law – may be either a value having existed prior to constitutional regulation or one formulated by the constitution-making power depending on whether it appears in an implied or express form in the basic law. However, this will be examined more closely only below, in point 3.4, since in order to establish the quality of solidarity as a constitutional value, it is necessary to explore the notion and legal relevance of solidarity first.

3.2 The notion of solidarity

3.2.1 *General interpretation of solidarity*

Solidarity[441] taken in its *most general* sense[442] means, on the one hand, the consciousness of individuals and groups of belonging together and, on the other hand (but stemming from this first mean-

---

[438] HCC Decision 47/2007. (VII. 3.) AB, ABH 2007-I. 620, 636.

[439] HCC Decision 47/2007. (VII. 3.) AB, ABH 2007-I. 620, 638.

[440] HCC Decision 47/2007. (VII. 3.) AB, ABH 2007-I. 620, 637.

[441] *Solidarietas* from the (Neo-Latin) word solidus (firm, well-founded): sharing of fate, community of fate. available at http://lexikon.katolikus.hu/S/szolidarit%C3%A1s.html

[442] *Magyar Nagylexikon [Hungarian Encyclopedia]*, Vol. 16. Magyar Nagylexikon Kiadó, Budapest, 2003, 876.

ing), joint and mutual commitment and assistance.[443] The appearance of solidarity as a *frame of mind* and as an *act* is based on the recognition of mutual dependence and on the established fact that mutual dependence between the members of a community gives rise to obligations.

The *scope of effect* or, rather, field of effect of solidarity extended primarily (and historically) to the micro- and small community (it existed in relations within the family, the religious and corporate community) – at a higher (universal) level it appeared only as a moral principle (command) (in religious tenets,[444] in theology and philosophy). Urbanization, industrialization and the appearance of

443 A similar approach: "In a wider sense, the well-founded belonging together of a group or society motivated from several sides; in a narrow sense, the undertaking of mutual obligations and mutual provision of assistance, by which each member of a group takes a stand for the group and the group takes a stand for them." available at http://lexikon.katolikus.hu/S/szolidarit%C3%A1s.html Concerning the definition of solidarity, see also: G. KARDOS: Szolidaritás, szubszidiaritás és a szociális jogok védelme [The Protection of Solidarity, Subsidiarity and Social Rights], in J. FRIVALDSZKY (ed.): *Szubszidiaritás és szolidaritás az Európai Unióban [Subsidiarity and Solidarity in the European Union]*, OCIPE Magyarország, Faludy Ferenc Akadémia, Budapest, 2006, 168. and K. ARATÓ: Szolidaritás és civil részvétel az Európai Unióban [Solidarity and Civil Participation in the European Union], in loc. cit. 143–144.

444 See Antal ÁDÁM: *Bölcselet, vallás, állami egyházjog [Philosophy, Religion, State Church Law]*, Dialóg Campus, Budapest–Pécs, 2007. Based on this work of Antal Ádám, if higlighting only the teachings of individual world religions, the following conclusions may be drawn. One requirement of Jewish religion is solidary charity (169). Judaism embodies the global solidarity of the Jewish people (171). An outstanding command of the Roman Catholic religion is love of one's fellow-beings, to which physical and spiritual works of mercy are attached (178). An important tenet of Protestantism is responsibility for the community (188–190). The third duty in the the Islamic religion is "obligatory alms-giving" (195). The divine attitudes expected of Buddhist people are: universal love and compassion for all living beings, delighting in other people's well-being and equanimity concerning one's own affairs (217). One command of the Sikh religion is to help the poor (226). Confucian ethics lays down as a requirement to care for others and exercize the virtue of humanity (228). The review of religious rules provides an exciting opportunity for the association of ideas, which Zoltán Nemessányi points out quoting Lord Atkin's reasoning given in the case of Donoghue (or McAlister) v Stevenson: the biblical rule that you are to "love thy neighbour" becomes in law: you must not injure your neighbour. In this case judicial practice transposes the religious requirement of

a service-providing state led to a definition of solidarity to be implemented at a higher level: to the presumption that society was a solidary unit. Within this scope, spontaneous mechanisms of solidarity gave way to the state's policy of solidarity and to a "system of compulsory solidarity".[445] The globalization of risks and dangers described in the introduction necessitated the recognition and influence of solidarity in a new dimension, as the motivating force behind international union and cooperation – institutionalized to varying degrees – which is based on the restriction of the sovereignty of states and reciprocity. In summary, one may consider as fields of effect of solidarity the sub-national level, the national level and also the supranational and international level. Solidarity implemented and operating at one level may enhance solidarity at the other levels, but it may also occur that the appearance of higher levels erodes solidarity that has existed in the small community, at the sub-state level.[446]

At the level of individual behaviour, solidarity may be perceived as a frame of mind and as an act. The *feeling* of solidarity – which is more than sympathy and compassion, because it means a feeling of responsibility based on fate shared from some aspect – is a precondition for solidary *activity*. Solidarity may be *directed* at persons (mainly in a community built on personal relations, e.g. in families, groups of friends or colleagues), or at issues (mainly in larger communities, e.g. fight against starvation, aid provision to victims of natural disasters).[447]

---

solidarity into law. Zolán NEMESSÁNYI: Rejtett képviselet az angol jogban [Hidden Representation under English Law], *JURA* № 2, 2008, 77.

445 Sz. HÁMOR: A szolidaritás világától a szép új világig? [From the World of Solidarity to the Brave New World?], *Esély* № 3, 2000, 4.

446 For example, the model of spending public goods elaborated by an international aid organization, the state or a private company may eliminate the generally more effective small community model based on solidarity, which had been developed by the users of the goods. See also inter alia, E. OSTROM: Collective Action and the Evolution of Social Norms, *The Journal of Economic Perspectives* Vol. 14, № 3, Summer, 2000, 153.

447 G. BOGNÁR and L. BOKROS: Verseny és szolidaritás [Competition and Solidarity], *BUKSZ* № 4, 2004, 382–383.

From the side of the individual, solidarity means that one voluntarily restricts the fulfilment and assertion of self-interest taking into consideration others' interests as well.[448] "The basic principle of conduct not based on self-interest can be altruism or equity; and it may be motivated by the improvement of others' welfare, the desire to give and goodwill directed toward the unknown members of society *(charitas)*, to the enhancement of social welfare. All these lead to the support of institutions serving others' interests – which are expected to be "unprofitable" for the individual.[449]

The system of solidary cohesion within the community presupposes the coordination of actions, which is based on joint consumption – resulting from the risk of material scarcity or uncertainty. This may cause the members of the community, whose aim is to satisfy needs based on equality within the community, to restrain their momentary self-interests and provide mutual assistance.[450] Solidarity within the group does not stem from the emotional or natural (biological) conditions of the members, but from common interests such as common needs, fight against poverty or oppression, or the achievement of some common goals.[451]

3.2.2 Disciplinary approaches to solidarity

Solidarity has relevance to numerous fields of social sciences. Before exploring the legal significance of the principle, it is worth reviewing briefly what aspects of solidarity are emphasized by other fields of science.

---

[448] B. Farkas: A szolidaritás a társadalmi-gazdasági szerveződésben [Solidarity in Social-Economic Organization] http://www.vigilia.hu/1999/9/9909far.html (2009.09.10.)

[449] B. Janky: Szolidaritás és jóléti preferenciák [Solidarity and Welfare Preferences], PhD- dissertation, manuscript, Budapest, 2002, 47. http://phd.lib.uni-corvinus.hu/83/01/janky_bela.pdf

[450] Ibid. 18.

[451] Solidarity with the members of the community or group may be based on shared political conviction, economic or political situation etc.

In *sociology* – mainly as a central notion of Durkheim's social theory – solidarity is the synopsis of social cohesion and two types of it may be distinguished. Mechanical solidarity corresponds basically to the traditional form of society defined by collective consciousness, in other words, it is based on common pre-defined criteria relating to some group (e.g. belonging to the given sex); while organic solidarity – which is based on interdependence – serves the integration of modern, functionally differentiated societies grounded on the division of labour.[452]

In accordance with this – as viewed by *political sociology* – solidarity represents a principle directed against isolation and massification, and emphasizes belonging together – that is, mutual responsibility for one another and joint obligation. Distinction may be made between group solidarity as the belonging together and joint action of persons of comparable social status who want to assert their common claims and interests jointly against others; and solidarity taken in a general sense oriented toward the common interests of all, toward the just order of society as a whole.

From the aspect of *political history*, in the workers' movement – in the beginning as a political slogan –, solidarity gave expression to the working class' self-consciousness and consciousness of belonging together, to their moral value serving as the foundation for their mutual aid institutions. In the workers' movement, solidarity provided opportunity for the members of the group to achieve freedom and social progress despite the fact that the members alone lacked the required power. It is also true of modern society that the individual can pursue political aims only if he joins forces with others (through interest organizations, trade unions, parties, civil initiatives). Beyond individual and group interests, there has grown a need for (global) solidarity extending to the whole world as the condition for a humane way of life and the survival of mankind in freedom and peace.

452 É. DURKHEIM: *A társadalmi munkamegosztásról* [On Social Division of Work], Osiris, Budapest, 2001, 69–80, 138–140. See also http://www.tankonyvtar.hu/filozofia/durkheim-szolidaritas-080904

In the approach of *economics,* the importance of solidarity is characterized by differing intensity in the dominant trends from the aspect of the apprehension and modelization of market economy.[453] The least space to solidarity is afforded in Adam Smith's theory, which oversimplifyingly proposed that, if everybody pursued their own interests in the economy, it would lead to the maximization of public good (through the "assistance" of an invisible hand). Consequently, if through the pursuit of individual interests the maximum of public good can be achieved, the role of solidarity in organizing society will become questionable. In contrast to this logic (following the world economic crisis), John Maynard Keynes considered that it was the state's task to interfere in market relations in order to increase employment. Parallel to this, state participation is also required to resolve social tensions and reduce inequalities, in other words, voluntary charity is not sufficient in this model. The value of solidarity was moved to the forefront as a result of the fact that the state provided welfare services for citizens through the redistribution of wealth. However, based on Milton Friedman's theory, (after the era known as the crisis of the welfare state) the idea reasserted itself that the socially detrimental effects of the operation of the market could basically be eliminated through civil solidarity and self-organization; it is not the state primarily that should provide remedy for them.[454]

The outlined disciplinary conceptions of solidarity are to be utilized by all means during legal interpretation, since they have been developed based on the examination of social reality from different aspects, and by its instrumental nature, law cannot disregard these results; at the same time, it flows from the function of law that dur-

---

[453] On this, see Farkas 'A szolidaritás a társadalmi-gazdasági szerveződésben'

[454] According to Beáta Farkas: "As neo-conservative and neo-liberal economists place the emphasis on providing proof for the optimal functioning of the self-regulating market, it goes without saying that the value of solidarity plays a subordinated role in their system." Farkas 'A szolidaritás a társadalmi-gazdasági szerveződésben'

ing regulation solidarity may acquire a peculiar relevance different from the above.

3.3 Solidarity as a legal value

Based on Ádám Antal's definition "the weight and hierarchical position of any value is determined or, at least, strongly influenced by the level of harmfulness of the danger, disadvantage, harm or lack of value constituting its opposite."[455] In our case it must be examined *what can be considered the opposite of solidarity,* in other words, what disadvantages and dangers may be caused by the lack of solidarity. In a socio-political sphere lacking the value of solidarity, one may reckon with the phenomena of isolation, separation, selfishness, hostility, massification, nivellization and inadequate assertion of interest. As a consequence of these phenomena – due to the lack of means or abilities, either through their own fault or through no fault of their own – certain members and groups of society get into a momentary or lasting disadvantageous situation; their living conditions may become desperately hard. From a legal aspect, one is to examine what subsidiary help the state or executive power (even one being established at the international level) may provide by its self-definition and participation, and by what legal means it may encourage the natural functioning of social solidarity.[456]

[455] ÁDÁM 'Bölcselet, vallás' 71.

[456] According to Pál Sonnevend: "State intervention [...] becomes justified and necessary in many areas only where solidarity between the individual people proves insufficient: state activity concerning the improvement of the situation of those at a disadvantage is of secondary importance anyway." P. SONNEVEND: Szolidaritás és jog [Solidarity and Law], available at http://www.vigilia.hu/1999/9/9909son.html. Concerning this, Lajos Bokros states the following: "If solidarity is raised to the level of social behavioral norm, its most beautiful form of implementation is constituted by voluntary social initiatives." L. BOKROS: Verseny és szolidaritás [Competition and Solidarity], Élet és Irodalom, Budapest, 2004, 29. However, this categorical imperative requires self-consciousness, independence and self-care (independent responsibility), the framework of which is set by democracy and market economy based on fair competition. This is adversely af-

The recognition and formulation of *solidarity rights,*[457] which may be regarded as a result of international legal development, contribute to the assertion of solidarity as a legal value. This circle comprises some modern rights (viewed by some as third generation rights) including the right to a healthy environment, sustainable development, proper feeding, consumer protection, the right to communication, protection of the future generations and the rights of the elderly as a manifestation of solidarity between the generations, as well as the right to peace, humanitarian aid or to the common heritage of humanity. The assertion of these rights requires active solidarity on the part of states and the international community; in the case of the major part of them one may regard as obligor all of the states taken together, while the part of obligee is taken by mankind as a whole. However, with a view to the present state of legal development, these rights can be enforced only to a low degree or hardly at all, since neither their content, nor their subjects and obligors are adequately defined.[458]

In law-making *states* may utilize and assert the principle of solidarity in various ways, although this mostly results in solidarity implemented with the help of the state, in other words, *rules prescribing citizens' solidarity toward each other* are rather rare. As exceptions to this one may regard the obligation to provide help (that is, the criminalization of the failure to provide help) and the obligation of support in family law.[459] The legal imprints of the moral minimum stemming from a family tie are parents' duty of childcare and education as well as the rights and duties of children. The state *may encourage* voluntary, civil *solidarity mechanisms,* e.g. by tax discounts on the aid provided for the needy and by announcing grants for

fected if the state forces people to undertake solidarity obligatorily and pushes self-care into the background. See Bokros ibid. 41.

457 V. Lamm and V. Peschka (eds.): *Jogi lexikon* [Lexicon of Law], KJK-KERSZÖV, Budapest, 1999, 563–564.

458 Petrétei 'Az alkotmányos demokrácia' 450. See also G. Halmai and G. A. Tóth (eds.): *Emberi jogok* [Human Rights], Osiris, Budapest, 2003, 88.

459 Sonnevend 'Szolidaritás'

charitable persons and organizations that carry out their activities in the interests of others.

Some sub-constitutional norms may contain *an element of solidarity as well* exceeding their primary objective, or at least, the idea of solidarity may also be detected among the problem impulses of the regulation.[460] One may consider as such obligations relating to the protection of the environment and nature, the protection of public health and emergency management. In the world of work one may mention social partnership, conciliation of interests, coalitional freedom and trade union activity as well as the exercise of the right to strike. Solidarity may function as significant motivation behind some pieces of crisis-legislation.[461] Finally, the public interest action relating to consumer protection – besides cost-effective litigation – and compulsory liability insurance – besides substituting for and distributing individual liability – may also be regarded, at least indirectly, as manifestations of solidarity flowing from a shared risk.

Non-legal means contributing to the implementation of norms carrying solidarity also include employment and social policies, anti-discrimination and labour market integration programmes and strategies.[462]

---

460 It is worth mentioning that in the Hungarian legal system relatively few normative provisions concerned solidarity expressly already before the FL. Some examples: the preamble of Act XCVI of 1993 on Voluntary Mutual Insurance Funds, the preamble of Act LXXVII of 1993 on the Rights of National and Ethnic Minorities, the basic principles and priorities of Parliamentary Resolution 29/2008. (III. 20.) OGY on the National Climate Change Strategy, Parliamentary Resolution 47/2007. (V. 31.) OGY on the National Strategy "Let it be better for Children!"

461 See Act XLVIII of 2009 on specific amendments required for the protection of citizens in a difficult situation caused by a house loan, Government Decree 136/2009. (VI. 24.) on supporting persons in a situation of crisis.

462 See e.g. Community programme for employment and solidarity – PROGRESS (2007–2013). http://europa.eu/scadplus/leg/en/cha/c11332.htm

3.4 Solidarity in the constitution

3.4.1 Solidarity as a constitutional value

Solidarity conceived as a constitutional value has three projections: political solidarity, social solidarity taken in a narrow sense and supra-national solidarity.

a) *Political solidarity* may be grasped, on the one hand, in the national consciousness of belonging together and its expression in the constitution and, on the other hand, in constitutional norms referring to cases and situations where the community-forming and cohesive force of some political issues is moved to the forefront. The former is supported, for example, by provisions laying down national sovereignty, the institution of citizenship, the emblems and symbols expressing belonging to the nation, and – if it is relevant to the given state – rules relating to the diaspora. The extent and form of appearance of this aspect of political sovereignty in the Constitution are influenced by the given political community's concept of "nation". More precisely, whether the constitutional order is dominated by the concept of "nation as state" or "nation as culture" (nation as language).[463] The other constitutional aspect of solidarity may be grasped in means intended for situations and events outside the law,[464] namely, in the rights relating to political participation and communication (especially, in the guarantee of the right to assembly and association, freedom of opinion and the right to petition).

b) The constitutional expression of *social solidarity* taken in a narrow sense[465] may be found in the principles of the social state, social market economy, the guarantee of social rights, the protection of

[463] PETRÉTEI 'Az alkotmányos demokrácia' 186–187.

[464] For example, a matter of political nature (internal or foreign political event) that evokes reaction from the community or a defined group who also intend to give expression to this in a demonstration or joint action.

[465] In a wider sense, social solidarity as an actuality outside law also serves as the foundation for political, social – taken in a narrow sense – and supranational solidarity.

social outcasts and the needy, which are implemented in the world of work and within the framework of the social care system. Social solidarity is a characteristic feature of the welfare state and it is related to the state's social welfare services functions; the purpose of laying it down in the Constitution may be to outline the legal guarantees of secure livelihood. If social solidarity is outlined in a paternalistic model or by paternalistic methods, its practical effect is usually to push individual self-care and responsibility-taking to the background.[466] Compulsory social solidarity also means the reorganization of relations of wealth to a certain degree, because people who have not borne the burden of averting risks also necessarily receive social benefits.[467] Therefore, the obligation of solidarity may be prescribed only based on the principle of equality and in compliance with the constitutional standard of the restriction of ownership.

The degree of solidarity manifested in the social security system depends on the size of the circle of members of the community involved in the system, the scope of the problems covered by it, the degree of intervention it leaves to the executive power and the degree of fairness of the model of redistribution applied by the system. Consequently, the distribution of risk is not determined individually but along a standard of equality adopted jointly by the whole society. Thus, problems constituting the subject of individual consideration earlier become politicized: what should happen in the case of illness, disability, old age, unemployment or parenthood is determined based on the principles of regularity, predict-

---

466 HÁMOR 'A szolidaritás világától' 3. According to Gábor Kardos: "Solidarity is if a person sympathizing with the situation of another person is also ready to act in his support. When the government carries out a financial transfer or redistribution through the taxation system and social policy with reference to solidarity, it quasi nationalizes this readiness. However, it is forced to do so because otherwise support for those in need could be implemented merely as voluntary care organized on a charitable basis. This way many people would be left without support." G. KARDOS: A szolidaritás határai [Limits of Solidarity], *Liget – literary and ecological journal* Vol. 21, № 3, 2008, 95.

467 A. TAKÁCS: A szociális jogok [Social rights], in G. HALMAI and G. A. TÓTH (eds.): *Emberi jogok* [Human Rights], Osiris, Budapest, 2003, 803.

ability and equality instead of eventuality and defencelessness.[468] All this leads to the recognition in the Constitution of the fact that individuals are not equal only in their civil and political rights but also in their risks. While the formal belonging together of the political community finds expression in citizenship, interdependence caused by personal and individual neediness and risk are manifested in social rights and institutions.

c) The requirement of *supranational* solidarity presents itself, on the one hand, in relation to global challenges. Among them mention could be made of managing climate change, combating poverty and famines, crisis management, ensuring sustainable development – all these require *global* solidarity on the part of mankind.[469] The assertion of the solidarity rights mentioned above already also presupposes global solidarity of the international community. On the other hand, organizations of defence and economic integration also emphasize the requirement of solidarity of participating states. This is manifested in the basic documents of the said organizations, e.g. it is implied in the North-Atlantic Treaty,[470] or expressly laid down in the Treaty on the European Union;[471] but Constitutions also usually give expression to commitment toward the international community and readiness to international cooperation.

[468] P. Baldwin: *The Politics of Social Solidarity,* Cambridge University Press, Cambridge, 1990, 2.

[469] Ban Ki Mun: A szolidaritás víziója [The Vision of Solidarity], *Figyelő* January 2009, 37.

[470] See the Preamble and Arts 3-5 of the North-Atlantic Treaty, available at http://www.nato.int/cps/en/natohq/official_texts_17120.htm.

[471] Preamble, Arts. 2-3, Art. 21, Art. 24, Art. 31 of the Treaty on the European Union (version incorporating the Lisbon Treaty); Preamble, Art. 67, Art. 80, Art. 122, Art. 194, Art. 222 of the Treaty on the Functioning of the European Union (consolidated version)

3.4.2 *Presence and interpretation of solidarity in constitutional law in Europe*

At this point it is worth examining how solidarity appears in the individual European constitutions and the founding treaties of the European Union.

a) The first group is made up of the – otherwise small number of – constitutions that *expressly lay down* the principle of solidarity. As example one may cite the preamble of the *Czech constitution,* which speaks about "equal and free citizens who are conscious of their duties towards others and their responsibility towards the whole". The *Polish constitution* provides an even simpler formulation of solidarity in its Article 20, which lays down, concerning the economic order, the principle of "a social market economy, based on solidarity, dialogue and cooperation between social partners", which is to be interpreted jointly with the basic principle of "a democratic state ruled by law and implementing the principles of social justice" laid down in Article 2. According to the preamble, the basic value of the Republic of Poland, among others, is the obligation of solidarity with others. Finally, mention could be made of the *Romanian constitution,* Article 1 of which – besides other values – also refers to solidarity taken in a political sense: "Romania is a sovereign, independent, unitary, and indivisible Nation State. The State foundation is laid on the unity of the Romanian people and the solidarity of its citizens."

b) The second group comprises constitutions that are *interpreted using* the principle of solidarity. Article 2 of the *Italian* constitution asserts that "The republic recognizes and guarantees the inviolable human rights, be it as an individual or in social groups expressing their personality, and it ensures the performance of the unalterable duty to political, economic, and social solidarity." The Italian theory of basic rights interprets individuals within the framework of a way of thinking founded on social dependence. In Article 2 the Constitution lays down two basic principles: the principle of personality *(il principio personalistico),* according to which natural persons have a sphere that cannot be violated by others and the principle of plurality *(il principio pluralistico)*, which protects individuals in their social relations. In addition to the general expression of the principle of plurality given in Article 2 (and Article 18 in the guarantee of the right to union), it is also specially formulated in the articles relating to social organizations having direct constitutional relevance (family, linguistic minority, religious communities, trade unions, political parties). *Solidarity* is not simply a programme principle, but *also influences civil law relations between citizens,* which is true of provisions relating to the family (Article 29), the right to health (Article 32), the right to work (Articles 35-36), the limits of the right to property (Articles 42 and 44), private economic enterprise (Article 41 (1)), workers' participation in the management of companies (Article 46), the system of cooperatives (Article 45) and the ability to acquire property (Article 47 (1)).[472] As the Italian constitution lists among basic constitutional principles the principle of equality (Article 3), the principle of solidarity and the right to work (Article 4), these principles provide guidance for legislature with establishing a social order in conformity with the constitution.[473]

Out of the state-organizing principles of the *German* basic law (GG), one may also mention the *creation of a social state* (GG, Articles 20 and 28), which, taken in a general sense, means protecting and helping weaker people. In a wider sense, however, it may be constructed as the possibility for everybody to share common goods, moreover, ensuring dignified conditions of existence. The GG supports this by the declaration of basic social rights, the special regulation of contributions to public revenues and the creation of equal

---

[472] In this sense, in Italy one may speak of the constitutionalization of civil law, which is manifested first of all in the decisions of the Constitutional Court relating to family law, labour law and the law of delict. The process of constitutionalization gained importance because the Constitutional Court moved away from the interpretation of general principles of constitutional law as mere programme norms.

[473] T. Drinóczi: Államszervezési elvek és államszervezet az Olasz Köztársaságban [Principles of State Organization and the Structure of State in the Republic of Italy], *Magyar Jog* № 11, 2007, 672–674.

opportunities.[474] However, the state – as a social state governed by the rule of law – does not only protect the individual from social risks but also encourages self-help and solidarity communities. Consequently, the GG's social state governed by the rule of law is not a "totally caring state" but, apart from the welfare of the individual, its aim is also to realize "responsible freedom".[475] The task of the German social state is to implement and maintain social justice. The protection of work and incomes earned by work as well as the guarantee of social security irrespectively of the individual's working capacity presuppose redistribution defined primarily by the principle of equality. This is grounded on the ethical principle of solidarity.[476] The guarantee of social justice by the state *transforms solidarity* to be borne by society *into a legal issue.* The socially just social system ensures everybody the possibility to contribute to the economy and culture in a self-determining way based on his own decision and performance.[477]

c) The principle of solidarity emphasized in the amended founding treaties of the *European Union* enhances – externally – the *identity* of the integrational *organization* (in other words, the fact that the integration of the member states forming an increasingly close union between themselves differs from other international organizations),[478] on the other hand – internally – it gives expression to the economic-social *cohesion between member states,* and to the com-

---

474 J. Zeller: Német Szövetségi Köztársaság [Federal Republic of Germany], in N. Chronowski and T. Drinóczi (eds.): *Európai kormányformák rendszertana [Systematics of European Forms of Government]*, HVG-ORAC, Budapest, 2007, 118–119.

475 T. Drinóczi: *Gazdasági alkotmány és gazdasági alapjogok [Economic Constitution and Basic Economic Rights]*, Dialóg Campus, Budapest–Pécs, 2007, 145.

476 P. Badura: *Staatsrecht*, C. H. Beck'sche Verlagsbuchhandlung, München, 1996, 256.

477 Ibid. 257.

478 P. Szilágyi: Csak akkor(?) és abban a mértékben(?)...: Szubszidiaritás és szolidaritás az Európai Unióban, Recenzió [Only if? and to the Extent(?)...: Subsidiarity and Solidarity in the European Union, Review], *Európai Jog* № 1, 2009, 63.

mitment of mutual assistance.[479] Internal solidarity is a natural consequence of the development of the community established amongst states, which, on the other hand, serves as a foundation e.g., for the free movement of labour, temporary derogations for acceding states concerning the fulfilment of some requirements or the expansion of transfers of resources.[480] The principle of social solidarity as the foundation for the social welfare system can also be found in the practice of the Court of Justice.[481] This practice is justified by the title of the *Charter of Fundamental Rights* summing up solidarity rights, which acquired legal force through the Treaty of Lisbon.[482] In this respect, attention must be drawn to the following idea of Gábor Kardos: "It is not unjustified to designate economic and social rights as solidarity rights. The reason for this is that the financial base of services provided on the basis of social rights is given by nationalized solidarity, which receives its resources from taxes. At the same time, the inclusion of the concept of solidarity in the summary of basic rights to be protected by the EU further emphasizes the importance of this value in the functioning of this institution."[483] Having regard to international legal development, the modern catalogue

---

[479] Some examples: The material manifestation of enhancing cohesion between the member states is the Solidarity Fund, which provides emergency relief in case of natural disasters. (O. Sebők: A szolidaritás alapja [The Basis of Solidarity], *Piac&Profit*, October 2007, 22–23.) Joint action against terror attacks and mutual assistance in case of a terrorist attack are ensured by the solidarity clause. See Art. 222 of the Treaty on the Functioning of the European Union (consolidated version).

[480] P. Balázs: A szolidaritás határai Európában [The Limits of Solidarity in Europe], *Esély* № 2, 2002, 5. In connection with the economic driving forces and political significance of solidarity, Árpád Gordos states that "the principle of solidarity is the suspension point of our European policy". Á. Gordos: A szolidaritás és a szubszidiaritás mint a közjó horizontális és vertikális szolgálatának alapelvei [Solidarity and Subsidiarity as the Basic Principles of the Horizontal and Vertical Service of Public Good], in 'Szubszidiaritás és szolidaritás az Európai Unióban' 182.

[481] A. Somek: Solidarity Decomposed. Being and time in European citizenship. *University of Iowa Legal Studies,* Research Paper 07-13, 2007, available at http://ssrn.com/abstract=987346, 4.

[482] Charter of Fundamental Rights of the European Union, Title IV. Articles 27–38. (OJ C 303/8-10, 14.12.2007).

[483] Kardos 'Szolidaritás, szubszidiaritás' 170.

of fundamental rights does not merely declare classical solidarity rights (oriented to the world of labour), but also attributes importance to solidarity between generations[484]; and also regulates environmental and consumption risks based on the universal principle of solidarity.[485]

3.4.3 *Solidarity-oriented provisions of the former Hungarian Constitution (Act XX of 1949)*

The former Hungarian Constitution did not expressly lay down the principle of solidarity; however, it contained several rules inspired by some aspects of solidarity. The solidarity-oriented rules, institutions and solutions of the legal system might be traced back to them. At the same time, it was – and still is – a problem that solidarity – similarly to other constitutional values – has become interiorized to a low degree in the members of the political community, to whom the constitution is addressed and whom it is about. As opposed to other constitutional values – such as the rule of law, democracy, parliamentarism, freedom, security, human rights etc. –, the value-character and preciousness of which could be (could have been) learnt by society in the two decades following the democratic political transformation, the value of solidarity could have taken root in the era of socialism too as a community-organizing factor. This is what happened, for example, in Poland and Czechoslovakia, where solidarity against the dictatorial state and regime had developed and influenced social practice before the years of political change. In contrast, in Hungary the Kádár era was favourable for achieving modest individual prosperity and influenced public atmosphere in the direction of self-interest pursuing behaviour. As a result of these circumstances, Hungary has a lower level

---

484 Art. 25 of the Charter of Fundamental Rights of the European Union (rights of the elderly).

485 Arts 37-38 of the Charter of Fundamental Rights of the European Union (protection of the environment, consumer protection).

of social solidarity, and consequently, also lower levels of law-abidance than other post-socialist countries with a similar line of development. On the other hand, there is a high demand for government intervention and high expectation of solutions of redistribution, in many cases without the recognition of the justified need for readiness to individual sacrifice. The outlined attitude of the political community may serve as explanation to the question why solidarity as a constitutional value has such a low impact on the actual state of reality in Hungary.

In spite of the above, from the aspect of Hungarian constitutional law, solidarity was considered a value that is independent of constitutional regulation, which, at the same time, may be served by several instrumental values laid down in the basic law or a lower level legal norm. The solidarity-oriented provisions of the Hungarian Constitution might also be analysed in political, international and social dimensions based on the system described above.

a) In the Constitution one might find only provisions giving expression to *political solidarity* indirectly, e.g., in the provision concerning the sense of responsibility for the fate of Hungarians living outside the borders (Article 6 (3) – responsibility clause), the institution of the Head of State designed to express national unity (Article 29), or the recognition of the rights of the national and ethnic minorities defined as participants in the sovereign power of the people (Article 68).[486] During the identification of solidarity norms it caused a problem that the basic law used the terms "people", "people representing a constituent part of the State" and "nation" as well (both in the form of subject and attribute). The expression "(Hungarian) people" denotes nation in a political sense having the meaning of nation as state, which also includes persons belonging to (national and ethnic) minorities. If the category of nation is used within the meaning of nation as culture, nation is both a narrower and wider category than political nation. It is narrower, because it

[486] Concerning political solidarity, see A. Zs. Varga: Alkotmányunk értékei. A fogalmi keretek [The Values of Our Constitution. A Notional Framework.], *Iustum Aequum Salutare* № 1, 2009, 97–100.

embraces only the part of the citizens of the state who share the same culture, speak the same language, have the same origins, identity etc. On the other hand it is wider, because it regards as part of the nation also those who live in other countries and are citizens of other states, but who otherwise belong to the nation based on their language, culture, origins etc. Because of the complicated nature of the notion of nation, the terms "people" and "citizenship" are rather applicable in constitutional law. Therefore – in this sense – "people" may be regarded as the indispensible element of the state, the source of state sovereignty and the community functioning as the vehicle of political solidarity.[487]

b) The *international dimension* of solidarity was manifested primarily in the foreign policy objectives of the state formulated in the Constitution (Article 6), the provision about the acceptance of international law (Article 7 (1)), the authorization relating to European integration (Article 2/A) as well as in compliance with certain policies (Article 57 (4)). Although solidarity with the international community and the other member states of the European Union was not expressly laid down by these provisions, nevertheless, it might be taken into account as an immanent value during the interpretation of the Constitution. Help with the latter was provided by the expressions: rejection of war and violence,[488] endeavour to cooperate, taking part in establishing European unity, joint exercise of authority, which presuppose solidarity with those concerned. Moreover, because readiness to international and supranational cooperation is expressed in the Constitution, the Constitutional Court, during

[487] Petrétei 'Az alkotmányos demokrácia' 185–188. A different view is held by e.g. János Zlinszky, who considers "people" an ethnic concept and "nation" a political category. J. Zlinszky: Tudjátok-e, mi a haza? [Do you know what motherland is?], in *Formatori Iuris Publici – Ünnepi kötet Kilényi Géza professzor 70. születésnapjára* [Special Volume Dedicated to the 70th Birthday of Professor Géza Kilényi], PPKE-JÁK, Szent István Társulat, Budapest, 2006, 599.

[488] This may also be regarded as the declaration of the right to peace, which may be grouped with the solidarity rights described above. See Zs. Balogh et al.: Az *Alkotmány magyarázata [Commentary of the Constitution]*, KJK-KERSZÖV, Budapest, 2003, 157.

its interpretational activity, used[489] the provisions of conventions containing accepted international obligations which give expression to and serve solidarity.[490]

c) The *rules* of the Constitution inspired by *social solidarity* and giving expression to the social responsibility of the state[491] were: providing support for those in need (Article 17), the protection of the young (Article 16), the right to social security (Article 70/E) and health (Article 70/D). In a wider sense and having regard to the tendencies of international legal development, solidarity may be associated with the right to a healthy environment (Article 18) and the right to access to culture (Article 70/F), freedom of coalition and the right to strike (70/C), parents' duty to educate their children (Article 66), and the obligation to contribute to public revenues, which constitutes the financial base of institutions of solidarity encouraged or organized by the state (Article 70/I).

With respect to the interpretation of the mentioned solidarity norms – expressed mostly in social rights – , determinative significance were attributed to *the right to human dignity, the prohibition of discrimination,* equal rights and opportunities;[492] while the background for their implementation is provided by the principle of market economy. According to the position of the Constitutional Court, apart from the declaration of *market economy,* the Constitution

---

489 For more detail concerning the role played by international law in the interpretation of the constitution, see László BLUTMAN: A nemzetközi jog használata az Alkotmány értelmezésénél [The Use of International Law during the Interpretation of the Constitution], *Jogtudományi Közlöny* № 7-8, 2009, 301–315.

490 See, for example, HCC Decision 357/B/2002 AB of the Constitutional Court (30 May 2006) dealing with the the protection of victims, in which the Constitutional Court also referred to the solidarity principle of the European Convention of 1983 on the Compensation of the Victims of Violent Crimes in its reasoning.

491 According to Sonnevend: "With regard to society-scale solidarity, the social responsibility of the state is what is laid down by the Constitution. In this context, two constitutional principles of central importance may serve as a starting point: respect for and protection of human dignity and the principle of citizens' equality before the law." SONNEVEND 'Szolidaritás' 1–2.

492 The above also serve as guarantees of social justice and tolerance (and social immunity). Solidarity is also connected with these values.

was neutral from the point of view of economic policy,[493] which meant that it was not committed to any model of market economy.[494] Social market economy, laid down in the preamble, was merely a state objective in the Republic of Hungary; therefore, it was not invoked concerning the principle of solidarity.[495]

In the present chapter, I do not provide a detailed analysis of the basic rights, fundamental duties and constitutional principles listed above, but merely mention the fact that, *in its practice, the Constitutional Court* invoked the principle of solidarity during its interpretational activity primarily in connection with the right to social security and the social security system guaranteeing this right.

The Court considered the *right to social security* a constitutional value: "The Constitution defines the right to social security as a terminal value (Constitution, Article 70/E), which – by way of the state's objective obligation to protect the institutions (maintenance of social insurance and social institutions) – ensures to those entitled to it the support required to live in old age, and in the case of sickness, disability, being widowed or orphaned and in the case of unemployment through no fault of their own. The instrumental values attached to the terminal value (the conditions for the establishment and operation of the institutions and for receiving the specific provisions) are set forth in statutes and other legal instruments relating to the institutions."[496]

Out of the connected "instrumental values", it was in the case of the characterization of the mixed nature and operation of the *social security system* and the services provided within its framework as

---

493 HCC Decision 33/1993. (V. 28.) AB, ABH (1993) 247, 249.

494 HCC Decision 21/1994. (IV. 6.) AB, ABH (1994) 117, 119.

495 If the Constitution contained, as a basic principle of the economic order, the requirement of social market economy or, in connection with market economy – similarly to the Polish Constitution – the principle of solidarity, then during the protection of the constitution, besides the requirements of fair distribution, social balance and the subsidiary responsibility of the state, the requirements of individual responsibility and foresight could also clearly unfold. Concerning this, see DRINÓCZI 'Gazdasági alkotmány' 165.

496 HCC Decision 47/2007. (VII. 3.) AB, ABH (2007)-I. 620, 637.

well as the created legal relations that the Constitutional Court invoked the principle of solidarity. State regulation of legal relations created within the framework of social security is governed by the principles of individual responsibility, self-care and social solidarity.[497] Social security, on the one hand, gives the insured persons some in-kind provisions based on the principle of solidarity, and on the other hand, it gives financial provisions to them adjusted to the amount of their payments.[498] The Court itself found the system mixed in a double sense: "Firstly, in the respect that the state meets its obligation of care laid down in the Constitution by operating both a compulsory social security system and a system of social provisions. In this dual system both insurance and solidarity are present. Secondly, the legal relation created by compulsory social security itself has a mixed nature too, because it contains both the elements of insurance and solidarity."[499] The principle of solidarity also played a role during the constitutional examination of the es-

[497] "In order to ensure the operability and financing of the social security system, there was a need for a comprehensive reform of the system. Since 1 January 1998 the pension system has been characterised by mixed financing: it consists of a distributive-impositional element (social security pension) and a capital backing element (private pension). The change is aimed at regulating legal relations created within the framework of social security in accordance with the requirements of individual responsibility and self-care and the principles of social solidarity." HCC Decision 5/1998. (III. 1.) AB, ABH (1998) 82, 87.

[498] "As applied in Art. 70/E of the Constitution, the notion of „social security" means a system based on legally compulsory membership and the compulsory payments of the members, providing both financial and in-kind services, the functioning of which is laid down by legal provision. In other words, state-operated social security is a supply system which gives insured persons in-kind provisions – based on the principle of solidarity – independently of the amount of the contributions, in case of the occurrence of events that are certain or highly probable to take place in a person's life, as well as financial provisions of differing amounts adjusted to the amount of the contributions paid by the insured persons, who are required to contribute a percentage of their income laid down by law to the maintenance of the social security system." HCC Decision 51/2007. (IX. 15.) AB, ABH (2007)-I. 652, 657.

[499] HCC Decision 35/1997. (VI. 11.) AB, ABH 1997. 200, 214.

tablishment of the obligation to pay a contribution,[500] and the amount of the contribution[501].

Finally, it could also be interesting to examine when the principle of solidarity played no role in the practice of the Constitutional Court. For example, in its decision on the wealth tax adopted in 2010,[502] the Constitutional Court does not mention it either as a reason or as an aspect of interpretation – despite the fact that, concerning the proportionality (fairness) of contributions to public revenues, social solidarity serves as a (not so hidden) underlying motivation.

3.4.4 *Solidarity and the Fundamental Law*

In the previous chapters of this book it was already discussed that in the field of international and social solidarity the FL gives a weaker standard than the Constitution. Instead, it puts emphasis on political solidarity by establishing the system of national cooperation, but the latter is also restricted to a nationalist and Hungarian ethnocentric concept.

---

[500] "Therefore, it may be deduced logically from the constitutionally acceptable principle of solidarity that based on the Constitution, the legislator is free to extend the obligation to pay a contribution to all incomes earned by work but derived from different sources, consequently, even to incomes gained by the insured persons within the framework of their legal relations in their second or third jobs, as employees, sole traders or partners. Otherwise, the principle that – within the framework of medical care – those of lower income are entitled to the same social security services as the insured persons paying higher contributions would not be constitutionally acceptable either. Therefore, if the extension of the obligation of contribution to include incomes gained within the framework of further employment and entrepreneurial legal relations is – at least partly – accompanied by an element of insurance, the taking into consideration of the principle of solidarity to a higher proportion in this circle is not in itself unconstitutional." HCC Decision 34/1997. (VI. 11.) AB, ABH (1997) 174, 187.

[501] In accordance with the principle of solidarity, contributions defined as percentages impose a heavier burden on people of higher incomes than those having lower incomes or no income at all; on the other hand, the quality of in-kind health insurance provisions is independent of the amount of the contribution paid. HCC Decision 197/B/2002. AB, ABH (2007) 1389, 1394–1395.

[502] HCC Decision 8/2010. (I. 28.) AB.

The 'rule by law' governance and the frequently amended new constitution of 2011/12 also reformulated the frameworks of the protection of human dignity and social solidarity. The decline of the standards in this field is spectacular and visible.

The recent case law of the Constitutional Court reaffirms the initial concerns, the dignity supported solidarity lost in the post-democratic transitions in the past seven years.

The Constitutional Court recognised in 2012 that the FL completely abandoned the approach of the former Constitution on right to social security, thus found necessary to distinguish and overrule the former case law. The Court emphasized that no fundamental rights are provided by the new constitutional regulation on social security, instead, only state duties and aims are prescribed in Article XIX.[503] This article mentions rights just in two cases, first the right to state pension of the elderly prescribed by law, and second the right to statutory subsidies in certain situations (maternity, illness, disability, handicap, widowhood, orphanage and unemployment for reasons outside of his or her control). These are far not enforceable right, their protection depends on the opportunities and economic situation of the state.[504] On the basis of the amendment to the former Constitution in 2011 and the new constitutional environment the Court found legitimate and just that the government reconstructed the system of early retirement, substituted the pensions with aids and allowances, which are completely ex gratia subsidies thus not even fall under the protection of private property. The constitutional protection of property is applicable to those social subsidies in the future where individual financial contribution justifies it. The ex gratia subsidies are subject to the legislative discretion thus they are not protected as fundamental or constitutional rights – the only criterion that they cannot based on arbitrary decision.[505] From

[503] HCC Decision 40/2012. (XII. 6.) AB, HCC Decision 9/2016. (IV. 6.) AB.

[504] HCC Decision 28/2015. (IX. 24.) AB.

[505] HCC Decision 32/2015. (XI. 19.) AB, reasoning [32], HCC Decision 25/2016. (XII. 21.) AB, reasoning [24]

the argumentation of the Court references to human dignity or social solidarity have totally disappeared.[506]

The level of protection of the social rights may be reduced by the state, argues the Court, and the state duties are restricted to – on the one hand – the establishment of an institutional system in which the constitutional rights may prevail, and – on the other – the statutory rights shall be outlined for the access to the social institutions. The Court noted that the FL just reaffirmed the limited economic capacity of the state and respected the fact that the former welfare model was unsustainable.[507] However, some kind of protection is still not excluded, because the certain situations enumerated by the FL – although do not generate subjective, justiciable fundamental rights but – create 'constitutional background' to the statutory rights.[508]

While the Constitutional Court was reluctant to find any unconstitutionality in the governmental reconstruction of the social security system, the European Court of Human Rights in a subsidiary way guarantees some remedy although the protection of social rights fall beyond the scope of the Convention. A recent case[509] concerned a social security benefit paid to the applicant, who had

---

506 See HCC Decision 40/2012. (XII. 6.) AB, press release: 'The Constitutional Court has declared that the adopted Article XIX of Fundamental Law and the still applicable Article 70/E para 5 of the previous Constitution authorise the law-maker expressly to reduce the pension or to modify it to social benefit if those who receive it are under the general retirement age, or even to terminate it in case of incapacity of work. Based on these regulations, the Hungarian Parliament adopted the Act that ensures health care insurance instead of retirement benefits for people with reduced ability to work. The Constitutional Court has declared that the Act contains transitional provisions because it took the previously declared age, the rate of disability and the previous forms of benefits into consideration when disposes the disbursement of benefits from 1 January 2012. Therefore, the concerned part of the Commissioner's petition has been dismissed. The Constitutional Court has declared as well that the regulation regarding the termination of eligibility for disability benefits does not infringe the Fundamental Law as the reasons of the termination are that the need thereof expires and an income necessary to minimal subsistence is ensured.'

507 HCC Decision 25/2016. (XII. 21.) AB, reasoning [21]

508 HCC Decision 28/2015. (IX. 24.) AB, reasoning [34]

509 Béláné Nagy v. Hungary (application № 53080/13), Judgment of 13 December 2016 (Grand Chamber)

received a disability benefit for almost ten years, which was then withdrawn. The claim to re-start the payments was dismissed, because a legislative change had meant that the applicant was no longer eligible to receive the benefit.

The ECtHR found in particular that Article 1 to Protocol 1 on protection of property had applied to the case, because the applicant had had a legitimate expectation that she would receive the pension, if she had satisfied the criteria set out in the former legislation. The refusal to grant her the benefit had been in accordance with the law (as it arose from the new legislation), and had been in pursuit of a legitimate purpose (saving public funds). However, it had not been proportionate: in particular, because it had involved the complete deprivation of a vulnerable person's only significant source of income, resulting from retrospectively effective legislation that had contained no transitional arrangements applicable to the applicant's case.

* * *

Summarizing the observations contained in the essay, one arrives at the conclusion that solidarity may have an impact on the existence, establishment or interpretation of several legal institutions. However, compulsory solidarity prescribed by the state is only a restricted means and may easily lead to paternalism.[510] Therefore,

[510] A Hungarian example of the declaration of political solidarity by the state is Political Statement 1/2010. (06. 16.) OGY of Parliament about National Cooperation, the posting of which in public institutions was ordered by Government Decision 1140/2010. (VII. 2.). Within the framework of this chapter it is impossible to give a thorough scholar analysis of the statement. However, it is worth mentioning that the statement recognizes the system of national cooperation founded by the parliamentary elections of April 2010, it sets as its objective to build up the system of national cooperation, which has both a political and an economic projection. The statement enumerates certain values (work, home, family, health, order) which "bind the members of the diverse Hungarian nation together". The content of the statement originally was a political declaration, but a certain extent it inspired the later constitution-making. By the constitutionalization of some of its elements, the state/governmental scale of values, styled as the new social contract, may acquire a certain degree of normativity. The 'system of

legal provisions expressing and implementing solidarity must be based on wide public social consensus. If the principle of solidarity is expressly laid down in the Constitution, this fact may encourage its assertion in legislation and the application of law because it enjoys the protection of the Constitutional Court. Moreover, the assertion of the principle of solidarity in (constitutional law) may contribute to the more effective implementation of social justice and tolerance as well as social immunity. Naturally, this presupposition is realistic only if the principle of solidarity laid down by the Constitution has real social legitimacy.

4 A nation torn apart by its constitution? From the perspective of minorities

The new Hungarian constitution has introduced unique and often criticized regulations regarding the rule of law, democracy and human dignity. This chapter evaluates the constitutional rules in the context of national identity and ethnicity, with special regard to those articles which are of discriminative nature and may lead to social exclusion. The first point is that – while the former Hungarian constitution was neutral regarding the values and applied the political nation concept – the new constitution does not clearly identify the political community to which it shall be applied, due to an inconsistent and controversial use of the concepts of political nation and cultural nation in the constitutional text. Using the category of nation in a cultural sense, the text allows for both a narrower and a wider meaning of membership than the category of

national coopearation' appeared in the National avowal (i.e. preamble) of the FL, but the Constitutional Court has not used it yet to the interpretation. See to this BERKES Lilla – FEKETE Balázs: Nemzeti Hitvallás: csupán díszítő szavak? [The National Avowal: Simply Words?], *Közjogi Szemle* № 1, 2017, and Balázs FEKETE: The National Avowal: More than a Conventional Preamble to a Constitution, in Z. SZENTE, F. MANDÁK and Zs. FEJES (eds.): *Challenges and Pitfalls in the Recent Hungarian Constitutional Development: Discussing the New Fundamental Law of Hungary*, Éditions L'Harmattan, Paris, 2015, 11–24.

political nation. Thus, because the definition of the 'nation' is rather controversial, it is unclear whether ethnic minorities fall under the same norms of political solidarity as the Hungarian majority. The second point is that the rights associated with the social solidarity might be interpreted restrictively. The possibility of penalizing homelessness or distributing social benefits on the basis of the 'usefulness of one's activity to the community' – again, combined with the ethnocentric nation concept – may in practice lead to social exclusion and indirectly sanction systematic discrimination against the largest Hungarian ethnic group, the Roma people, the members of which are most likely to live in poverty.

Constitutions try to contribute to, and at the same time they are the evidence of the constitutional identity of the given political community.[511] If the constitution drafting is a discoursive, democratic, representative and transparent process, it may help to close the gaps of the society, otherwise those gaps remain tenacious and anchored by the constitution.

Before analysing the text of the FL from the perspective of nation and ethnicity, it is worth to recall how far national and ethnic minorities were involved into the Hungarian constitution-making. Formally all minority self-governments and the parliamentary commissioner for ethnic and national minority rights (special ombudsperson) were invited to send proposals to the new constitution during the summer of 2010. Finally the special parliamentary commissioner and four – out of thirteen – minority self-governments (the Bulgarian, the German, the Croatian and the Ruthenian) submitted their recommendations. A common point was that they supported the elimination of the dual term (national and ethnic minorities) from the constitutional text and the introduction of a single term (nationalities) partly for historical reasons and partly for the better expression of equality of national minorities. They also recommended the extension of individual minority rights by precise enumeration, strengthening the special commissioner's constitu-

511 G. J. Jacobsohn: Constitutional identity, *The Review of Politics* № 3, 2006, 363.

tional position, guaranteeing the status of minority self-governments, and finding the solution for parliamentary representation.[512] At this stage the expert and interest groups received no feedbacks from the parliamentary ad hoc committee, and their substantive participation was not provided for. As it was outlined earlier in this book, the effective constitution-making period was very short, and in reality neither the academic institutions, expert organizations, civilians, nor minorities and other groups of the society were involved into the process. From the expressed proposals of the national and ethnic minorities the need for a parliamentary representation and the change of denomination, however, were taken into consideration. In return, the minorities lost their special, independent parliamentary commissioner[513] and the chance for better defined rights.

It is also interesting to have a look at the number of the members of national and ethnic minorities, which has increased to 555,507 from 313,832 between 2001 and 2011.[514] The reason for the difference may be the better advertisement of the census and the introduction of the minority electoral registration.[515] The actual number

---

512 A. L. PAP: Észrevételek a kisebbségek parlamenti képviseletének szabályozásához az új alkotmányban [Remarks on the parliamentary representation of minorities in the new constitution], *Pázmány Law Working Papers* № 27/2011, 2–3.

513 Hungary was one of very few European states that has established a specialized Ombudsman for the protection of minorities. The Parliamentary Commissioner (Ombudsman) for the Rights of National and Ethnic Minorities was first elected in 1995 and was independent from both the judiciary and the executive power, reporting exclusively to parliament. The powers of this body were based on the former Hungarian Constitution of 1989 and it assumed an important function in the formulation of laws and policies regarding minority protection.

514 The data of the national census in 2001 and 2011. For a comparative table see Table 1. However, this data is criticized by experts, for methodological problems of the survey and for measurement multiple ties.

515 As Minority Rights Group International assessed: "Critics contended from the late 1990's that as the right to participate in minority self-government elections was open to all Hungarian citizens, i.e. it was based on the general right to vote at local elections, and did not depend on effective membership of a minority, many minority representatives were not from the relevant minority. The abuse of minority self-governments for political or other purposes was also addressed by modifying the system of minority elections. Article 70 of the former Constitution was amended in 2002 (entering into force in May 2004) so that only persons

– based on voluntary and anonymous confession of the residents – is more than 5 per cent of the total population. As the data on belonging to a national or ethnic minority are sensitive and their confession is voluntary on the census questionnaire, almost 1.5 million people omitted the question. Thus the above mentioned number is far not exact; other estimates – which are naturally not based on self-confession of the concerned – put just the proportion of the Roma minority at 5 to 10 per cent of the total population. The regulation of national minority rights may directly affect approx. 10 per cent of the population.[516] Neither this significant number of the citizens, nor other groups of society were directly represented in the 2011 constitution making process in Hungary. In the following the examination focuses on the political and societal status of national and ethnic minorities as it is reflected in the FL.

Table 1 – number of nationalities – voluntary confession on censuses 1980-2011

Source: http://www.ksh.hu/nepszamlalas/tables_regional_00[517]

	Number			
	1980	1990	2001	2011
	Total			

belonging to minorities can elect their self-governments and to stand as candidates in those elections. According to this legislation, those who decide to run in elections for minority self-governments are required to register with the head of the local election office and declare their ethnic identity. However, the declared ethnic identity may not be questioned by the state organs." http://minorityrights.org/country/hungary/ <http://www.minorityrights.org/?lid=5804>

516 A. Magicz: Re-regulation of National Minority Rights, in *Their Shield is the Law – The Ombudsman's Protection for Vulnerable Groups* (eds. Barnabás Hajas and Máté Szabó), Office of the Commissioner for Fundamental Rights, Budapest, 2013, 27.

517 The significant change of number between 1980 and 1990 does not mean the exponential increase of the number of births in the Roma ethnic group, it just means that the number of voluntary confessions increased.

Hungarian	10638974	10142072	9416045	8314029
National and ethnic minorities				
Bulgarian	..	..	1358	3556
Gipsy (Romany, Bea)[1]	6404	142683	189984	308957
Greek	..	..	2509	3916
Croatian	13895	13570	15597	23561
Polish	..	..	2962	5730
German	11310	30824	62105	131951
Armenian	..	..	620	3293
Romanian	8874	10740	7995	26345
Ruthenian	..	..	1098	3323
Serbian	2805	2905	3816	7210
Slovakian	9101	10459	17693	29647
Slovenian	1731	1930	3025	2385
Ukrainian	..	..	5070	5633
National and ethnic minorities together	..	..	313832	555507
Arabic	..	..	1396	4537
Chinese	..	..	2275	6154
Russian	..	..	2341	6170
Vietnamese	..	..	958	3019
Other	16369	19640	36472	28068
Did not wish to answer, no answer	–	–	570537	1455883
Total	..	..	10343856	10 373 367
Population	10709463	10374823	10198315	9937628

4.1 Conceptualisation of the Hungarian people and nation in the Fundamental Law

It is problematic, from the perspective of the principle of democracy and popular sovereignty, that the FL does not clearly identify the political community to which it shall be applied, because the use of the concepts of political nation and cultural nation is inconsistent and controversial in the constitutional text. Article B of FL refers to the 'people' as the source of public power,[518] and the preamble – at least according to its closing sentence – is written on behalf of citizens.[519] Both statements are the proofs of the political nation approach. At the same time, the opening sentence of the preamble called National avowal puts the Hungarian nation into the centre,[520] without defining who belongs to the nation, and the text of the preamble later also refers to the "intellectual and spiritual unity of our nation torn apart".[521] In the first part of the FL, under the title "Foundation", Article D uses the expression of "one single Hungarian nation".[522] This wording seems to support the cultural nation concept; i.e. the cultural and linguistic belonging together irrespective of territorial unity, which became common – in sense of ethno-nation – in Central Eastern Europe during the 19th

518 Article B(3)-(4) of the FL: "The source of public power is the people. The people shall exercise their power through their elected representatives or, in exceptional cases, directly."

519 Closing sentence of the preamble: "We, the citizens of Hungary, are ready to found the order of our country upon the common endeavours of the nation."

520 A. L. PAP: Who Are "We, the People"? Biases and Preferences in the Hungarian Fundamental Law, in Z. SZENTE, F. MANDÁK, ZS. FEJES (eds.): *Challenges and Pitfalls in the Recent Hungarian Constitutional Development: Discussing the New Fundamental Law of Hungary*. Éditions L'Harmattan, Paris, 2015, 35–73.

521 Preamble, opening sentence: "WE, THE MEMBERS OF THE HUNGARIAN NATION, at the beginning of the new millennium, with a sense of responsibility for every Hungarian, hereby proclaim the following: (...)"; Preamble, thesis 6-8: "We promise to preserve the intellectual and spiritual unity of our nation torn apart in the storms of the last century. We proclaim that the nationalities living with us form part of the Hungarian political community and are constituent part of the State. We commit to promoting and safeguarding our heritage, our unique language, Hungarian culture, the languages and cultures of nationalities living in Hungary, along with all man-made and natural assets of the Carpathian Basin."

522 Article D of the FL: "Bearing in mind that there is one single Hungarian nation that belongs together, Hungary shall bear responsibility for the fate of Hungarians living beyond its borders, and shall facilitate the survival and development of their communities; it shall support their efforts to preserve their Hungarian identity, the assertion of their individual and collective rights, the establishment of their community self-governments, and their prosperity in their native lands, and shall promote their cooperation with each other and with Hungary."

century.[523] From this perspective the recognition of the "nationalities living with us" shifts the emphasis to their difference (from the majority), or their secondary status.[524]

Under the constitutional theory, the term of (Hungarian) people refers to the political nation in the meaning of state-nation to which also the national and ethnic minorities belong. Under the state-nation concept all the citizens living in a given territory belong to the nation, irrespective of their ethnic belonging, cultural diversity or different mother-tongue. This egalitarian nation concept is characteristic to the common law countries and French constitutionalism, and its roots lie in the civil enlightenment. It is recognised by the FL as well, when it states that the "nationalities living with us form part of the Hungarian political community" and they "shall be constituent parts of the State" (see the preamble and Article XXIX).[525] However, the preamble of the FL makes a very clear grammatical distinction between the 'nation' – although it is not unambiguous who this nation exactly is – and the 'minorities': the 'nation' is 'we', the minorities – living with 'us' – are 'they'. This is a linguistically very manifest exclusion of the minorities from the 'we' (whatever that represents in this context), and this exclusion makes it necessary to reintegrate them at least into the state in Article XXIX and in the preamble – but not into the nation. It is problematic, because the preamble clearly puts the nation above the state.[526]

---

523 G. BRUNNER: *Nationality problems and minority conflicts in Eastern Europe: strategies for Europe,* Gutersloh Bertelsmann Foundation Publishers, 1996, 9–10., Cs. PÁKOZDI – M. SULYOK: The Birth of a »New Nation«? Mapping progressive approaches to the nation-concept based on the Hungarian Fundamental Law, *Miskolc Journal of International Law* № 2, 2011, 43–55., H. KÜPPER: Paternalista kollektivizmus és liberális individualizmus között: az új magyar Alaptörvényben rögzített emberkép normatív alapjai, *Közjogi Szemle* № 3, 2012, 9.

524 B. MAJTÉNYI: The Nation's Will as Trump in the Hungarian Fundamental Law, *European Yearbook on Human Rights* 2015, 250.

525 N. CHRONOWSKI: The new Hungarian Fundamental Law in the light of the European Union's normative values, *Revue Est Europa* № spéciale 1, 2012, 135.

526 H. KÜPPER: *Ungarns Verfassung vom 25. April 2011, Einführung – Übersetzung – Materialien,* Peter Lang, Frankfurt/Main, 2012, 55–56.

Using the category of nation in cultural sense, on the one hand has a narrower, on the other hand, however, a wider meaning than the political nation. It has narrower meaning, because it comprises only those citizens who belong to the majority national-ethnic group of the country with the same culture, language, identity, historic fate perception etc. At the same time, it has a wider meaning, as it identifies as belonging to the nation also those who live in other countries and are citizens of other states, but their language, culture and origin bind them to Hungary. These ethnic ties are underpinned with Article D on the responsibility for Hungarians living outside the borders, and Article G on the constitutional protection of descent principle (*ius sanguinis*) in citizenship law – the combination of them supports the preferential naturalization of ethnic Hungarians living abroad without any effective territorial link to the country.[527]

Thus, because defining the 'nation' is rather controversial,[528] under Hungarian constitutional law it would be better to use the term of 'people' or 'citizens'. That also means that one can consider the (Hungarian) people as indispensable component of the state, as well as a community bearing the political solidarity.[529] From this perspective, it is extremely controversial that the FL specifies the subject of the constitution making power three ways. At the beginning of the preamble it refers to the "members of the Hungarian nation" – it is not clear yet whether in political or in cultural sense[530] –, at the end of the preamble speaks about citizens of Hungary, and then at the very end, in the postamble it turns out that the FL was adopted by the members of Parliament elected in 2010. If the con-

527 Zs. KÖRTVÉLYESI: Az »egységes magyar nemzet« és az állampolgárság, *Fundamentum* № 2, 2011, 49–50.

528 A. JAKAB: Defining the Borders of the Political Community: Constitutional Visions of the Nation, Manuscript, 2012, 43–44., B. MAJTÉNYI: Alaptörvény a nemzet akaratából, *Állam- és Jogtudomány* № 1, 2014, 80. According to Küpper, the FL applies the concept of ethno-nation. KÜPPER 'Paternalista kollektivizmus' 9.

529 PETRÉTEI 'Az alkotmányos demokrácia' 185–188.

530 According to Körtvélyesi, the text of the preamble refers to the cultural nation. Zs. KÖRTVÉLYESI: From »We the People« to »We the Nation«, in *Constitution for a Disunited Nation* (ed. Gábor Attila TÓTH), CEU Press, Budapest, 2012, 113–114.

stituent was the Hungarian nation, which shares the public power with the nationalities living in Hungary (or with 'us'), then the nationalities were not subject of the constituent power.[531] If the constitution making power is vested in the people in the sense of political community, and the nationalities form part of this community, they must have been subject of the constituent power.

The unique solution of the FL differs from those constitutions of the Central-European region, which could also legitimately reflect to the cultural nation context upon historical reasons. For a short comparison it is enough to refer to the Constitutions of the Polish and Slovak Republics. The Polish Constitution of 1997 makes clear in its preamble and Article 41 that the Polish Nation as the bearer of the sovereignty is composed of all equal citizens of the Republic.[532] Although the constitution refers to the Poles outside borders and to the rights of ethnic minorities, the main principle is the political nation concept with minor cultural elements. In the Slovakian Republic with its significant number of citizens belonging to Hungarian national minority, the constitution defines Slovak people as all

---

[531] A. L. Pap: Észrevételek a nemzetiségek parlamenti képviseletének szabályozásához az Alaptörvényben, a választójogi törvényben és a nemzetiségek jogairól szóló törvényben, in *Vol. 1. of Alkotmányozás Magyarországon 2010–2011* (eds. András Jakab and Tímea Drinóczi) Pázmány Press, Budapest–Pécs, 2013, 434., 437.; B. Majtényi: Legislative Stupidities in the New Hungarian Constitution, *Peace Human Rights* № 1, 2012, 108.

[532] Polish Constitution of 1997, Preamble: "We, the Polish Nation – all citizens of the Republic, (...) Equal in rights and obligations towards the common good – Poland, (...) Bound in community with our compatriots dispersed throughout the world, (...) Hereby establish this Constitution of the Republic of Poland as the basic law for the State, based on respect for freedom and justice, cooperation between the public powers, social dialogue as well as on the principle of aiding in the strengthening the powers of citizens and their communities." Article 41: "Supreme power in the Republic of Poland shall be vested in the Nation." Article 35: "The Republic of Poland shall ensure Polish citizens belonging to national or ethnic minorities the freedom to maintain and develop their own language, to maintain customs and traditions, and to develop their own culture."

Slovak citizens, together with national and ethnic minorities who is the subject of the constituent power.[533]

4.2 Parliamentary representation of minorities (nationalities) in Hungary

Article XXIX of the FL recognises nationalities living in Hungary as "constituent parts of the State", and Article 2 prescribes that „Nationalities living in Hungary shall contribute to Parliament's work as defined by a cardinal act".

In 1992 – before the adaption of the Act on the Minority Rights (1993) – on the basis of the former Constitution the Hungarian Constitutional Court declared that the legislature had created an unconstitutional situation with its failure to ensure minorities' representation. Whilst the Court accepted that parliamentary representation is not a precondition for the enforcement of the rights of nationalities, it stated that it would be the most effective means towards this end. The Act of 1993 on the Minority Rights guaranteed the political representation through local and nation-wide self-governments. To restrain ethno-business,[534] after a thorough academic and constitutional discourse the minority registration was introduced in 2005 on minority self-government elections. The

---

533 "We, the Slovak People, Bearing in mind the political and cultural heritage of our predecessors, the experience gained through centuries of struggle for our national existence, and statehood, (...) Together with members of national minorities and ethnic groups living in the Slovak Republic, (...) we, the citizens of the Slovak Republic, have, herewith and by our representatives, adopted this Constitution" Preamble, Constitution of the Slovak Republic 1992.

534 Before 2005 in the absence of minority electoral registration every citizens had the right to vote and stand as a candidate on minority self-governmental elections. As the minority self-governments received fiscal support from the central budget, some candidates decided to make a good use of the system without belonging to the national or ethnic minority they represented. See also Majtényi: What has happened to Our Model Child? The Creation and the Evolution of the Hungarian Minority Act, *European Yearbook of Minority Issues* Vol. 6, 2005/2006, 411–412.

registration is voluntary and based on self-determination, its baseline is the free choice on the (national or ethnic) identity – thus it cannot really prevent the abuse of minority rights.

After the 2010 parliamentary elections, the governing coalition almost immediately expressed its strong will for the introduction of minority representation in the parliament. The former Constitution (Act XX of 1949) was amended, and besides reducing the number of the seats in the parliament from 386 to 200 it was also prescribed that a maximum of 13 surplus mandates shall be guaranteed to minorities.[535] It was a strong political declaration of intents, but at the end of the day the FL adopted another solution. The shortcoming of the fixed number of minority mandates was clear: it suggested that the number of recognised minorities is constant and the recognition of a new minority would require a constitutional amendment as well. Thus this construction was put aside during the constitution-making. The final text of the FL does not guarantee parliamentary representation of the minorities explicitly, it just ensures a potential contribution to the work of the parliament. There are altogether 199 seats in the parliament (106 mandates for individual constituencies, 93 mandates for lists), and the nationalities may compete for preferential mandates during the general parliamentary elections. If a nationality list gets a preferential mandate, the number of party list mandates is accordingly reduced.

The representation of the nationalities now is guaranteed by the Acts on parliamentary elections (2011 and 2013),[536] and the new legal framework was applied first in April 2014. The ruling parties and their think-tanks assess the new regulation a great success, which remedies a twenty-year-old deficiency of the Hungarian political system. However the new solution is not unambiguous and

535 The former Constitution was amended on 25 May 2010, but the cited rule never came into force, and the FL finally repealed the former Constitution. Thus the amendment was just an ad-hoc demonstration of political will.

536 Act CCIII of 2011 on the election of the members of National Assembly (Sections 7-18), and Act XXXVI of 2013 on electoral procedure (especially Sections 86–87, 255–257).

as it was endorsed during the legislative rush of the Hungarian parliament, the expert advises were not considered during the elaboration of the system. One of the core problems is who belongs to a nationality. The FL does not specify the notion of nationality or the conditions of being member of a national or ethnic group.[537] Under the new Act on Nationalities (2011) a person belonging to a nationality shall not be necessarily Hungarian citizen, but in respect of voting rights the citizenship is a requirement.[538] Another – dogmatically and practically confusing – problem is that the ethnic (nationality) representation is integrated into the political representative system of the unicameral parliament, disrupting its political character, but in turn, with the risk of politicization.[539] A nationality MP will get necessarily into the attraction of political party factions, and finally will represent mainstream political interest instead of specific minority interest. Furthermore, the nationality voters are forced to choose among their political or minority preferences. If they choose the nationality preference, automatically exclude themselves from voting to party lists.

The Act on parliamentary election links both active and passive voting rights of nationalities to registration on the nationalities' electoral roll. When registering, the voter must explicitly state whether s/he wishes to vote in the election of MPs on party lists, i.e. refuses the possibility of the extension of nationality registration to parliamentary elections, or the vice versa, s/he wishes to extend the nationality registration to the parliamentary elections. In the former case, s/he can vote for a party list, in the latter case for a nationality list beside the single constituency candidate. By choosing

---

537 A. L. Pap: Recognition, representation and reproach: new institutional arrangements in the Hungarian multiculturalist model, in Balazs Vizi, Norbert Toth, Edgar Dobos (eds.): *Beyond International Conditionality: Local Variations of Minority Representation in Central and South-Eastern Europe,* Nomos, Baden-Baden, 2017. 101–136.

538 Pap 'Észrevételek' 428–429. See also Sections 1 and 170 of the Act CLXXIX of 2011 on the rights of nationalities.

539 G. Kurunczi: A nemzetiségek parlamenti képviseletének kérdéséről, *Közjogi Szemle* № 1, 2014, 58.

the nationality-preference, the voter's potential to express political preference wanes to the half compared to a non-nationality voter. The formal equality rule triumphs over the substantive: every voter has two votes, but some of the voters have initially less chance to influence the political composition of the parliament.

Exclusively the nation-wide nationality self-governments may set up nationality lists, thus other actors – e.g. minority associations or ethnic parties – have no influence on the composition of the lists, and cannot recommend candidates. On the 2014 parliamentary election all nationalities successfully entered their lists. They cannot cooperate, joint nationality lists are prohibited.

The new electoral legislation provides nationalities with the opportunity to obtain preferential mandates. Under the preferential quota one nationality mandate is guaranteed for the quarter of the votes cast necessary to gain a list mandate. The exact number always depends on the participation, but taking into account the number of the members of nationalities and the nature of the new electoral system, estimates suggested long before the 2014 parliamentary elections that a preferential mandate can be obtained with approx. 20,000-24,000 votes. The turn-outs justified the estimates, none of the nationalities had the chance for own MPs in 2014, as the willingness of the citizens to register as nationality voters was extremely low, and 22,022 vas the limit of a nationality preferential mandate.[540] No more than one preferential mandate may be won from each nationality's list, but theoretically if more than 5 per cent of all votes are cast for a nationality list, then other candidates may enter parliament from that list – but it is completely illusory considering that the total proportion of all nationalities together is approx. 5 per cent of the inhabitants according to the voluntary confessions. The Act states that if a nationality does not obtain a preferential mandate, it may send the top candidate on its list to parliament as a spokesperson, who is not a full MP, just participates in the work of parliament with consultative rights. In 2014 all of the nationalities

[540] See Tables 2 and 3.

delegated spokespersons to the National Assembly. This institution fits better to the unicameral political representation system of the Hungarian parliament, although it does not offset that those citizens who sacrificed their vote for a party list have the possibility only to elect a representative with limited status.[541]

Table 2 – Voters registered as members of a national minority

Source: National Election Office,

http://www.valasztas.hu/hu/ogyv2014/766/766_5_3.html

Number of voters in the nationalities' electoral (2014)

National minority	Total number of voters registered as members of a national minority	Registration is extended to the parliamentary elections	
		20 March 2014	6 April 2014
Bulgarian	232	101	104
Greek	483	135	140
Croatian	3727	1535	1623
Polish	711	130	133
German	23543	13749	15209
Armenian	455	186	184
Roma	25498	18150	14271
Romanian	1852	635	647
Ruthenian	993	599	611
Serbian	673	320	349
Slovakian	3120	1214	1317
Slovenian	461	194	199
Ukrainian	544	453	502

Table 3 – Scores of Nationalities on 2014 parliamentary elections

541 Kurunczi 'A nemzetiségek parlamenti' 62.

Source: National Election Office,
http://www.valasztas.hu/hu/ogyv2014/861/861_0_index.html

All votes cast for nationality and party lists	5 047 363
5% threshold	252 369
Limit of nationality preferential mandate	22 022
Number of nationality preferential mandate	0
Number of nationalities' spokespersons	13

List	Type of list	Votes	Proportion
German Nationality Self Government (MNOÖ)	Nationality	11 415	0.23 %
Hungarian Gipsy Party (MCP)	Party	8810	0.17 %
Roma Nationality Self Government	Nationality	4048	0.08 %
Croatian Nationality Self Government	Nationality	1212	0.02 %
Slovakian List	Nationality	995	0.02 %
Romanian Nationality Self Government (ORÖ)	Nationality	463	0.01 %
Ruthenian Nationality Self Government (MROÖ)	Nationality	362	0.01 %
Ukrainian Nationality Self Government	Nationality	293	0.01 %
Serbian Nationality Self Government (SZOÖ)	Nationality	236	0.0 %
Slovenian Nationality Self Government	Nationality	134	0.0 %
Armenian Nationality Self Government	Nationality	110	0.0 %
Hungarian Greeks	Nationality	102	0.0 %
Polish Nationality Self Government	Nationality	99	0.0 %
Bulgarian Nationality Self Government	Nationality	74	0.0 %

4.3 Human dignity, equality and solidarity - lost in transition

During the Hungarian constitution making in 2011 it occurred – and the Hungarian Government inquired from the Venice Commission – whether and to what extent it was necessary to incorporate the EU Charter of Fundamental Rights (hereinafter: Charter) into the national constitution. The Venice Commission emphasised that "up-dating the scope of human rights protection and seeking to adequately reflect, in the new Constitution, the most recent developments in the field of human rights protection, as articulated in the EU Charter, is a legitimate aim and a signal of loyalty towards European values". However, the Commission also underlined, that the incorporation of the Charter as a whole or of some parts of it could lead to legal complications, thus "it would be more advisable (...) to consider the EU Charter as a starting point or a point of reference and source of inspiration in drafting the human rights and fundamental freedoms chapter of the new Constitution."[542]

The adopted FL in its relevant Chapter ("Freedom and Responsibility") incorporated some sentences of the Charter, but – compared to the Charter and especially after the Fourth Amendment of the FL in 2013 – the content of the rights enumerated by the FL is less detailed and the text raises the possibility of wider limitation of rights. Furthermore, the context of the two bills of rights are completely different. It is worth referring also to the preamble of the FL, according to which "individual freedom can only be complete in cooperation with others". The Charter applies a completely different approach, and emphasises in its preamble that the Union "places the individual at the heart of its activities". It raises the individuals' responsibility only in connection with the enjoyment of

[542] European Commission For Democracy Through Law (Venice Commission) Opinion № 614/2011, Strasbourg 28 March 2011, Opinion on Three Legal Questions Arising in the Process of Drafting the New Constitution of Hungary, Points 21, 25–28, 32.

rights.[543] While the approach of the FL – taking also into consideration the numerous basic obligations – is communitarian and nationalist, the Charter focuses on the philosophy of individual freedom and supports pluralism.[544]

The difference is not accidental. In the last decade the Hungarian society has become more and more closed, exclusive, disunited, and discrimination, segregation, xenophobia, hate speech has become part of everyday life with the support of political populism.[545] In the field of the most important human values the FL legalised and reaffirmed unprecedented solutions based on unacceptable societal practise.

While most of the national and ethnic minorities are integrated into the society, the target group of the above mentioned phenomena is the Roma people. The facts are well known. As Minority Rights Group International reported "the marginalization of the Roma population increased. (...) Roma were among those most affected by Hungary's difficult transition period from socialism to a market-based economy and many lost their employment following economic decline and privatization of state industries. (...) Living conditions for Roma communities continue to be significantly worse than for the general population. Roma are significantly less educated and have below average income and life expectancy. The unemployment rate for Roma is estimated at 70 per cent, more than 10 times the national average, and most Roma live in extreme poverty. (...) Widespread discrimination against Roma continues in education, housing, penal institutions, employment and access to public institutions (...) especially Roma children suffer from stigmatization, exclusion and socio-economic disparities,

---

543 Charter Preamble: "Enjoyment of these rights entails responsibilities and duties with regard to other persons, to the human community and to future generations."

544 Also refers to this European Commission For Democracy Through Law (Venice Commission) Opinion № 621/2011, Strasbourg 20 June 2011, Opinion on the New Constitution of Hungary, Point 57.

545 I. Gy. TÓTH: *Bizalomhiány, normazavarok, igazságtalanságérzet és paternalizmus a magyar társadalom értékszerkezetében*, TÁRKI, Budapest 2009, 13.

notably related to housing, unemployment, access to health services, adoption and educational facilities because of their ethnic status."[546] The low clearly came in 2008 and 2009: "According to media reports and information provided by the Hungarian Chief of Police and the European Roma Rights Centre (ERRC) and the Open Society Institute, since the beginning of 2008 there have been 15 incidents of Roma houses being firebombed with Molotov cocktails, and two attacks on Roma homes with hand grenades. During this time, at least five people of Roma origin have been murdered and more seriously injured in these and other incidents involving stabbings and beatings. (…) On 23 February 2009 a Roma father and his five-year-old son were shot dead in an attack on a family home in Tatárszentgyörgy, a village 40 miles south-east of Budapest, and two children were injured when the house was set on fire."[547]

Against this background, it is worth to assess how the FL reflects on the problems. Several of its provisions are deepening the gap between the Roma minority and the majority of the society, either by sanctioning poverty, or having an anti-egalitarian character and implicitly addressing Roma people.[548]

The FL in its Article XV regulates the equality rights in order of the EU Charter, however without applying the latter's up-to-date solutions. Article XV lacks any mention of the prohibition of discrimination on the ground of sexual orientation,[549] genetic features, age,[550] ethnic origin or membership of a national minority. Although the FL prohibits any discrimination on the grounds of race, colour

---

546 http://minorityrights.org/minorities/roma-8/

547 http://minorityrights.org/minorities/roma-8/

548 K. Kovács: Equality: the missing link, in *Constitution for a Disunited Nation* (ed. G. A. Tóth) CEU Press, Budapest, 2012, 186.

549 See the Opinion № 621/2011 of Venice Commission, Points 76–80. It is important to note in this context that the Hungarian Act CXXV of 2003 on Equal Treatment and Promotion of Equal Opportunities forbids discrimination based on factors that include sexual orientation and sexual identity in the fields of employment, education, housing, health and access to goods and services as yet.

550 The prohibition of discrimination on the ground of age has an increasing significance in the case law of the CJEU, see e.g. C–144/04. Werner Mangold v Rüdiger Helm, Judgment of 22 November 2005 [ECR 2005, I–9981], or C-499/08.

and national origin, but taking into consideration the special situation of ethnic and national minority groups in Hungary an updated constitutional text should contain the legal consequences of the facts. In the context of the FL the 'national origin' refers the more to the majority nation, and does not really imply to minorities.[551] Article XV(2) of the FL is an open-ended provision, thus during its interpretation the legislator, the courts of law and the Constitutional Court will be able to extend the grounds of non-discrimination, still it would have been reasonable to name expressly the mentioned grounds. The equality of men and women in Article XV(3) of the FL can be considered laconic compared to the Charter. The FL only declares gender equality but does not specify it to employment, work, pay, marriage and family relations, although in practice discrimination appears in these relations most frequently. While Articles 25-26 of the Charter contain positive rights of the elderly and disabled people, the FL in its Article XV(5) only promises the protection by the state in form of special measures. It is worthwhile to mention that Roma minority is not mentioned among the target groups of affirmative action.[552]

After the Fourth Amendment to the FL, Article XV(4) reads as follows in the official translation: "By means of separate measures, Hungary shall promote the achievement of equality of opportunity and social inclusion." The Hungarian text, however, applies the word 'felzárkózás' – catching up, instead of 'befogadás' – inclusion. The difference is revealing. The term 'social catching up' created constitutional bases for school segregation, the most affected by which are the Roma children.

As an evidence, the Hungarian Supreme Court in April 2015 declared that segregation of the Roma in parochial schools is legal. The Chance for Children Foundation (CFCF), a Hungarian organisation that campaigns for Roma education rights and was applicant

---

Ingeniørforeningen i Danmark v Region Syddanmark, Judgment of 12 October 2010.

551 CHRONOWSKI 'The new Hungarian Fundamental Law' 130–131.

552 KOVÁCS 'Equality' 193–194.

in the case, reported: "Although the previous decisions by the Hungarian courts established on two instances that the school in Nyíregyháza segregates Roma children unlawfully, therefore this practice should be stopped, the Hungarian Supreme Court (Kúria) has taken a very different view on this case: dismissed CFCF's claims."[553] Antecedents of decision: "On 28 February 2014 the Court of Nyíregyháza delivered the first instance judgment. In 2007, as a result of CFCF's court action and extensive negotiations, Nyíregyháza closed its segregated school in the Guszev settlement and provided a free school bus for Roma children who were integrated to mainstream primary schools in the city centre. Integration of children of the lower grades turned out to be successful, while for children of upper grades it was not. In 2011, the new mayor decided to have the school reopened as part of the Greek Catholic Church's primary school. He provided the school building for free and committed substantial local funds for extra financial help. (…) The Greek Catholic Church maintains a nursery, primary and a secondary school in the city centre which are considered elite schools. The Church has long been present in the settlement offering Roma missionary services. The segregated school was reopened in September, 2011. Altogether 16 children of first grade enrolled to the 're-segregated' school."[554]

CFCF sued both the Church and the Hungarian state for introducing segregation. The Court of first instance established that "the Church segregated its pupils on a school level, and that the municipality segregated Roma students by handing over the school building to the Church. The Court also noted that the religious education provided by the Church in the segregated school could not justify racial segregation. The Court pointed out that parents of the children enrolled to the Roma school did not choose the school because of the religious education it provided but because of its location and the fact that many Roma children were harassed in

[553] Chance for Children Foundation, The Nyíregyháza resegregation case, http://www.cfcf.hu/en/ny%C3%ADregyh%C3%A1za-resegregation-case
[554] Ibid.

other schools. The Court prohibited the continuation of the illegal activity, therefore it ban the Church to launch new classes in the segregated school. The Court however dismissed CFCF's claim on termination of segregation by arguing that the Court could not order the closing down of the school completely because it would have violated the parent's right to freely choose education for their children and that it would have effected public law relationships which fall beyond the scope of civil litigation. The Court of second instance upheld the decision of the court of first instance. On 22 April 2015 the Supreme Court repealed the judgment of the court of first instance and dismissed the applicant's claims. The Supreme Court argued that the Greek Catholic Church has successfully justified the segregation by proving that it provided religious education and that parents have freely chosen the school and exercised their freedom of religion. (...) The Supreme Court took the position that the fact that the Greek Catholic Church conducted Roma pastoral care (pastoration) justified its decision to open a school in a Roma settlement and to maintain a Roma-only school, because it could not conduct Roma pastoral care in a school where the ethnic composition of the students was different."[555]

The case clearly illustrates that the FL is not proper legal norm to prevent segregation. The argumentation and logic of the Hungarian Supreme Court reminds to the ancient judgment of the SCOTUS in Plessy v Fergusson (1896) about "separate but equal" doctrine, which was overruled in the landmark Brown v Board of Education (1954). In the meantime, the Hungarian government communicates that this judgment was the victory of the new "delicate segregation" policy.

At this point it seems necessary to reflect once more that the FL eliminated the dual definition of 'national and ethnic minorities' and introduced – for historical reasons and upon the demands of some minorities – the word 'nationalities' instead, which falls short in reflecting the fact that in Hungary, beside the national minorities,

---

555 Ibid.

also two ethnic minorities are recognised – the Roma and the Ruthenian.[556] As to the linguistic and cultural rights, any commitment for protection of minority languages can be found only in the preamble of the FL, while the protection of the Hungarian language – as official language – and sign language is a clear obligation for the state (see Article H of the FL). However, the FL contains in its chapter on fundamental rights also language rights of nationalities.[557] The former Constitution clearly asserted the Hungarian state's obligation to ensure the fostering of the cultures of minorities, the use of their native language, etc. The FL uses the term 'respect' in connection with these rights of nationalities, but avoids the use of terms 'promote' or 'protect' in Article XXIX. Furthermore, only the rights to express and preserve one's (minority) identity and the use of names in their native languages are formulated as individual rights, i.e. rights of persons belonging to nationalities. The other rights respected by the FL – just as the promotion of their own culture, the use of their native language, the education in their native language – seem to belong to minority communities.[558] The Fourth Amendment to the FL Article XXIX(3) has introduced the conditionality of recognition as a national minority on the level of constitution: "A cardinal Act may provide that recognition as a nationality shall be subject to a certain length of time of presence and to the initiative of a certain number of persons declaring to be members of the nationality concerned." As the Amicus Brief to the Venice Commission explains: "The amendment explicitly indicates that the recognition of a group as a nationality can be limited to

---

[556] Pap 'Észrevételek' 432.

[557] "The Venice Commission finds regrettable that Art. H, which regulates the protection of Hungarian language as the official language of the country, does not include a constitutional guarantee for the protection of the languages of national minorities. It however notes that Article XXIX guarantees the right to the use of these languages by Hungary's 'nationalities' and understands this provision as implying also an obligation for the State to protect these languages and to support their preservation and development (see also the Preamble and Article Q of the Constitution)." Opinion № 621/2011 of Venice Commission, Point 45.

[558] See also Opinion № 621/2011 of Venice Commission, Point 82.

those groups that have held national status already for a certain period of time, which appears to limit the ability of new groups to Hungary to claim such status. In addition, the recognition of a nationality may be made contingent on a minimum number of members of the nationality residing in Hungary, which limits the ability of smaller groups to claim nationality status. This may not sound terribly important, until one recognizes the rights that may not be claimed unless one is a member of a recognized nationality."[559]

By introducing the right to self-defence in the constitutional provisions (Article V), the boundaries of the individual and state responsibility become uncertain. The relationship between the new right and the monopoly of the state to enforce the constitution and the legislation as outlined in Article C(3) of FL remains an open question.[560] It can be presupposed that the former is an exception to the latter rule, however, this solution is rather unfortunate in case of a constitutional provision, because the constitutional text should be unambiguous, without exception rules. Furthermore, it is also open to debate, what the relationship between the right to self-defence and the norm on justified defence in the Criminal Code is. Beyond the jurisprudential uniqueness, Article V clearly target the Roma population, whose members are living in great poverty and in need they commit petty offences against property.[561]

Among the rights guaranteeing free communication, the freedom to express one's opinion originally was formulated in the FL similarly to the former Constitution, but the Fourth Amendment to the FL introduced serious bans on speeches violating human dignity, the dignity of the Hungarian nation or minority groups.[562] This is

---

559 G. Halmai and K. L. Scheppele et al.: *Amicus Brief for the Venice Commission on the Fourth Amendment to the Fundamental Law of Hungary*, Princeton, 2013, 56.

560 Article V of FL: "Every person shall have the right to repel any unlawful attack against his or her person or property, or one that poses a direct threat to the same." Article C(3) of FL: "The State shall have the exclusive right to use coercion in order to enforce the Fundamental Law and legislation."

561 Kovács 'Equality' 190.

562 Article IX(5) of the FL: "The right to freedom of speech may not be exercised with the aim of violating the dignity of the Hungarian nation or of any national,

the only point in the constitution where ethnicity became relevant, but the wording and the enumeration is still not in line with the non-discrimination rule of Article XV(2). Even the Venice Commission found it contradicting European standards, because "the provisions on the dignity of communities are too vague and the specific protection of the 'dignity of the Hungarian nation' creates the risk that freedom of speech in Hungary could, in the future, be curtailed in order to protect Hungarian institutions and office holders".[563] The constitutional bans on free expression support the preservation of the disproportionate, impartial and controversial judicial practice in the field of hate-crimes that has been characterised by protecting the Hungarian majority against the Roma minority.[564]

In the previous chapter the low constitutional standards of the protection of social solidarity was already discussed. It is worth adding here that the uncertain measure of 'usefulness of activity to the community' in Article XIX(3) reflects to the prejudices and stereotypes of the majority society that Roma people live on social subsidies, and creates constitutional basis for the government's community service programme.[565]

* * *

Although the FL seemingly, on the surface recognizes the constitutional values of dignity, equality and solidarity, an in-depth analysis brings out the contradictions, the non-egalitarian and abusive messages. The FL is unsuitable for the integration of the political community and the Hungarian society, it does not address the problem

---

ethnic, racial or religious community. Persons belonging to such communities shall be entitled to enforce their claims in court against the expression of an opinion which violates the community, invoking the violation of their human dignity, as provided for by an Act."

563 Opinion № 720/2013 of the Venice Commission, Point 141.

564 L. Balogh, H. Dinók and A. L. Pap: A jog által láthatatlan? A gyűlölet-bűncselekmények szabályozási kérdései és gyakorlati problémái, *Fundamentum* № 4, 2012, 95.

565 Kovács 'Equality' 191.

of ethnicity, and does not even try to close the gaps, prevent from segregation and discrimination.[566] The adjective 'ethnic' appears only once throughout the text; the ethnicity questions are hidden into the historic term 'nationality'. In fact, this constitution was not created with the intention of uniting the political nation.

566 A. L. Pap: Az illiberális multikulturalizmus magyar modellje: a magyar kisebbségi jog változása 2010–2016 (I. rész), *Közjogi Szemle* Vol. 9, № 2, 2016, 39–47.

EPILOGUE

Despite the continued reliance on the rule of law and the respect of fundamental rights in the Fundamental Law as the foundational principles of the Hungarian state, there have been a number of significant systemic developments which indicate that in the new constitutional order the ability of the government to rule by law enjoys priority over the idea that for government to be constitutional it must be constrained by law. The controversial practices followed in amending the constitutional text, the limitations imposed on the review powers of the Constitutional Court, and the evident subordination of the constitutional order as defended by the Constitutional Court to the political regime offer clear indications of this significant shift in Hungarian constitutionalism.[567]

Backsliding – i.e. providing lower than the former constitutional standards – may be external or internal. It is external, if the international or supranational legislation or case law raises concerns by eroding the higher national standards, and it is internal if the national constitution or judiciary erodes the minimum-standards of the international or European community.[568]

At this stage in Central and Eastern Europe the internal backsliding is threatening the common European values, and the Hungar-

---

567 Varju and Chronowski 'Constitutional backsliding' 296 et sqq., A. L. Pap: *Democratic Decline in Hungary: Law and Society in an Illiberal Democracy,* Routledge, 2018.

568 Aziz Huq and Tom Ginsburg: How to lose a constitutional democracy, *Vox* 21 February 2017, www.vox.com/the-big-idea/2017/2/21/14664568/lose-constitutional-democracy-autocracy-trump-authoritarian

ian illiberal practices[569] already cross-fertilised other countries: Poland as well follows the illiberal path. The developments undermining rule of law show significant similarities, as the ruling parties of both counties commenced attack on the constitutional courts. The actions taken against the courts are fostering the impression that a fight took place in both countries between the majoritarian democracy and the rule of law in the form of a parliament versus constitutional court struggle, where the former represents the majority rule and the latter the guardian of rule of law. After all, the constitutional landscape allows the assumption that the courts lost the game.[570]

In Poland the procedural constitutionality was the field of the battle – in the lack of supermajority the Polish government not easily get rid of constitutional control, and had to find different measures from the Hungarian by challenging the election of constitutional court judges, and changing the rules of procedure of the court. While the Hungarian government created constitutional basis for the changes, the Polish entered even into open violation of the constitution.[571]

The European fora and especially the EU institutions are not able to effectively intervene when a member state does not observe the rule of law and respect for human rights voluntarily. The infringement procedures are of narrow scope, the parliamentary scrutiny is just a political tool of persuasion and the opinions of the Venice Commission are although prestigious but not legally binding. The EU Commission had some successful actions in case of the Hungar-

---

569 A. L. Pap: Constitutional identity? The Hungarian model of illiberal democracy, in M. Steven Fish, Graeme Gill and Milenko Petrovic (eds.): *A quarter century of post-communism assessed,* Palgrave Macmillan, London, 2017, 161–186.

570 Zoltán Szente: Die politische Orientierung der Mitglieder des ungarischen Verfassungsgerichts zwischen 2010 und 2014, *Jahrbuch für Ostrecht* Vol. 18, № 1, 2016, 45–67.; Renáta Uitz: Poland, Hungary and Europe: Pre-Article 7 Hopes and Concerns, *VerfBlog,* 2016/3/14, http://verfassungsblog.de/poland-hungary-and-europe-pre-article-7-hopes-and-concerns/.

571 Á. Lukonits: A demokrácia eszközeivel a demokrácia ellen Lengyelországban és Magyarországon, *Közjogi Szemle* Vol. 9, № 1, 2016.

ian and Polish government but could not really restrain the systemic changes and the renegade governments can easily circumvent the rule of law requirements by constitutional amendments or by chilling judiciary and constitutional review.

It is clear that the crisis chain started in 2008 with the credit crunch, and followed by economic depression, refugee crisis and exit strives of the member states requires a deliberate and considered bailout mechanism. The Hungarian and Polish experience indicates the renewal of legal fetisism and the rule by law solutions instead of the observance of rule of law.[572] At the end of the day this pattern of member state disobedience can easily undermine the European community of law. The ideal way of change would be a more effective Article 7 procedure,[573] a generally binding bill of rights, and a more federalised structure – otherwise the constitutional identity claims of the member states will subvert the consent in the common European values.

---

572 Some authors identify these developments as 'political constitutionalism' against 'legal constitutionalism' (see e.g. K. Pócza: Alkotmányozás Magyarországon és az Egyesült Királyságban, *Kommentár* № 5, 2012, 40. I. Stumpf: *Erős állam – alkotmányos korlátok,* Századvég, Budapest, 2014, 244–249.), but the theory and practice of the former does not justify its applicability to the Polish and Hungarian constitutional environment. See Ágnes Kovács: Fényevők? A hazai alkotmányelmélet esete a politikai konstitucionalizmussal, *Fundamentum* Vol. 19, № 2-3, 2015, 19–40. Blokker and Halmai classifies the Hungarian situation as 'populist' constitutionalism. Paul Blokker: Populist Constitutionalism, *VerfBlog* 2017/5/04, http://verfassungsblog.de/populist-constitutionalism/; Gábor Halmai: The Hungarian Constitutional Court and Constitutional Identity, *VerfBlog* 2017/1/10, http://verfassungsblog.de/the-hungarian-constitutional-court-and-constitutional-identity/.

573 Article 7 TEU demands the clear and present danger of the violence of the EU values for the initiation of the Council's procedure and decision. It can be presumed that in practice it would mean multitudinous or at least numerous proceedings and/or omissions leading to foreseeable and certain violation of Article 2 of TEU in a given member state. As Article 7 has never been applied, it also allows the presumption that the actors would be very cautious and circumspect with initiating such procedure. And finally, the margins of appreciation can be supposed to be wide in cases falling into the scope of constitutional identity of member states. See also Halmai 'Perspectives' 165–168.

BIBLIOGRAPHY

Ádám Antal: *Alkotmányi értékek és alkotmánybíráskodás* [Constitutional Values and the Practice of the Constitutional Court]. Osiris, Budapest 1998

Ádám Antal: Biztonság, felelősség, kötelesség [Security, Responsibility, Duty]. *Jogtudományi Közlöny* 2005/7-8

Ádám Antal: *Bölcselet, vallás, állami egyházjog* [Philosophy, Religion, State Church Law]. Dialóg Campus, Budapest-Pécs 2007

Ádám Antal: A rendőrség az alkotmányi értékek között [The Police and Constitutional Values]. In Gy. Gaál and Z. Hautzinger (eds.): *Tanulmányok a „Rendészet és rendvédelem – kihívások a XXI. században.* Magyar Hadtudományi Társaság Határőr Szakosztály Pécsi Szakcsoportja, Pécs 2008

Ádám Antal: Vallás, vallásszabadság és egyház Magyarország Alaptörvényének, továbbá „A lelkiismereti- és vallásszabadság jogáról, valamint az egyházak, vallásfelekezetek és vallási közösségek jogállásáról" szóló 2011. évi C. törvény figyelembe vételével. (17) *JURA* 2011/2

Ádám, Antal: On novel goals and tasks of the public power. In: Bogusław Banaszak (ed.): *Festschrift für Professor Kazimierz Działocha.* Wroczlaw 2012

Arató Krisztina: Szolidaritás és civil részvétel az Európai Unióban [Solidarity and Civil Participation in the European Union]. In: J. Frivaldszky (ed.): *Szubszidiaritás és szolidaritás az Európai Unióban* [Subsidiarity and Solidarity in the European Union]. OCIPE Magyarország – Faludy Ferenc Akadémia, Budapest 2006

Arnold, Denis G.: Transnational Corporations and the Duty to Respect Basic Human Rights. (20) *Business Ethics Quarterly* July 2010/3

Arnold, Rainer: Fundamental Rights in the European Union. In: Nadiezda Siskova (ed.): *The Process of Constitutionalisation of the EU and Related Issues.* Europa Law Publishing, Amsterdam-Groningen 2008

Badura, Peter: *Staatsrecht.* C. H. Beck'sche Verlagsbuchhandlung, München 1996

Baldwin, Peter: *The Politics of Social Solidarity.* Cambridge University Press, Cambridge 1990

Balogh Lídia – Dinók Henriett – Pap András László: A jog által láthatatlan? A gyűlölet-bűncselekmények szabályozási kérdései és gyakorlati problémái. *Fundamentum* 2012/4

Barnard, Catherine: The 'Opt-out' for the UK and Poland from the Charter of Fundamental Rights: Triumph or Rhetoric over the Reality. In: S. Griller – J. Ziller (eds.): *The Lisbon Treaty. EU Constitutionalism without a Constitutional Treaty?* Springer, Wien, New York 2008

Benhabib, Seyla: *Another Cosmopolitanism, with the Commentaries by Jeremy Waldron, Bonnie Honig, Will Kymlicka* (ed. Robert Post), Oxford University Press, Oxford 2006

Berkes Lilla – Fekete Balázs: Nemzeti Hitvallás: csupán díszítő szavak? [The National Avowal: Simply Words?]. (10) *Közjogi Szemle* 2017/1

Besselink, Leonard F. M.: National and constitutional identity before and after Lisbon. (6) *Utrecht Law Review* 2010/3

Besselink, Leonard F. M.: General Report. In: *The Protection of Fundamental Rights Post-Lisbon: The Interaction between the Charter of Fundamental Rights of the European Union, the European Convention on Human Rights and National Constitutions* (ed. Julia Laffranque). Tartu University Press, Tallinn 2012

Besselink, Leonard – Claes, Monica – Reestman, Jan-Herman: A Constitutional moment: Acceding to the ECHR (or not). (11) *European Constitutional Law Review* 2015/1

Bilchitz, David: The Ruggie Framework: An Adequate Rubric for Corporate Human Rights Obligations? (7) *SUR international journal on human rights* June 2010/12

Blokker, Paul: Populist Constitutionalism. *VerfBlog* 2017/5/04 http://verfassungsblog.de/populist-constitutionalism/

Blutman László: Az alkotmányos és európai alapjogok viszonya. In: Bodnár László (szerk.): *EU-csatlakozás és alkotmányozás.* SZTE ÁJK Nemzetközi Jogi Tanszék, Szeged 2001

Blutman László – Chronowski Nóra: Az Alkotmánybíróság és a közösségi jog: alkotmányjogi paradoxon csapdájában I. *Európai Jog* 2007/2

Blutman László: A nemzetközi jog használata az Alkotmány értelmezésénél [The Use of International Law during the Interpretation of the Constitution]. *Jogtudományi Közlöny* 2009/7-8

Blutman László: *Az Európai Unió joga a gyakorlatban.* HVG-ORAC, Budapest 2010

Blutman, László – Chronowski, Nóra: Hungarian Constitutional Court: Keeping Aloof from European Union Law. (5) *International Constitutional Law* 2011/3

Blutman László: Az Alkotmánybíróság és az alkotmány feletti normák: könnyű liaison elkötelezettség nélkül? [Constitutional Court and Supraconstitutional Norms: An Airy Liaison Without Commitments?] *Közjogi Szemle* 2011/4

Blutman László: A nemzetközi jog érvényesülése a magyar belső jogban: két előkérdés [The functioning of international law in Hungarian internal law: two preliminary questions]. In: Blutman László – Csatlós Erzsébet – Schiffner Imola: *A nemzetközi jog hatása a magyar joggyakorlatra* [The effect of international law on Hungarian legal practice]. HVG-ORAC, Budapest 2014

Bogdandy, Armin von: *Doctrine of Principles.* Jean Monnet Working Paper Series [2003] 9/03

Bogdandy, Armin von: Founding Principles of EU Law: A Theoretical and Doctrinal Sketch. (16) *European Law Journal* 2010/2

Bogdandy, Armin von: How to protect European Values in the Polish Constitutional Crisis. *VerfBlog* 2016/3/31 http://verfassungsblog.de/how-to-protect-european-values-in-the-polish-constitutional-crisis/

Bogdandy, Armin von: European Law Beyond 'Ever Closer Union' – Repositioning the Concept, its Thrust, and the ECJ's Comparative Methodology. (22) *European Law Journal* 2016/3

Borowsky, Martin: Kapitel VII. Allgemeine Bestimmungen. In: J. Meyer (ed.): *Kommentar zur Charta der Grundrechte der Europäischen Union.* Nomos, Baden-Baden 2003

Bragyova, András: No New(s), Good News? The Fundamental Law and the European law. In: Gábor Attila Tóth (ed.): *Constitution for a Disunited Nation.* CEU Press, New York 2012

Brunner, Georg: *Nationality problems and minority conflicts in Eastern Europe: strategies for Europe.* Gutersloh Bertelsmann Foundation Publishers 1996

Buhmann, Karin: Business and Human Rights: Analysing Discursive Articulation of Stakeholder Interests to Explain the Consensus-based Construction of the 'Protect, Respect, Remedy UN Framework'. (1) *International Law Research* 2012/1

Callewaert, Johan: The European Convention on Human Rights and European Union Law: a Long Way to Harmony. *European Human Rights Law Review* 2009/6

Callewaert, Johan: Unionisation vs. conventionisation. The Relationship between EU Law and the European Convention on Human Rights and its Impact on the Domestic Legal System of the EU Member States. In: *Conference on the Europeanisation of Public International Law: The Status of International Law in the EU and its Member States. Universiteit van Amsterdam.* 2005 September 2. Collection of Documents

Canaris, Claus-Wilhelm: Grundrechte und Privatrecht. *Archiv für die civilistische Praxis* 184(3) 1984

Cherednychenko, Olha O.: Fundamental rights and private law: A relationship of subordination or complementarity? (3) *Utrecht Law Review* 2007/2

Chronowski Nóra – Drinóczi Tímea – Kocsis Miklós – Zeller Judit: 6. cikk. In: Osztovits András (szerk.): *Az Európai Unióról és az Európai Unió működéséről szóló szerződések magyarázata 1.* Complex, Budapest 2011

Chronowski, Nóra: Integration of European Human Rights Standard – the Accession of EU to the ECHR. In: *Efektywność europejskiego systemu ochrony praw człowieka* (red. Jerzy Jaskiernia). Adam Marszałek, Toruń 2012

Chronowski, Nóra: The new Hungarian Fundamental Law in the light of the European Union's normative values. R*evue Est Europa numéro spéciale* 2012/1

Chronowski, Nóra – Csatlós, Erzsébet: Judicial Dialogue or National Monologue? – the International Law and Hungarian Courts. (1) ELTE *Law Journal* 2013/1

Chronowski, Nóra: The Fundamental Law Within the Network of Multilevel European Constitutionalism. In: *Challenges and Pitfalls in the Recent Hungarian Constitutional Development* (eds. Zoltán Szente – Fanni Mandák – Zsuzsanna Fejes). L'Harmattan, Paris 2015

Chronowski, Nóra – Varju, Márton: Two Eras of Hungarian Constitutionalism: From the Rule of Law to Rule by Law. (8) *Hague J Rule Law* 2016/2

Chronowski Nóra – Vincze Attila: Önazonosság és európai integráció – az Alkotmánybíróság az identitáskeresés útján. (72) *Jogtudományi Közlöny* 2017/3

Costa, Jean-Paul: The Relationship between the European Convention on Human Rights and European Union Law – A Jurisprudential Dialogue between the European Court of Human Rights and the European Court of Justice. Lecture at the King's College London, 7 October 2008. In: *Background Documentation. Fundamental Rights Protection in EU Law under the Lisbon Treaty*. ERA Trier, 22-23 April 2010

Cram, Ian: Resort to foreign constitutional norms in domestic human rights jurisprudence with reference to terrorism cases. (68) *Cambridge Law Journal* 2009/1

Csatlós, Erzsébet: The Red Star Story and the ECtHR in the Hungarian Legal Practice. (15) *Jogelméleti Szemle* 2014/4

Dine, Janet: *Companies, International Trade and Human Rights*. CUP, Cambridge 2007

Donnelly, Jack: *Universal Human Rights in Theory and Practice*. Cornell University Press, New York 2003

Donnelly, Jack: The Relative Universality of Human Rights. (29) *Human Rights Quarterly* 2007/2

Dougan, Michael: Judicial review of Member State action under the general principles and the Charter: defining the "scope of Union law". (52) *Common Market Law Review* 2015/5

Drinóczi Tímea: *Államszervezési elvek és államszervezet az Olasz Köztársaságban* [Principles of State Organization and the Structure of State in the Republic of Italy]. Magyar Jog 2007/11

Drinóczi Tímea: *Gazdasági alkotmány és gazdasági alapjogok* [Economic Constitution and Basic Economic Rights]. Dialóg Campus, Budapest-Pécs 2007

Drinóczi, Tímea: Constitutional dialogue theories – extension of the concept and examples from Hungary. *Zeitschrift für öffentliches Recht* (68) 2013/1

Durkheim, Émile: *A társadalmi munkamegosztásról* [On Social Division of Work]. Osiris, Budapest 2001

Ehlers, Dirk: *Fundamental Rights and Freedoms*. De Gruyter, Berlin 2007

Engle, Eric: Third Party Effect of Fundamental Rights (Drittwirkung). (5) *Hanse Law Review* 2009/2

Erkollar, Alptekin – Oberer, B. J.: Responsible Business: The European Union is Driving Forward the European Strategies on Corporate Social Responsibility. *Journal of EU Research in Business* 2012. Article ID 360374

Falk, Richard: Interpreting the Interaction of Global Markets and Human Rights. In: *Globalization and Human Rights* (ed. Alison Brysk). University of California Press, Berkeley – Los Angeles – London 2002

Fekete, Balázs – Czina, Veronika: *Article 7 of the Treaty on European Union – is it really a nuclear weapon?* http://hpops.tk.mta.hu/en/blog/2015/04/article-7-of-the-treaty-on-european-union

Fekete, Balázs: The National Avowal: More than a Conventional Preamble to a Constitution. In: Zoltán Szente, Fanni Mandák, Zsuzsanna Fejes (eds.): *Challenges and Pitfalls in the Recent Hungarian Constitutional Development: Discussing the New Fundamental Law of Hungary*. Éditions L'Harmattan, Paris 2015

Fekete, Balázs: How to Become a Judge in Hungary? From the Professionalism of the Judiciary to the Political Ties of the Constitutional Court. In: Sophie Turenne (ed.): *Fair Reflection of the Society in Judicial Systems: a Comparative Analysis.* Springer, Heidelberg/London/New York 2015

Fossum, John Erik – Menéndez, Agustín José: The Constitution's Gift? A Deliberative Democratic Analysis of Constitution Making in the European Union. (11) *European Law Journal* 2005/4

Galgano, Francesco: *Globalizáció a jog tükrében* [Globalisation through the prism of law]. HVG-ORAC, Budapest 2006

Ginsburg, Tom – Chernykh, Svitlana – Elkins, Zachary: Commitment and Diffusion: Why Constitutions Incorporate International Law. *University of Illinois Law Review* 2008

Grimm, Dieter: Zur Bedeutung nationaler Verfassungen in einem vereinten Europa. In: Detlef Merten – Hans-Jürgen Papier (eds.): *Handbuch der Grundrechte in Deutschland und Europa.* C.F. Müller 2009

Győrfi Tamás – Jakab András: Jogállamiság. In: A. Jakab (ed.): *Az Alkotmány kommentárja.* Századvég, Budapest 2009

Gyulavári, Tamás – Hős, Nikolett: Retirement of Hungarian Judges, Age Discrimination and Judicial Independence: A Tale of Two Courts. (42) *Industrial Law Journal* 2013/3

Habermas, Jürgen: *Between Facts and Norms.* Polity Press, Cambridge 1996

Halmai Gábor – Tóth Gábor Attila (eds.): *Emberi jogok* [Human Rights]. Osiris, Budapest 2003

Halmai, Gábor – Scheppele, Kim Lane (eds.): Amicus Brief for the Venice Commission on the Transitional Provisions of the Fundamental Law and the Key Cardinal Laws, February 2012. http://halmaigabor.hu/dok/426_Amicus_Cardinal_Laws_final.pdf NOTE 292

Halmai, Gábor – Scheppele, Kim Lane et al.: Amicus Brief for the Venice Commission on the Fourth Amendment to the Fundamental Law of Hungary. Princeton 2013. 1–83. http://halmaigabor.hu/dok/437_Amicus_Brief_on_the_Fourth_Amendment4.pdf

Halmai, Gábor: *Perspectives on Global Constitutionalism. The Use of Foreign and International Law.* Eleven, The Hague 2014

Halmai, Gábor: The Hungarian Constitutional Court and Constitutional Identity. *VerfBlog* 2017/1/10 http://verfassungsblog.de/the-hungarian-constitutional-court-and-constitutional-identity/

Hámor, Szilvia: A szolidaritás világától a szép új világig? [From the World of Solidarity to the Brave New World?] (3) *Esély* 2000

Jacobsohn, Gary Jeffrey: Constitutional identity. *The Review of Politics* 2006/3

Jakab, András: Defining the Borders of the Political Community: Constitutional Visions of the Nation, Manuscript, 2012. 1–54. http://ssrn.com/abstract=2045648

Jakab, András – Sonnevend, Pál: Continuity with Deficiencies: The New Basic Law of Hungary (9) *European Constitutional Law Review* 2013/1

Jakab, András: Supremacy of the EU Charter in National Courts in Purely Domestic Cases. http://www.verfassungsblog.de/de/ungarn-was-tun-andras-jakab/#.Un652RAtb5R

Jakab, András: The EU Charter of Fundamental Rights as the Most Promising Way of Enforcing the Rule of Law against EU Member States. In: C. Closa and D. Kochenov (eds.): *Reinforcing Rule of Law Oversight in the European Union.* Cambridge University Press, Cambridge 2017

Johansen, Stian Øby: EU law and the ECHR: the Bosphorus presumption is still alive and kicking – the case of Avotiņš v. Latvia, http://eulawanalysis.blogspot.hu/2016/05/eu-law-and-echr-bosphorus-presumption.html

Joseph, Sarah: *Corporations and Transnational Human Rights Litigation.* Hart Publishing, Oxford and Portland, Oregon 2004

Kardos, Gábor: Szolidaritás, szubszidiaritás és a szociális jogok védelme [The Protection of Solidarity, Subsidiarity and Social Rights]. In: J. Frivaldszky (szerk.): *Szubszidiaritás és szolidaritás az Európai Unióban* [Subsidiarity and Solidarity in the European Union]. OCIPE Magyarország – Faludy Ferenc Akadémia, Budapest 2006

Kardos, Gábor: A szolidaritás határai [Limits of Solidarity]. (21) *Liget – literary and ecological journal* 2008/3

Kiss, György: *Alapjogok a munkajogban* [Fundamental Rights in Labour Law]. JUSTIS, Pécs 2010

Klug, Heinz: Constitutional Transformations: Universal Values and the Politics of Constitutional Understanding. In: Charles Sampford – Tom Round (eds.): *Beyond the Republic. Meeting the Global Challenges to Constitutionalism.* Leichhardt, NSW, The Federation Press 2001

Knox, John H.: Horizontal Human Rights Law. *The American Journal of International Law* 2008/1

Knox, John H.: The Ruggie Rules: Applying Human Rights Law to Corporations. In: *The UN Guiding Principles on Business and Human Rights: Foundations and Implementation* (ed. Radu Mares). Martinus Nijhoff Publishers, Leiden, Boston 2012

Kovács Ágnes: Fényevők? A hazai alkotmányelmélet esete a politikai konstitucionalizmussal, (19) *Fundamentum* 2015/2-3

Kovács, Kriszta: Equality: The Missing Link. In: *Constitution for a Disunited Nation* (ed. Gábor Attila Tóth). CEU Press, Budapest 2012

Körtvélyesi Zsolt: Az »egységes magyar nemzet« és az állampolgárság. *Fundamentum* 2011/2

Körtvélyesi, Zsolt: From »We the People« to »We the Nation«. In: *Constitution for a Disunited Nation* (ed. Gábor Attila Tóth) CEU Press, Budapest 2012

Kukorelli István: Hány éves az Alaptörvény? A régi-új kérdése az Alaptörvényben. *Iustum Aequum Salutare* 2016/4

Kurunczi Gábor: A nemzetiségek parlamenti képviseletének kérdéséről. (7) *Közjogi Szemle* 2014/1

Küpper, Herbert: *Ungarns Verfassung vom 25. April 2011. Einführung – Übersetzung – Materialien.* Peter Lang Verlag, Frankfurt/Main 2012

Küpper, Herbert: Paternalista kollektivizmus és liberális individualizmus között: az új magyar Alaptörvényben rögzített emberkép normatív alapjai. (5) *Közjogi Szemle* 2012/3

Lavranos, Nikolaos: UN Sanctions and Judicial Review. In: Jan Wouters – André Nollkaemper – Erika de Wet (eds.): *The Europeanisation of International Law. The Status of International Law in the EU and its Member States.* T.M.C. Asser Press, The Hague 2008

Lavranos, Nikolaos: The ECJ's Judgments in Melloni and Åkerberg Fransson: Une ménage à trois difficulté. *European Law Reporter* 2013/4

Law, David S. – Versteeg, Mila: The Evolution and Ideology of Global Constitutionalism. (99) *California Law Review* 2011; APSA 2010 Annual Meeting Paper; 5th Annual Conference on Empirical Legal Studies Paper; Washington University in St. Louis Legal Studies Research Paper № 10-10-01. Available at http://ssrn.com/abstract=1643628

Lebeck, Carl: The European Court of Human Rights on the relation between ECHR and EC-law: the limits of constitutionalisation of public international law. *Zeitschrift für öffentliches Recht* 2007/62

Leisinger, Klaus M.: Business and human rights. In: *The Future of Sustainability* (ed. Marco Keiner). Springer 2006

Lock, Tobias: The future of the European Union's accession to the European Convention on Human Rights after Opinion 2/13: is it still possible and is it still desirable? (11) *European Constitutional Law Review* 2015/2

Lopez, Carlos – Shea, Ben: Negotiating a Treaty on Business and Human Rights: A Review of the First Intergovernmental Session. (1) *Business and Human Rights Journal* 2016/1

Lukonits Ádám: A demokrácia eszközeivel a demokrácia ellen Lengyelországban és Magyarországon. (9) *Közjogi Szemle* 2016/1

Magicz, András: Re-regulation of National Minority Rights. In: *Their Shield is the Law. The Ombudsman's Protection for Vulnerable Groups* (ed. Barnabás Hajas – Máté Szabó). Office of the Commissioner for Fundamental Rights, Budapest 2013

Majtényi, Balázs: What has happened to Our Model Child? The Creation and the Evolution of the Hungarian Minority Act. (6) *European Yearbook of Minority Issues* 2005/2006

Majtényi, Balázs: Legislative Stupidities in the New Hungarian Constitution. *Peace Human Rights* 2012/1

Majtényi Balázs: Alaptörvény a nemzet akaratából. *Állam- és Jogtudomány* 2014/1

Majtényi, Balázs: The Nation's Will as Trump in the Hungarian Fundamental Law. *European Yearbook on Human Rights* 2015

Mares, Radu (ed.): *The UN Guiding Principles on Business and Human Rights: Foundations and Implementation.* Martinus Nijhoff Publishers, Leiden, Boston 2012

Mares, Radu: Business and Human Rights After Ruggie: Foundations, the Art of Simplification and the Imperative of Cumulative Progress. In: *The UN Guiding Principles on Business and Human Rights: Foundations and Implementation* (ed. Radu Mares). Martinus Nijhoff Publishers, Leiden, Boston 2012

Mathisen, Karoline L.: The Impact of the Lisbon Treaty, in particular Article 6 TEU, on Member States' obligations with respect to the protection of fundamental rights. *University of Luxembourg Law Working Paper Series*, Paper number 2010-01, 29 July, 2010

Mészáros Bence: Kiemelt jelentőségű ügyek, alkotmányos aggályok – új különeljárás a büntetőeljárási törvényben. (4) *Közjogi Szemle* 2011/3

Methven O'Brien, Claire – Mehra, Amol – Blackwell, Sara – Bloch Poulsen-Hansen, Cathrine: National Action Plans: Current Status and Future Prospects for a New Business and Human Rights Governance Tool. (1) *Business and Human Rights Journal* 2016/1

Meyer, William H.: *Human Rights and International Political Economy in Third World Nations: Multinational Corporations, Foreign Aid, and Repression*. Praeger, Westport 1998

Mohay, Ágoston – Sándor-Szalay, Erzsébet: Hungary. In: J. Laffranque (ed.): *The Protection of Fundamental Rights Post-Lisbon: The Interaction between the Charter of Fundamental Rights of the European Union, the European Convention on Human Rights and National Constitutions*. Tartu University Press, Tallinn 2012

Molnár Tamás: Az új Alaptörvény rendelkezései a nemzetközi jog és a belső jog viszonyáról. In: Drinóczi Tímea– Jakab András (eds.): *Alkotmányozás Magyarországon 2010-2011*. PPKE JÁK – PTE ÁJK 2013

Myjer, Egbert: Csatlakozhat-e az Európai Unió az Emberi jogok és alapvető szabadságok védelméről szóló Európa Tanács-i Egyezményhez? *Magyar Jog* 2007/3

Nagy, Csongor István: Est-ce que l'union europeénne devrait avoir le pouvoir de forcer les états membres à respecter les droits de l'homme? Une analyse prospective relative à l'application de la charte des droits fondamentaux aux états membres. *Revue de droit international et de droit comparé* 2017/3

Naszladi, Georgina: The Hungarian Constitutional Court's judgement concerning the preliminary ruling procedure – comments on a rejection order. *Pécs Journal of International and European Law* 2015/1

Nemessányi Zoltán: Rejtett képviselet az angol jogban [Hidden Representation under English Law]. *JURA* 2008/2

Nipperdey, Hans Carl: Die Grundprinzipien des Wirtschaftsverfassungsrechts. *Deutsche Rechtszeitschrift* 5, 1950

Ostrom, Elinor: Collective Action and the Evolution of Social Norms. (14) *The Journal of Economic Perspectives* 2000/3

Ottmann, Juliane: The Concept of Solidarity in National and European Law: The Welfare State and the European Social Model. *Vienna Journal on International Constitutional Law* 2008/1

Pap, András László: *Democratic Decline in Hungary: Law and Society in an Illiberal Democracy*. Routledge 2018

Pap, András László: Constitutional identity? The Hungarian model of illiberal democracy. In: M Steven Fish, Graeme Gill, Milenko Petrovic (eds.): *A quarter century of post-communism assessed*. Palgrave Macmillan, London 2017

Pap, András László: Recognition, representation and reproach: new institutional arrangements in the Hungarian multiculturalist model. In: Balazs Vizi, Norbert Toth, Edgar Dobos (eds.): *Beyond International Conditionality: Local Variations of*

Minority Representation in Central and South-Eastern Europe. Nomos, Baden-Baden 2017

Pap András László: Az illiberális multikulturalizmus magyar modellje: a magyar kisebbségi jog változása 2010-2016 (I. rész). (9) *Közjogi Szemle* 2016/2

Pap, András László: Who Are "We, the People"?: Biases and Preferences in the Hungarian Fundamental Law. In: Zoltán Szente, Fanni Mandák, Zsuzsanna Fejes (eds.): *Challenges and Pitfalls in the Recent Hungarian Constitutional Development: Discussing the New Fundamental Law of Hungary.* Éditions L'Harmattan, Paris 2015

Pap András László: Észrevételek a nemzetiségek parlamenti képviseletének szabályozásához az Alaptörvényben, a választójogi törvényben és a nemzetiségek jogairól szóló törvényben. In: *Alkotmányozás Magyarországon 2010-2011. I.* (eds. Jakab A., Drinóczi T.) Pázmány Press, Budapest-Pécs 2013

Pap András László: Észrevételek a kisebbségek parlamenti képviseletének szabályozásához az új alkotmányban. *Pázmány Law Working Papers* 2011/27

Pákozdi, Csaba – Sulyok, Márton: The Birth of a »New Nation«? Mapping progressive approaches to the nation-concept based on the Hungarian Fundamental Law. *Miskolc Journal of International Law* 2011/2

Peers, Steve: The EU's Accession to the ECHR: The Dream Becomes a Nightmare. (16) *German Law Journal* 2015

Pernice, Ingolf: The Treaty of Lisbon and Fundamental Rights. In: S. Griller – J. Ziller (eds.): *The Lisbon Treaty. EU Constitutionalism without a Constitutional Treaty?* Springer Verlag, Wien 2008

Petrétei József: *Az alkotmányos demokrácia alapintézményei* [Basic institutions of constitutional democracy]. Dialóg Campus, Budapest-Pécs 2009

Petrétei József: *Magyarország alkotmányjoga I. Alapvetés, alkotmányos intézmények.* Kodifikátor Alapítvány, Pécs 2013

Pócza Kálmán: Alkotmányozás Magyarországon és az Egyesült Királyságban. *Kommentár* 2012/5

Pokol Béla: *A jurisztokratikus állam.* Dialóg Campus, Budapest 2017

Rosas, Allan: When is the EU Charter of Fundamental Rights Applicable at National Level? (19) *Jurisprudence* 2012/4

Ruggie, John: Protect, Respect and Remedy – A Framework for Business and Human Rights. (3) *Innovations* 2008/2

Ruggie, John G.: *Just Business: Multinational Corporations and Human Rights.* Norton, New York – London 2013

Sajó, András: Erosion and Decline of the Rule of Law in Post-communism: An Introduction. In: A. Sajó (ed.): *Out of and Into Authoritarian Law.* Kluwer Law International, The Hague, London, New York 2003

Sánches, Sara Iglesias: The Court and the Charter: The impact of the entry into force of the Lisbon Treaty on the ECJ's approach to fundamental rights. (49) *Common Market Law Review* 2012/5

Samp, Rich: Supreme Court Observations: Kiobel v. Royal Dutch Petroleum & the Future of Alien Tort Litigation. http://www.forbes.com/sites/wlf/2013/

04/18/supreme-court-observations-kiobel-v-royal-dutch-petroleum-the-future-of-alien-tort-litigation/

Sarmiento, Daniel: Who's Afraid of the Charter? The Court of Justice, National Courts and the New Framework of Fundamental Rights Protection in Europe. (50) *Common Market Law Review* 2013/5

Schima, Bernhard: EU fundamental rights and Member State action after Lisbon: putting the ECJ's case law in its context. (38) *Fordham International Law Journal* 2015/4

Schutter, Olivier de: Transnational Corporations and Human Rights: An Introduction. *Global Law Working Paper* 01/05, Symposium – Transnational Corporations and Human Rights, NYU School of Law

Schutter, Olivier de: Towards a New Treaty on Business and Human Rights. (1) *Business and Human Rights Journal* 2016/1

Simons, Marco: Post-Kiobel roundup: Apartheid case is not dismissed, but may soon be; some positive decisions from other courts (September 10, 2013), http://www.earthrights.org/blog/post-kiobel-roundup-apartheid-case-not-dismissed-may-soon-be-some-positive-decisions-other

Sólyom, László: Introduction to the Decisions of the Constitutional Court of the Republic of Hungary. In: L Sólyom/G Brunner (eds.): *Constitutional Judiciary in a New Democracy. The Hungarian Constitutional Court.* University of Michigan Press, Ann Arbor, 2000

Sólyom, László: The Rise and Decline of Constitutional Culture in Hungary. In: A. von Bogdandy, P. Sonnevend (eds.): *Constitutional Crisis in the European Constitutional Area.* Hart Publishing, Oxford 2015

Somek, Alexander: Solidarity Decomposed. Being and time in European citizenship. *University of Iowa Legal Studies Research Paper* 07-13, 2007

Sonnevend, Pál – Jakab, András – Csink, Lóránt: The Constitution as an Instrument of Everyday Party Politics: The Basic Law of Hungary. In: *Constitutional Crisis in the European Constitutional Area. Theory, Law and Politics in Hungary and Romania* (eds. Armin von Bogdandy – Pál Sonnevend). C.H. Beck – Hart – Nomos, Oxford/Portland, Oregon 2015

Steindorff, Ernst: *Persönlichkeitsschutz im Zivilrecht.* Müller, Heidelberg 1983

Stieglitz, Edgar: *Allgemeine Lehren im Grundrechtsverständnis nach der EMRK und der Grundrechtsjudikatur des EuGH.* Nomos Verlagsgesellschaft, Baden-Baden 2002

Stumpf István: Erős állam – alkotmányos korlátok. Századvég, Budapest 2014

Sulyok Gábor: 6. § [Nemzetközi kapcsolatok]. In: Jakab András (szerk.): *Az Alkotmány kommentárja.* Századvég, Budapest 2009

Sulyok Gábor: A nemzetközi jog és a belső jog viszonyának alaptörvényi szabályozása. *Jog Állam Politika* 2012/1

Sulyok, Gábor: Incorporation of International Law into Domestic Law under the Fundamental Law of Hungary. In: Péter Smuk (ed.): *The Transformation of the Hungarian Legal System 2010-2013.* CompLex, Budapest 2013

Szalayné Sándor, Erzsébet: Konvergenz der Grundrechte und Grundfreiheiten in der Europäischen Union. In: Chronowski Nóra (ed.): *Adamante Notare – Essays in Honour of Antal Ádám on the Occasion of His 75th Birthday.* PTE ÁJK, Pécs 2005

Szalayné Sándor Erzsébet: Új távlatok az európai alapjogvédelemben. Hatályba lépett az Egyezmény 14. Kiegészítő Jegyzőkönyve. (3) *Közjogi Szemle* 2010/3

Szente, Zoltán: The interpretive practice of the Hungarian Constitutional Court – A critical view. *German Law Journal* 2013/8

Szente, Zoltán: Breaking and making constitutional rules. The constitutional effects of the world economic and financial crisis in Hungary. In: Xenophon Contiades (ed.): *Constitutions in the Global Financial Crisis: A Comparative Analysis.* Farnham, Ashgate 2013

Szente Zoltán: Az Alkotmánybíróság döntése Magyarország Alaptörvényének Átmeneti rendelkezései alkotmányosságáról: az Alaptörvény integritása és az alkotmányozó hatalom korlátai. (4) *Jogesetek Magyarázata* 2013/1

Szente, Zoltán: The Decline of Constitutional Review in Hungary – Towards a Partisan Constitutional Court? In: *Challenges and Pitfalls in the Recent Hungarian Constitutional Development* (eds. Zoltán Szente – Fanni Mandák – Zsuzsanna Fejes). L'Harmattan, Paris 2015

Szente, Zoltán: Die politische Orientierung der Mitglieder des ungarischen Verfassungsgerichts zwischen 2010 und 2014. (18) *Jahrbuch für Ostrecht* 2016/1

Szentgáli-Tóth, Boldizsár: *The Scope of Qualified Law: Comparative Analysis. 22nd International Academic Conference, Proceedings,* ISBN 978-80-87927-21-2, IISES, Lisbon, 22 March 2016

Szilágyi, Emese: Hungarian Constitutional Court: Transparency and Business Activities of the State. (10) *Vienna Journal On International Constitutional Law* 2016/3

Takács, Albert: A szociális jogok [Social rights]. In: G. Halmai and G. A. Tóth (eds.) *Emberi jogok* [Human Rights]. Osiris, Budapest 2003

Takács, Tamara: Human rights in trade: The EU's experience with labour standards conditionality and its role in promoting labour standards in the WTO'. In: J. Wetzel (ed.): *The EU as a 'Global Player' in the Field of Human Rights.* Routledge 2012

Tévar, Nicolás Zambrana: Shortcomings and Disadvantages of Existing Legal Mechanisms to Hold Multinational Corporations Accountable for Human Rights Violations. (4) *Cuadernos de Derecho Transnacional* 2012/2

Thym, Daniel: Separation versus Fusion – or: How to Accommodate National Autonomy and the Charter? Diverging Visions of the German Constitutional Court and the European Court of Justice. (9) *European Constitutional Law Review* 2013/3

Tomuschat, Christian: *Human Rights: Between Realism and Idealism.* Oxford University Press, Oxford 2003

Tóth István György: *Bizalomhiány, normazavarok, igazságtalanságérzet és paternalizmus a magyar társadalom értékszerkezetében.* TÁRKI, Budapest 2009

Tóth Gábor Attila: *Túl a szövegen. Értekezés a magyar alkotmányról.* Osiris, Budapest 2009

Trstenjak, Verica: General Report: The Influence of Human Rights and Basic Rights in Private Law. In: Verica Trstenjak – Petra Weingerl (eds.): *The Influence of*

Human Rights and Basic Rights in Private Law. Springer International, Heidelberg/ New York/Dordrecht/London 2016

Tushnet, Mark: The Inevitable Globalization of Constitutional Law. (50) *Virginia Journal of International Law* 2009/1

Uitz, Renáta: Collective Constitutional Learning in Europe: European Courts Talk to Hungary (Again). *VerfBlog* 2014/4/10 http://verfassungsblog.de/collective-constitutional-learning-in-europe-european-courts-talk-to-hungary-again/

Uitz, Renáta: Poland, Hungary and Europe: Pre-Article 7 Hopes and Concerns. *VerfBlog* 2016/3/14 http://verfassungsblog.de/poland-hungary-and-europe-pre-article-7-hopes-and-concerns/

Varga Zs. Andás: Alkotmányunk értékei. A fogalmi keretek [The Values of Our Constitution. A Notional Framework]. *Iustum Aequum Salutare* 2009/1

Varju, Márton: *European Union human rights law.* Edward Elgar Publishing, Cheltenham 2014

Varju, Márton – Chronowski, Nóra: Constitutional backsliding in Hungary. *Tijdschrift voor Constitutioneel Recht* 2015/4

Vega, Connie de la – Mehra, Amol – Wong, Alexandra: *Holding Businesses Accountable for Human Rights Violations – Recent Developments and Next Steps.* Dialogue on Globalisation, Friedrich Ebert Stiftung 2011

Vincze, Attila – Varju, Márton: Hungary: the New Fundamental Law. (18) *European Public Law* 2012/3

Vincze, Attila: Wrestling with constitutionalism: the supermajority and the Hungarian Constitutional Court. (8) *Vienna Journal on International Constitutional Law* 2014/1

Vincze Attila: Az osztrák Alkotmánybíróság döntése az Alapjogi Charta alkalmazandóságáról. (3) *Alkotmánybírósági Szemle* 2013/1

Vincze, Attila: Der EuGH als Hüter der ungarischen Verfassung – Anmerkung zum Urteil des EuGH v. 6.11.2012, Rs. C-286/12 (Kommission/Ungarn). *Europarecht* 2013/3

Vincze, Attila: Judicial independence and its guarantees beyond the nation state – some recent Hungarian experience. (56) *Journal of the Indian Law Institute* 2014/2

Vincze Attila: Odahull az eszme és a valóság közé az árnyék: a szuverenitás-átruházás az alkotmánybíróság esetjogában [The shadow falls between the idea and the reality: transfer of sovereignty in the case-law of the Constitutional Court]. *MTA Law Working Papers* 2014/23

Vincze, Attila: Dismissal of the President of the Hungarian Supreme Court: ECtHR Judgment Baka v. Hungary. (21) *European Public Law* 2015/3

Voßkuhle, Andreas: Az emberi jogok védelme a bíróságok európai együttműködésében [Protection of human rights in the European cooperation of courts]. *Alkotmánybírósági Szemle* 2013/1

Vörös, Imre: The constitutional landscape after the fourth and fifth amendments of Hungarian Fundamental Law. *Acta Juridica Hungarica* 2014/1

Weiler, Joseph: Fundamental Rights and Fundamental Boundaries: on Standards and Values in the Protection of Human Rights. In: Nanette A. Neuwahl – Allan

Rosas (eds.): *The European Union and Human Rights.* Martinus Nijhoff, The Hague – Boston – London 1995

Weissbrodt, David: Business and Human Rights. (74) *University of Cincinnati Law Review* 2005/1

Weschka, Marion: Human Rights and Multinational Enterprises: How Can Multinational Enterprises Be Held Responsible for Human Rights Violations Committed Abroad? (66) *ZaöRV* 2006/3

Wettstein, Florian: *Multinational Corporations and Global Justice.* Stanford University Press, Stanford, California 2009

Zeller Judit: Német Szövetségi Köztársaság [Federal Republic of Germany]. In: N. Chronowski and T. Drinóczi (eds.): *Európai kormányformák rendszertana* [Systematics of European Forms of Government]. HVG-ORAC, Budapest 2007

Zeller, Judit: Nichts ist so beständig... Die jüngsten Novellen des Grundgesetzes Ungarns im Kontext der Entscheidungen des Verfassungsgerichts. (59) *Osteuropa Recht* 2013/3

Zlinszky János: Tudjátok-e, mi a haza? [Do you know what motherland is?] In: *Formatori Iuris Publici – Ünnepi kötet Kilényi Géza professzor 70. születésnapjára* [Special Volume Dedicated to the 70th Birthday of Professor Géza Kilényi]. PPKE-JÁK, Szent István Társulat, Budapest 2006

L'Harmattan France
5-7 rue de l'Ecole Polytechnique
75005 Paris
T.: 33.1.40.46.79.20
Email: diffusion.harmattan@wanadoo.fr

L'Harmattan Italia SRL
Via Degli Artisti 15
10124 TORINO
T.: (39) 011 817 13 88 / (39) 348 39 89 198
Email: harmattan.italia@agora.it

Cover design: László Kára
Layout design: Zsanett Kállai
Printing: Robinco Ltd.,
Manager: Péter Kecskeméthy

www.ingramcontent.com/pod-product-compliance
Lightning Source LLC
Chambersburg PA
CBHW071338230926
51846CB00009B/249